THE
GEOFFREY
BOYCOTT
FILE

Complete match-by-match
record of Geoffrey Boycott's
career 1962-81,including
the England tour of
India, 1981-82

THE GEOFFREY BOYCOTT FILE

STEVEN SHEEN

Hamlyn

London · **New York** · **Sydney** · **Toronto**

To my parents Norman and Marion Sheen,
to Sue Murphy and to Peter Arnold: thanks
for the help

Acknowledgement
The photographs on the cover were supplied by Patrick Eagar

Text checked and approved by Geoffrey Boycott

Published by
The Hamlyn Publishing Group Limited
London · New York · Sydney · Toronto
Astronaut House, Feltham, Middlesex, England

ISBN 0 600 34675 7

Printed in Great Britain by
Fakenham Press Limited, Fakenham, Norfolk

Contents

One-day Games

Gillette Cup   154

Nat West Trophy   161

John Player League   161

Benson and Hedges Cup   176

One-day Internationals   184

Opposite: A triumphant Geoff Boycott on the balcony at Trent
Bridge, Nottingham, after England had won the Third Test
against Australia in 1977. Boycott scored 107 and 80 not out.
Greg Chappell, Australia captain, is on the left.

Introduction

Geoffrey Boycott's Career So Far

Geoffrey Boycott was born on Monday, 21 October 1940, in Fitzwilliam, near Pontefract, Yorkshire. He was the eldest of three sons, his father being a miner. Young Geoffrey's interest in cricket was boosted at the age of ten when he won a newspaper competition with a score of 45 out of a team total of 52 and took six wickets for ten runs. The prize was a Len Hutton bat. Uncle Albert Speight helped with his development as a cricketer when he suggested that every member of the family contribute 2/6d (12½p) towards a winter's coaching in the Indoor School at Rothwell. The coach was Johnny Lawrence, who had been a batsman-leg spinner with Somerset.

The first captaincy post Boycott held was of his junior school at Fitzwilliam and later he captained Hensworth Grammar School. He also played for various other local school elevens. At 10 he joined Ackworth and at 13 played in the Yorkshire Council League. He had progressed by the age of 15 to playing for Yorkshire Schoolboys and for two league clubs, in Barnsley and Leeds. From these clubs he moved rapidly to the Yorkshire 2nd XI, for whom he first played in 1971.

Boycott made his first appearance in first class cricket against Pakistan on Saturday 16 June 1962, at the age of 21 years 239 days, and was selected for the two following matches. For the rest of that season his only appearances were when injuries and Test calls affected the Yorkshire team. He made his big impact in 1963, scoring his first century in the Whitsuntide Roses match against Lancashire. He scored 145, the innings going as follows: 4 4 2 3 4 1 2 2 1 4 2 1 4 4 1 2 2 4 4 1 4 1 1 4 4 4 2 4 4 4 1 2 1 1 4 1 4 2 4 4 1 2 4 2 2 2 1 3 1 2 4 4 2 2 4 1. During the summer of 1963 Boycott gave up his job as a wages clerk for the Ministry of Pensions in the Civil Service. He was awarded his Yorkshire County Cap on Wednesday, 2 October 1963, one year 108 days after making his debut, and was voted Young Cricketer of the Year by the Cricket Writers' Club. He represented England for the first time in 1964, against Australia at Trent Bridge.

In the 1960s and 1970s the five feet ten inches tall right-handed batsman was the most phenomenal scoring machine, getting more runs than any other batsman. The technique was flawless and perfection was the aim. He used a lightweight bat of two pounds 4½ ounces for flexibility. His cover drive was compared to those of the true greats of the game such as Hammond and Hutton, and was diagrammed in many coaching manuals. On fast pitches he played the shot off the back foot through the square cover area and on slow pitches the shot would go between cover and mid-off.

Boycott was an accumulator of runs and can be compared with Don Bradman for his appetite to get them. With his right hand low on the bat, the back swing not very high, genuine power was hard to create, so timing became a necessity. A shot that was prominent during the 1970s and 1980s was the leg push played into the mid-wicket region when the ball pitched around middle or middle and leg stump. There were not many strokes that he did not play, and to the middle 1970s he even played the hook shot, but he cut this shot out of his repertoire after getting out a couple of times in Test matches with it. Boycott was never better than when facing spin bowling, and would use his feet to go down the wicket and drive through the covers. He played Lance Gibbs with great precision and scored heavily off him.

Boycott worked hard to improve his batting. Never was a player more dedicated or one who spent more hours in the nets. Every year he went back to Johnny Lawrence to check his batting.

A weakness he has never overcome is poor running between the wickets, although he insists his reputation for this is based purely on a bad spell he had in the early 1970s. He suffered a serious back injury during a Test match at Edgbaston in 1968, and has had a number of broken bones in fingers and hands.

Boycott takes the game seriously. On 18 October 1965, when the MCC plane to Australia stopped at Colombo Airport, Sri Lanka, on the way, the seventeen players were asked to complete forms for the immigration office. One question was 'what is the purpose of your visit?' Fifteen answered 'to play cricket,' one put 'holiday' and Boycott put 'business'. At a cricket ground he will often say to the media 'I'm here to play cricket and that's all.' When the MCC tour of South Africa in the winter of 1968/69 was cancelled, Boycott changed from spectacles to contact lenses and joined the Mark McCormack Organisation, who specialise in promoting sportsmen.

Only four batsmen scored a thousand runs in each season of the 1970s: G. Boycott, A. Jones, D. Amiss and G. Turner. Ten players scored 2,000 runs in a season and only G. Boycott, D. Amiss and G. Turner achieved this feat twice. A bowler prized the wicket of Boycott more than that of any other batsman. If the team were in a crisis, he would often be keeping one end going. Other world-class cricketers such as C. Lloyd, V. Richards, G. Chappell, Zaheer Abbas and Barry Richards played brilliant innings but could not match Boycott's great consistency.

Boycott has faced all the best bowlers the world offered during the 1960s and 1970s and coped with them all. Some of the bowlers he has faced are: Bedi, Chandrasekhar, Croft, Garner, Gibbs, Gleeson, Griffith, Hadlee, Hall, Holding, Intikhab Alam, Lillee, McKenzie, Pollock, Procter, Ramadhin, Rice, Roberts, Sobers, Snow, Statham, Thomson, Underwood and Willis.

Over the years Boycott has taken some knocks from the fast bowlers, but has not allowed them to affect his concentration. When he was struck on the head by a lifting ball from Peter Clough, a six feet five inches fast bowler, during the game with the Combined Universities at Adelaide in 1979, Boycott left the field with bruising behind his left ear but was able to bat again the following day.

During Boycott's career he bowled relatively few overs, but was a very accurate and reliable bowler and could have been a lot better if given the chance to bowl more, or had he not spent all his time perfecting his batting. When he became captain he hardly ever bowled himself. His unusual characteristic was to bowl with his cap on, the only bowler during the 1970s to do so.

By sheer application and practice he improved his fielding until he had a very safe pair of hands. His usual fielding positions were cover, mid-off, mid-on, third man or long leg, where he usually drew applause for neatness and accuracy and strength in returning the ball to the wicket-keeper.

There can be few cricketers who have aroused controversy like Geoff Boycott. Whatever he does on and off the field has always been reported in the press. The media often asked him provocative questions, hoping he would give them a good story. During a television interview held just before the England party departed for the West Indies in 1981, the reporter asked if captain Botham had ever asked Boycott for advice concerning tactics. Boycott's reply was 'If he does he always gets the benefit of my help. But I haven't known him bother to ask much have you?' He explained this later by saying that Botham is a very strong willed person who doesn't ask help from anybody. There have been problems on the cricket field, too. In the sixth Test against Australia at Adelaide in 1971 Boycott was dissatisfied with an umpiring decision which adjudged him to be run out. Unfortunately, his feelings got the better of him and he threw his bat to the ground, Greg Chappell picking up the bat and returning it. Boycott was booed by the 22,000 crowd while leaving the pitch. On 10 December 1978, in the England tour match with Western Australia, Hughes played a ball from Botham and was hit on the pad, being given not out after an appeal. Boycott walked towards the bowler's end from mid-off and called umpire Don Weser a 'cheat'. Weser asked him to repeat what he had said, and he did without thinking. After the day's play manager Doug Insole said he thought Boycott should apologise, and he did.

The 1970–71 tour of Australia saw Boycott at his greatest, finishing top of both the Test and tour batting averages, and with the most runs. He would surely have broken Wally Hammond's record of 1,553 runs for a tour of Australia if not for two events, the first arising in a match with Queensland. Boycott retired hurt after scoring 124. He had a slight strain, and with a Test match coming up it was decided not to risk any aggravation. Typically, he was unable just to throw his wicket away. The second event occurred in a one-day game just before the seventh Test, on a rain affected green pitch at Sydney. Boycott was hit on his left wrist by the third ball of the game from Graham McKenzie, and it was later discovered that he had broken a bone. This caused him to miss the rest of the tour and he returned to England, 18 runs short of the record.

The greatest unanswered question of the 1970s is why Boycott declined to play Test cricket from 1974 to 1977, a total of 30 Tests. The answer must await Boycott's autobiography. When the England captaincy became vacant for the tour to the West Indies in 1973–74, the two main candidates appeared to be Boycott and Tony Greig, and it was a surprise when Mike Denness was chosen. It was during the third Test of this tour, at Bridgetown, that Boycott was dropped from opening to bat at number four, for the only time in his Test career.

Boycott did become captain of England, although only as substitute, when Mike Brearley broke his arm in Pakistan in 1978. He was never captain by right and this has been difficult for him to accept as he always would have liked the opportunity of being captain.

During his career he has played some long, slow innings. In

1967 he scored 246 not out against India at Headingley, spending nearly six hours over the first hundred. The total innings lasted 573 minutes, just over nine and a half hours, and Boycott scored one six and 29 fours from 555 balls, the scoring strokes being 2 4 4 2 1 1 1 1 1 3 2 1 1 1 4 1 4 3 1 2 1 4 4 1 1 4 1 1 1 2 1 2 2 1 2 1 4 1 1 4 4 1 1 1 1 1 2 2 1 1 1 2 4 1 4 4 4 1 1 1 1 2 1 1 4 1 1 4 1 1 1 2 2 1 2 1 1 2 4 4 3 1 1 1 1 4 1 1 4 4 1 4 1 2 1 4 2 1 1 1 1 4 1 4 1 1 4 1 1 1 1 2 4 1 1 1 1 1 1 2 1 6 1 1 4 1 4 1. This innings was his highest score in Test cricket and is also the highest total in an England–India Test series. Before the match the selectors had asked players for a positive approach to batting. Unfortunately, Boycott was not positive enough for the selectors who dropped him for the second Test as a disciplinary measure. After another slow innings of 106 in 1969 against the West Indies at Lord's, which saved the game, the Press thought Boycott might be disciplined again, but this time no action was taken. A reason could have been that he had recently changed from spectacles to contact lenses and was granted time to adjust.

The postscript to this is that if he had played these innings in the late 1970s or 1980s nothing would have been said as the general batting of the England team was so poor.

In a special meeting in November 1970 Boycott was voted by the Yorkshire committee to be the 21st captain since 1863. This had been one of his greatest ambitions since an early age. The committee notified Boycott while he was on the MCC tour in Australia. It was a difficult time in Yorkshire's history because after a successful decade many of their top and experienced players had left or retired. Trueman, Close, Illingworth, Stott, Binks and Taylor, all difficult players to replace, had gone. The only experienced players, apart from Boycott, left on the York-shire books were Hampshire, Nicholson, Padgett, Sharpe and Wilson.

In Boycott's first match as captain for Yorkshire against War-wickshire in 1971 he scored a century in only 34 scoring strokes: 5 4 2 4 1 4 2 4 2 4 4 4 1 2 1 2 2 4 1 4 1 1 4 3 4 4 6 2 4 1 4 2 1 6 1 4 4 1, a total of 81 in boundaries.

Boycott lost the captaincy shortly after the end of the 1978 season. The Yorkshire committee decided to change captains in search of a trophy. Boycott was considered too defensive. He claims more matches were won with him as captain than with any of the substitute captains who took over when he was injured or on Test duty. The committee had almost changed the captaincy the year before, but had voted narrowly in Boycott's favour. During his eight-year reign as captain Yorkshire did not win any major honours, and their highest position in the Championship was second in 1975. They were runners-up to Leicestershire in the first Benson and Hedges final of 1972.

When in 1978 England's party for the Australian tour was announced, Boycott found himself bypassed as vice-captain. The job was given to Bob Willis. Just one year earlier Boycott had taken over the England captaincy from injured Mike Brearley in Pakistan.

Before the England party was due to leave for Australia there was a Special General Meeting to censure the Committee and to try to reinstate Geoff Boycott as Yorkshire captain. It was held on 9 December 1978 at the Royal Hall in Harrogate, and was organised by the Members Reform Group. The meeting lasted three hours before the Reform Group lost the vote, most of which were by proxy, by 4,826 votes to 2,602, a majority of 2,224 not to re-appoint him.

In the three years after he had been ousted as captain, Yorkshire did not win anything or even look as if they would.

Boycott's Record as Captain
In all matches for Yorkshire

Result	1971	1972	1973	1974	1975	1976	1977	1978	TOTAL
Won	4	3	0	6	10	5	7	5	40
Lost	4	1	3	5	1	4	1	1	20
Drawn	10	6	7	7	8	3	9	8	58
								TOTAL	118

For MCC and England   Tests 1977–78

	1977–78		P	NZ
Won	3		0	1
Lost	1		0	1
Drawn	4		1	1
TOTAL	8	TOTAL	1	3

Grand Total

Won	43
Lost	21
Drawn	62
TOTAL	126

Matches in County Championship

Result	1971	1972	1973	1974	1975	1976	1977	1978	TOTAL
Won	4	3	0	4	9	4	6	5	35
Lost	4	1	3	5	1	4	1	1	20
Drawn	9	6	5	6	8	3	8	6	51
								TOTAL	106

Yorkshire position each year in the County Championship

1971	13	1975	2
1972	10	1976	8
1973	14	1977	12
1974	11	1978	4

One-day Matches

Gillette Cup

Result	1971	1972	1973	1974	1975	1976	1977	1978	TOTAL
Won	0	0	0	1	0	0	0	2	3
Lost	1	1	1	1	1	1	1	1	8
								TOTAL	11

John Player League

Result	1971	1972	1973	1974	1975	1976	1977	1978	TOTAL
Won	4	6	7	7	9	5	2	4	44
Lost	5	3	3	2	5	5	6	4	33
No Result	0	0	0	1	0	0	4	0	5
								TOTAL	82

Yorkshire position each year in the John Player League

1971	15 equal	1975	7
1972	4	1976	15
1973	2	1977	13 equal
1974	7 equal	1978	7

Benson and Hedges Cup

Result	1972	1973	1974	1975	1976	1977	1978	TOTAL
Won	4	3	2	3	2	2	1	17
Lost	1	1	2	2	1	2	3	12
							TOTAL	29

One-day Internationals

Result	1978	TOTAL
Won	1	1
Lost	1	1
	TOTAL	2

Grand Total in One-day Matches

Won	65
Lost	54
No Result	5
TOTAL	124

When in 1977 Kerry Packer planned World Series Cricket it was announced that one of the first players asked to sign was Boycott, who turned down a substantial offer, saying that it might interfere with him playing for Yorkshire.

The 1978–79 tour to Australia proved to be a bad one for Boycott. His mother died and he lost the Yorkshire captaincy, two shattering blows within a couple of days just before the touring party left. In Australia he was very limited in his stroke play, mainly because he used a two-eyed stance, which restricted his off-side play. His reflexes seemed to be a bit slow and he was dismissed several times leg before wicket to the faster bowlers. This was the only one of his ten tours in which he did not score a century. For the only time in his career he batted at number eleven against South Australia at Adelaide. Boycott thought this funny, comparing himself to Wilfred Rhodes who started his career at number eleven and ended up as number one.

Boycott was one of the last English batsmen to don a protective helmet.

Before the 1978–79 tour started Boycott had scored more Test runs than the rest of the tour party put together, 5,675 to 5,435, showing a tremendous difference in Test experience between himself and the other players.

In 1981 Boycott played in his hundredth Test at Lord's and was given a standing ovation by the large crowd. After sporting handshakes from Dennis Lillee and Kim Hughes he tried to score a hundred to celebrate the occasion, as did Cowdrey in his hundredth Test, but had to be satisfied with 60 in the second innings.

At the end of the 1981 season Boycott's Yorkshire future was in doubt because of comments he made when he was left out of various games towards the end of the season. He announced to the Press that he was '. . . not getting a fair deal from the team manager and wanted to sort it out with him at the end of the season.' On 9 September manager Ray Illingworth suspended him and ordered Boycott to leave the dressing room. Yorkshire County Cricket Club later released results of a straw poll of the players indicating that they did not want Boycott to play again for Yorkshire and certainly not as captain. Boycott, on the other hand, has always said 'I want to play for Yorkshire and no one else.'

The 1981–82 tour of India provided Boycott with many records. He obtained a record aggregate of Test runs, and will probably remain the top Englishman for many years. The record took about 450 hours from 1964 to 1982.

Boycott has obtained every score from 0 to 100 except 67, 91 and 96.

Boycott has many strings to his bow. He has provided expertise for BBC television commentaries of the one-day games, has written books on his tours, contributed articles to boy's comics and compiled a coaching manual. He also advertises cricket equipment for the Slazenger company.

Boycott's Hundredth Hundred

Boycott has openly admitted that his greatest and proudest moment was when he scored his hundredth hundred. He is the only batsman to date to achieve the feat in a Test match. He became only the third player to score his ninety-ninth and hundredth hundred in consecutive innings, the others being Don Bradman and Colin Cowdrey. Boycott became the eighteenth player (the third Yorkshireman) to score 100 hundreds.

The innings started at 11.31 a.m. on Thursday, 11 August 1977 and ended at 4.55 p.m. on Friday, 12 August. During the course of it he scored 191 in 629 minutes from 471 balls in 86 scoring strokes. The century came at 5.49 p.m. on 11 August when Boycott on-drove Greg Chappell for four. The scoring strokes went as follows: 2 3 1 2 4 1 3 2 4 4 4 4 1 1 1 4 3 4 4 1 3 2 1 1 1 4 2 4 4 4 1 1 2 1 4 1 2 2 1 1 1 4 1 4 1 4 1 3 1 1 2 1 2 1 4 2 1 2 1 2 1 1 2 2 4 4 1 3 2 1 2 3 1 1 1 1 4 5 1 2 4 1 1 4 1 1 4 2; 1 five, 23 fours, 7 threes, 18 twos

FOURTH T...

8p

ENGLAND v...

THURSDAY, FRIDAY, SATURDAY, MONDAY & TU...

ENGLAND WON BY A...

ENGLAND

	First Innings		Second Innings
*1—J. M. Brearley c Marsh b Thomson ...	0		
2—G. Boycott c Chappell b Pascoe	191		
3—R. A. Woolmer c Chappell b Thomson	37		
4—D. W. Randall lbw b Pascoe	20		
5—A. W. Greig b Thomson	43		
6—G. R. J. Roope c Walters b Thomson	34		
7—I. T. Botham b Bright	0		
†8—A. P. E. Knott lbw Bright	57		
9—D. L. Underwood c Bright b Pascoe ...	6		
10—M. J. Hendrick c Robinson b Pascoe .	4		
11—R. G. D. Willis not out	5		
Extras...	39		Extras...
Total...	**436**		Total...

FALL OF WICKETS

First Innings:	1-0	2-82	3-105	4-201	5-275	6-398	7-398	8-412	9-42...
Second Innings:	1 -	2-	3-	4-	5-	6-	7-	8-	9-

Bowling Analysis	Overs	Mdns.	Runs	Wkts.	Overs	Mdns.	Runs	Wkts
J. R. Thomson	34	7	113	4				
M. H. N. Walker	48	21	97	0				
L. S. Pascoe	34.4	10	91	4				
K. D. Walters	3	1	5	0				
R. Bright	26	9	66	2				
G. Chappell	10	2	25	0				

* Denotes Captain

† Denotes Wicket-Keepe...

Umpires:
W. E. ALLEY & W. L. BUDD

Scorers
E. I. LESTER & D. SHERWOO...

PREVIOUS RESULTS IN THE SERIES

First Test — Lords — MATCH DRAWN.
Second Test — Old Trafford — ENGLAND won by 9 wickets.
Third Test — Trent Bridge — ENGLAND won by 7 wickets.

T MATCH

AUSTRALIA

8p

)AY, 11th, 12th, 13th, 15th & 16th AUGUST, 1977

NINGS AND 85 RUNS

AUSTRALIA

First Innings		Second Innings	
1—R. B. McCosker run out	27	c Knott b Greig	12
2—I. C. Davis lbw Hendrick	0	c Knott b Greig	19
*3—G. Chappell c Brearley b Hendrick	4	c Greig b Willis	36
4—D. W. Hookes lbw Botham	24	lbw Hendrick	21
5—K. D. Walters c Hendrick b Botham	4	lbw Woolmer	15
6—R. D. Robinson c Greig b Hendrick	20	b Hendrick	20
*7—R. W. Marsh c Knott b Botham	2	c Randall b Hendrick	63
8—R. Bright not out	9	c Greig b Hendrick	5
9—M. H. N. Walker c Knott b Botham	7	b Willis	30
0—J. R. Thomson b Botham	C	b Willis	0
1—L. S. Pascoe b Hendrick	0	not out	0
Extras...	6	Extras...	27
Total...**103**		Total...**248**	

FALL OF WICKETS

First Innings:	1-8	2-26	3-52	4-57	5-60	6-77	7-87	8-100	9-100
Second Innings:	1-31	2-35	3-63	4-97	5-130	6-167	7-179	8-244	9-245

Bowling Analysis	Overs	Mdns.	Runs	Wkts.	Overs	Mdns.	Runs	Wkts.
R. G. D. Willis	5	0	35	0	14	7	32	3
M. J. Hendrick	15.3	2	41	4	22.5	6	54	4
I. T. Botham	11	3	21	5	17	3	47	0
A. W. Greig					20	7	64	2
R. A. Woolmer					8	4	8	1
D. L. Underwood					8	3	16	0

Hours of Play: First Second Third and Fourth Days, 11-30 a.m. to 6-30 p.m.
Fifth Day, 11-00 a.m. to 5-30 p.m. or 6-00 p.m.

Lunch: 1-30 p.m. to 2-10 p.m.   Tea: 4-15 p.m. to 4-35 p.m.

NEXT MATCH IN YORKSHIRE
YORKSHIRE v. LANCASHIRE at Bradford
20th, 22nd and 23rd August, 1977

Completed copies of this Score Card (20p each post free) are available from
Morton & Wright Ltd., The Sports Printers, 67-79 Kirkstall Road, Leeds LS3 1LP

and 37 singles. The timetable for Boycott's hundredth hundred was:

50 in 176 minutes from 119 balls with   8 fours
100 in 320 minutes from 235 balls with 14 fours
150 in 493 minutes from 360 balls with 19 fours

Boycott, at 36 years 295 days, was the fourth youngest to achieve this feat, behind:

W. Hammond	32 years 359 days
D. Compton	34 years 19 days
L. Hutton	35 years 23 days

From debut to hundredth hundred took Boycott 15 years 57 days. He is the third quickest to achieve the feat, behind:

| H. Sutcliffe | 13 years 43 days |
| W. Hammond | 14 years 299 days |

Other players would have been quicker than they were, had it not been for the First and Second World Wars.

It took Boycott 645 innings to complete his hundredth hundred, putting him fourth behind:

D. Bradman	295 innings
D. Compton	552 innings
L. Hutton	619 innings

Reading the Tables

In the following innings by innings section, Boycott's match appearances are numbered in chronological order with the result of each match indicated after the date.

The total or totals of Boycott's side are given first, followed by details of his scores and dismissals. Then come the opposing side's totals, followed by the number of catches Boycott made. Details of the catches, i.e. the victims and the bowlers off whom the catches were made are in brackets. Last, if Boycott bowled, is his bowling analysis, with the names of his victims, the manner of their dismissal and the fieldsmen involved (if any).

In lists and tables which include all matches, Test matches are printed in CAPITAL LETTERS.

In the classified tables, the number of catches Boycott took each season, or on each ground, etc, are included in the tables of his innings.

Seasons of winter tours are indicated thus: 1970–71, etc.

In some tables the following abbreviations are used:

A for Australia; S A for South Africa; I for India; W I for West Indies; N Z for New Zealand; P for Pakistan; C for Ceylon (now Sri Lanka).

An asterisk represents not out.

First-class Matches

1962

Geoffrey Boycott made his debut in first class cricket at the age of 21 years 239 days in the tour match against Pakistan. He scored 4 in each innings. He was later to get revenge against Pakistan by scoring three Test centuries and averaging over 84 against them. In this, his first season, he opened against Pakistan, Derbyshire, Essex and Kent but batted in the middle order against Northamptonshire. He started 1963 batting in the middle order, finally establishing himself as an opener in the second half of 1963. His scoring was inconsistent. He obtained the first duck in his career in his last innings of the season against Kent.

A suggestion that Boycott was a poor runner between wickets came in the first two matches when he ran out two colleagues for which, according to Wisden, his captain reprimanded him.

1 Yorkshire v **Pakistan**
at Bradford *June 16, 18, 19*
Drawn

246 *b* D'Souza 4
137 *ct* Imtiaz *b* D'Souza 4

285 1ct (Alim-ud-Din *b* Bolus)
26–0 0ct

2 Yorkshire v **Northamptonshire**
at Northampton *June 20, 21, 22*
Northamptonshire won by 6 wickets

157 *ct* Allen *b* Lightfoot 6
193 *not out* 21

201 0ct
152–4 0ct

3 Yorkshire v **Derbyshire**
at Chesterfield *June 23, 25, 26*
Drawn

279 *ct* Taylor *b* Smith 47
61–2 *not out* 30

309 0ct
214–5d 0ct

4 Yorkshire v **Essex**
at Sheffield *July 28, 30, 31*
Yorkshire won by an innings and 44 runs

363–9d *lbw* Greensmith 20

207 1ct (Preston *b* Fearnley)
112 1ct (Edmeades *b* Close)

5 Yorkshire v **Kent**
at Middlesbrough *August 1, 2, 3*
Yorkshire won by 3 wickets

251 *lbw* Halfyard 18
230–7 *b* Melville 0

344–7d 0ct
136 1ct (Leary *b* Close)

1963

In his second season with Yorkshire and his first full season in the County Championship, Boycott scored his first first-class century against the arch enemy Lancashire, a team he was to score very heavily against in the future. His score was 145, which included 23 fours, and he shared in a 4th wicket partnership of 249 with Stott. Boycott's second century was also against Lancashire; he thus scored hundreds in both home and away fixtures.

A total of 1,628 runs was scored at an average of 45·22, which included three hundreds and eleven fifties. His other century came against Leicestershire, when he scored 165 not out. This looked promising for the future. Boycott and Taylor shared in a hundred partnership for the 1st wicket in both innings against Leicestershire. Boycott's first attempts at bowling were not too successful, his analysis being two overs for twenty runs. He did not bowl again for Yorkshire for another two seasons.

At the end of the season Geoff Boycott was awarded his county cap and voted Young Cricketer of the Year by the Cricket Writers Club.

6   Yorkshire v Cambridge University
at Cambridge   *May 1, 2, 3*
Drawn

235–8d   *ct* Briggs   *b* Miller   16

120   1*ct* (Pritchard   *b* Wilson)
198–5   1*ct* (Kerslake   *b* Close)

7   Yorkshire v Northamptonshire
at Northampton   *May 4, 6, 7*
Yorkshire won by 7 wickets

339   *b* Milburn   8
105–3   *did not bat*

137   0*ct*
303   1*ct* (Milburn   *b* Trueman)

8   Yorkshire v Gloucestershire
at Bradford   *May 18, 20, 21*
Drawn

187   *b* Mortimore   9

80   0*ct*
54–5   0*ct*

9   Yorkshire v Kent
at Gravesend   *May 29, 30, 31*
Yorkshire won by 22 runs

263   *ct* Catt   *b* Dye   27
187–9d   *not out*   21

199   1*ct* (Leary   *b* Close)
229   1*ct* (Wilson   *b* Close)

10   Yorkshire v Lancashire
at Sheffield   *June 1, 2, 3*
Yorkshire won by an innings and 110 runs

384–6d   *b* Greenhough   145

151   0*ct*
123   0*ct*

11   Yorkshire v Somerset
at Harrogate   *June 5, 6, 7*
Yorkshire won by an innings and 39 runs

352   *ct* Virgin   *b* Rumsey   37

202   1*ct* (Langford   *b* Wilson)
111   1*ct* (Virgin   *b* Ryan)

12   Yorkshire v Derbyshire
at Chesterfield   *June 8, 10, 11*
Yorkshire won by an innings and
56 runs

404–4d   *lbw* H. Jackson   25

238   0*ct*
110   0*ct*

13   Yorkshire v Somerset
at Taunton   *June 15, 17, 18*
Drawn

222   *ct* Stephenson
b Doughty   76
241   *lbw* Doughty   53

271–8d   0*ct*
13–1   0*ct*

14   Yorkshire v Gloucestershire
at Bristol   *June 19, 20, 21*
Drawn

63–2d   *did not bat*
173–7   *not out*   49

126–2d   0*ct*
154–4d   0*ct*

15   Yorkshire v Worcestershire
at Bradford   *June 22, 24, 25*
Drawn

213–9   *b* Carter   50

307   0*ct*

16   Yorkshire v Glamorgan
at Sheffield   *June 26, 27, 28*
Yorkshire won by 10 wickets

218   *ct* Pressdee   *b* Wheatley   0
63–0   *did not bat*

185   0*ct*
95   0*ct*

17   Yorkshire v Nottinghamshire
at Nottingham   *June 29, July 1, 2*
Drawn

126   *ct* Moore   *b* Gillhouley   21

267   0*ct*
8–0   0*ct*

18   Yorkshire v Middlesex
at Leeds   *July 6, 8, 9*
Middlesex won by 6 wickets

147   *lbw* Bick   14
147–7d   *b* Bick   66

47   0*ct*
251–4   0*ct*

19   Yorkshire v Surrey
at The Oval   *July 13, 15, 16*
Drawn

149   *not out*   50
180–6d   *lbw* Sydenham   8

168–4d   0*ct*
19–0   0*ct*

20   Yorkshire v Sussex
at Bradford   *July 17, 18, 19*
Yorkshire won by 10 wickets

188   *ct* Langridge   *b* Bates   2
28–0   *not out*   5

103   0*ct*
112   0*ct*

21   Yorkshire v Surrey
at Sheffield   *July 20, 22, 23*
Drawn

246   *b* Loader   0
21–4   *ct* McIntyre   *b* Lock   2

225   0*ct*
230–3d   1*ct* (Edrich
b Illingworth)   2–0–20–0

22   Yorkshire v Glamorgan
at Cardiff   *July 24, 25, 26*
Yorkshire won by an innings and
66 runs

332–7d   *ct* Pressdee
b Shepherd   80

88   0*ct*
178   1*ct* (A. Jones   *b* Wilson)

23   Yorkshire v Worcestershire
at Worcester   *July 27, 29*
Worcestershire won by an innings
and 57 runs

166   *ct* Graveney   *b* Slade   32
129   *ct*   Richardson
b Slade   37

352–7d   0*ct*

24   Yorkshire *v* Warwickshire
at Scarborough   *July 31, August 1, 2*
Yorkshire won by 92 runs

301   *b* Cartwright   62
172   *b* Edmonds   28

269   2*ct* (Miller   *b* Trueman, A. Smith   *b* Close)
112   0*ct*

25   Yorkshire *v* Lancashire
at Manchester   *August 3, 5, 6*
Drawn

345–8d   *ct* Clayton
b Statham   113
63–1   *not out*   20

237   0*ct*

26   Yorkshire *v* Derbyshire
at Leeds   *August 7, 8*
Yorkshire won by 7 wickets

152   *ct* Taylor   *b* Rhodes   12
60–3   *ct* Carr   *b* Morgan   0

123   0*ct*
85   0*ct*

27   Yorkshire *v* West Indies
at Sheffield   *August 10, 12, 13*
West Indies won by an innings and 2 runs

260   *ct* Allan   *b* King   71
96   *lbw* Hall   13

358–9d   0*ct*

28   Yorkshire *v* Nottinghamshire
at Bradford   *August 14, 15, 16*
Drawn

176–9d   *ct* Millman
b Forbes   24
20–0   *not out*   8

55   0*ct*
214   1*ct* (Bolus   *b* Wilson)

29   Yorkshire *v* Middlesex
at Lord's   *August 17, 19, 20*
Drawn

144   *ct* Murray   *b* Moss   90

145–8   0*ct*

30   Yorkshire *v* Essex
at Clacton   *August 21, 22, 23*
Drawn

160   *ct* Taylor   *b* Bailey   4
125–8d   *lbw* Knight   1

83   0*ct*
151–7   0*ct*

31   Yorkshire *v* Leicestershire
at Scarborough   *August 24, 26, 27*
Yorkshire won by an innings and 111 runs

337–5d   *not out*   165

124   0*ct*
102   0*ct*

32   Yorkshire *v* Leicestershire
at Leicester   *August 28, 29, 30*
Yorkshire won by 269 runs

250   *b* Spencer   38
221–5d   *b* Spencer   64

133   0*ct*
69   0*ct*

33   Yorkshire *v* MCC
at Scarborough   *August 31, September 1, 2*
Drawn

110   *lbw* Knight   7
265–8   *ct* Andrew
b Gillhouley   75

290   0*ct*

1964

Boycott showed to all in 1964 that he was the most promising player in the country and would be on the cricket scene for some years. By this time he was being compared to Len Hutton. Boycott had the same style and way of accumulating runs.

This proved to be a very successful season for him. He not only scored 2,110 runs at an average of 52·75, hitting six centuries, but also was selected for his first Test match against Australia. This match was marred because he broke a finger whilst fielding in Australia's first innings, and thus missed the second innings and the following Test. By the end of the series, however, Boycott had established himself as a world-class batsman, scoring his maiden Test century at the Oval, 113 in five hours. His aggregate for the four Tests was 291, at an average of 48·50; not bad for his opening Test series.

The season started slowly with mediocre scores for MCC, but by the end of May Boycott was in fine form scoring hundreds against Middlesex, Lancashire, Leicestershire, the Australians (twice) and Gloucestershire, the last providing him with his highest score of the year, 177 which included 2 sixes and 23 fours in 340 minutes.

Boycott was involved in ten century partnerships, two of them double centuries: 236 with Taylor for the first wicket against Lancashire, and an unbroken stand of 205 for the fourth wicket with Sharpe against Leicestershire.

His only duck of the season came at Worcester where he was dismissed third ball by England fast bowler Jack Flavell. Worcestershire later proved to be the county he had most trouble with.

At the end of the season he was selected for his first tour abroad, to South Africa.

34 Yorkshire _v_ MCC
at Lord's
April 29, 30, May 1
Drawn

257 _b_ Barber 36

212–9d 0ct
8–0 0ct

35 MCC _v_ Surrey
at Lord's _May 2, 4, 5_
Drawn

210 _b_ Sydenham 7
183–1d _lbw_ Sydenham 4

200–9d 0ct
193–7 0ct

36 Yorkshire _v_ Essex
at Hull _May 6, 7, 8_
Yorkshire won by 7 wickets

167 _ct_ Edmeades _b_ Hobbs 19
146–3 _ct_ Hilton _b_ Smith 77

206 0ct
106 1ct (Barker _b_ Illingworth)

37   Yorkshire *v* **Kent**
at Bradford   *May 9, 11, 12*
Kent won by 14 runs

102–3d   *not out*   53
200   *ct* Cowdrey
b Underwood   30

249   1*ct* (Denness   *b* Trueman)
67–3d   1*ct* (Richardson   *b* Ryan)

38   Yorkshire *v* **Middlesex**
at Leeds   *May 13, 14, 15*
Yorkshire won by 10 wickets

413   *ct* Clark   *b* Hooker   151
29–0   *not out*   17

309–6d   0*ct*
132   0*ct*

39   Yorkshire *v* **Lancashire**
at Manchester   *May 16, 18, 19*
Drawn

354–3d   *ct* Clayton
b Shuttleworth   131
81–1d   *ct* Clayton   *b* Higgs   46

284–9d   0*ct*
129–7   0*ct*

40   Yorkshire *v* **Worcestershire**
at Worcester   *May 20, 21, 22*
Drawn

177   *lbw* Flavell   0
118–4   *b* Coldwell   7

281–6d   0*ct*

41   MCC *v* **Australians**
at Lord's   *May 23, 25, 26*
Australia won by 9 wickets

229   *ct* Grout   *b* Hawke   63
224   *ct* Grout   *b* McKenzie   17

358–6d   0*ct*
99–1   0*ct*

42   Yorkshire *v* **Leicestershire**
at Leicester   *May 30, June 1, 2*
Drawn

270–3   *not out*   151

127   0*ct*

43   ENGLAND *v* **AUSTRALIA**
1st Test at Nottingham
June 4, 5, 6, 8, 9   Drawn

216–8d   *ct* Simpson
b Corling   48
193–9d   *did not bat*

168   0*ct*
40–2   0*ct*

44   Yorkshire *v* **Glamorgan**
at Leeds   *June 20, 22, 23*
Yorkshire won by an innings and
39 runs

288–9d   *ct* Evans   *b* I. Jones   7

55   0*ct*
194   0*ct*

45   Yorkshire *v* **Surrey**
at Bradford   *June 27, 29, 30*
Drawn

273   *run out*   46
292   *ct* Stewart   *b* Harman   15

358   0*ct*

46   ENGLAND *v* **AUSTRALIA**
3rd Test at Leeds   *July 2, 3, 4, 6*
Australia won by 7 wickets

268   *ct* Simpson   *b* Corling   38
229   *ct* Simpson   *b* Corling   4

389   0*ct*
111–3   0*ct*

47   Yorkshire *v* **Glamorgan**
at Swansea   *July 8, 9, 10*
Yorkshire won by 51 runs

263   *ct* Slade   *b* Pressdee   83
107–5d   *ct* Hughes
b Shepherd   9

116   1*ct* (Wheatley   *b* Wilson)
203   0*ct*

48   Yorkshire *v* **Derbyshire**
at Chesterfield   *July 11, 13, 14*
Drawn

326   *b* Jackson   6

203   0*ct*
176–5   0*ct*   1–0–1–0

49   Yorkshire *v* **Nottinghamshire**
at Scarborough   *July 15, 16, 17*
Yorkshire won by 8 wickets

278   *ct-b* Forbes   75
81–2   *lbw* Gillhouley   1

198   0*ct*   2–1–4–0
160   0*ct*

50   Yorkshire *v* **Northamptonshire**
at Sheffield   *July 18, 20, 21*
Drawn

203   *lbw* Milburn   10
209–7d   *ct* Milburn   *b* Scott   39

176   0*ct*
89–4   0*ct*

51   ENGLAND *v* **AUSTRALIA**
4th Test at Manchester   *July 23, 24, 25, 27, 28*   Drawn

611   *b* McKenzie   58

656   0*ct*   1–0–3–0
4–0   0*ct*

52   Yorkshire *v* **Lancashire**
at Leeds   *August 1, 3, 4*
Yorkshire won by an innings and 131 runs

352   *lbw* Ramadhim   62

101   0*ct*
120   0*ct*

53   Yorkshire *v* **Gloucestershire**
at Sheffield   *August 5, 6, 7*
Drawn

319   *ct* Meyer
b Mortimore   28

127   0*ct*
210   0*ct*

54   Yorkshire *v* **Australians**
at Bradford   *August 8, 10, 11*
Australians won by 81 runs

222   *ct* Simpson   *b* McKenzie   54
241   *ct* Jarman   *b* McKenzie   122

315–7d   1*ct* (Veivers   *b* Close)
229–5d   1*ct* (Booth   *b* Illingworth)

55   ENGLAND *v* **AUSTRALIA**
5th Test at The Oval
August 13, 14, 15, 17, 18
Drawn

182   *b* Hawke   30
381–4   *ct* Redpath
b Simpson   113

379   0*ct*

56   President of MCC's XI *v*
Australians
at Lord's   *August 19, 20, 21*
Drawn

193–9d   *b* Hawke   23
179–7   *ct* Sub (Booth)
b Martin   53

162   0*ct*
258–6d   0*ct*

57   Yorkshire *v* **Surrey**
at The Oval   *August 22, 24, 25*
Surrey won by 57 runs

207   *ct* Storey   *b* Arnold   78
184   *ct* Edrich   *b* Pocock   26

307   0*ct*
141–8d   0*ct*

58   Yorkshire *v* **Warwickshire**
at Harrogate   *August 26, 27, 28*
Drawn

281   *b* Cartwright   68
216–6   *not out*   15

355–7d   0*ct*   1–0–1–0
211–2d   0*ct*   12–3–46–0

59   Yorkshire *v* **Gloucestershire**
at Bristol   *September 2, 3*
Yorkshire won by an innings and 294 runs

425–7d   *ct* Allen
b Graveney   177

47   0*ct*
84   0*ct*

60   An England X I v Sir Frank Worrell's X I
at Lord's   *September 14, 15, 16*   Drawn

208   *ct* Murray   *b* Griffith   13

83–2   0*ct*

1964–65 MCC Tour of South Africa

On Boycott's first tour abroad, he made a significant contribution by scoring over 1,000 runs at an average of 56·75, as well as bowling 94 overs, a lot for an opening batsman who did not bowl regularly. He twice took three wickets in an innings.

The tour started with moderate scores for Boycott but from the fifth match onwards he was unstoppable, being one of England's top scorers. Against Eastern Province he scored 193 not out, sharing in a fourth wicket partnership of 278 with M. J. K. Smith. Boycott followed this with 106 against Western Province and passed fifty in the next two matches, 73 in the first Test at Durban and then 81 against South African Universities. Both matches MCC won by an innings. The next two Tests proved unsuccessful, with low scores on two good pitches where plenty of runs were scored, but the last five games all produced scores of over fifty. He scored 76 not out in his second innings against South Africa in the fourth Test, followed by 114 versus an Invitation X I, which included many of the Test team. Two of his three wickets in this match were among South Africa's best batsmen, namely, Graeme Pollock and Colin Bland. The tour ended with the fifth Test, in which Boycott recorded his first Test century abroad, scoring 117, the highlight of his tour.

MCC finished the tour undefeated, and this proved to be the last time MCC were to tour South Africa, because of political problems.

61   MCC v Rhodesia
at Salisbury   *October 24, 25, 26, 27*
MCC won by 5 wickets

298   *ct* de Caila   *b* Partridge   17
209–5   *b* Partridge   4

281   0*ct*
225   0*ct*

62   MCC v South African Colts
at Benoni   *October 30, 31,*
November 2   Drawn

267   *ct* Macaulay   *b* Tillim   38
241–8   *ct-b* Crookes   53

398   0*ct*
161   1*ct* (MacKay-Coghill
b Hobbs)

63　MCC v Transvaal
at Johannesburg　*November 6, 7, 9*
MCC won by an innings and 82
runs

464–9d　*ct* Carr　*b* Motley　17

125　1*ct* (Fullerton　*b* Titmus)
257　0*ct*

64　MCC v Natal
at Durban　*November 13, 14, 16, 17*
MCC won by 10 wickets

445　*lbw* Goddard　14
19–0　*not out*　8

360–9d　0*ct*
102　0*ct*

65　MCC v Eastern Province
at Port Elizabeth　*November 20,
21, 23*
MCC won by an innings and 150
runs

447–7d　*not out*　193

133　0*ct*
164　0*ct*

66　MCC v Western Province
at Cape Town　*November 27, 28,
30, December 1*　Drawn

441　*b* Budge　106
228–6d　*ct* Ferrandi　*b* Meeding　0

357　0*ct*
158–8　0*ct*

**67　ENGLAND v SOUTH
AFRICA**
1st Test at Durban
December 4, 5, 7, 8
England won by an innings and
104 runs

485–5d　*lbw* Partridge　73

155　0*ct*
226　0*ct*

**68　MCC v South African
Universities**
at Pietermaritzburg
December 12, 14, 15

MCC won by an innings and 112
runs

356　*lbw* Steyn　81

114　1*ct* (Dumbrill　*b* Hobbs)
130　0*ct*

**69　ENGLAND v SOUTH
AFRICA**
2nd Test at Johannesburg
December 23, 24, 26, 28, 29
Drawn

531　*ct* Lindsay　*b* P. Pollock　4

317　0*ct*
336–6　0*ct*　5–3–3–0

**70　ENGLAND v SOUTH
AFRICA**
3rd Test at Cape Town
January 1, 2, 4, 5, 6
Drawn

442　*ct* Barlow　*b* Bromfield　15
15–0　*not out*　1

501–7d　0*ct*
346　0*ct*　20–5–47–3
(G. Pollock bowled, Bland bowled,
Burke *ct* Barber)

71　MCC v Border
at East London　*January 9, 11, 12*
MCC won by 9 wickets

407–5d　*ct* A. Wilkins　*b* Wild　56
54–1　*not out*　23

215　0*ct*
244　1*ct* (Ackerman　*b* Cartwright)

72　MCC v Orange Free State
at Bloemfontein　*January 15, 16, 18*
MCC won by 7 wickets

199–7d　*ct* Richardson
b Macaulay　73
143–3　*ct* Macaulay　*b* Riley　27

170　0*ct*
171–9d　0*ct*

**73　ENGLAND v SOUTH
AFRICA**
4th Test at Johannesburg
January 22, 23, 25, 26, 27
Drawn

384   *ct* Barlow   *b* Partridge   5
153–6   *not out*   76

390–6d   0*ct*   8–1–25–0
307–3d   0*ct*

74   MCC *v* Invitation XI
at Cape Town   *February 5, 6, 8, 9*
Drawn

326   *ct* Gamsy   *b* Botten   114
205–7   *ct* Gamsy   *b* Trimborn   13

437   0*ct*   12–2–36–0
316–7d   1*ct* (Steyn   *b* Cartwright)
21–6–69–3
(Bland   *ct* Allen, G. Pollock
ct Sub (Barrington), Van der
Merwe bowled)

75   ENGLAND *v* SOUTH AFRICA
5th Test at Port Elizabeth
February 12, 13, 15, 16, 17
Drawn

435   *ct* Van der Merwe
b Bromfield   117
29–1   *ct* Waite   *b* Macaulay   7

502   1*ct* (Goddard
b Allen)   26–7–69–1 (Barlow
ct Parfitt)
178   1*ct* (Goddard
b Thomson)   2–0–13–1
(Macaulay   *ct* Titmus)

1965

After a very successful tour of South Africa a lot was expected from Boycott, but unfortunately, he could not produce any sort of form. Just when he was set to get a big score he would be dismissed. It was the only season apart from his first that he did not score a single century. He did collect eleven fifties in scoring 1,447 runs, averaging 35·29.

Boycott scored two nineties – 95 versus Somerset, which included 15 fours, and 92 against Surrey with one six and 9 fours, being dismissed by Ken Barrington. Hampshire are a team Boycott has a low average against, and they accounted for him cheaply, for 0 and 5. In the county match with Kent at Gillingham Boycott shared in two ninety partnerships for the first wicket with Philip Sharpe, the scores being 99 and 94. It was a poor Test season for him, his highest score being 76 against New Zealand.

Boycott's running between the wickets was in question again, and he was run out on four occasions, in the tour match with South Africa being dismissed twice in this manner.

One of his best innings this season was in the Gillette Cup Final: 146 against Surrey.

He did enough to suggest to the selectors that he was capable of recapturing his form on the tour of Australia and New Zealand, for which he was selected.

76   Yorkshire *v* **MCC**
at Lord's   *April 28, 29, 30*
Drawn

194   *ct* Lewis   *b* Allen   46
188–3   *lbw* Allen   22

197   0*ct*   3–1–5–1 (Murray
bowled)

77   Yorkshire *v* **Cambridge
University**
at Cambridge   *May 1, 3*
Yorkshire won by an innings and
66 runs

295–9d   *ct* Hughes
b McLachlan   79

130   1*ct* (P. Close   *b* Nicholson)
99   0*ct*

78   Yorkshire *v* **Gloucestershire**
at Harrogate   *May 5, 6, 7*
Yorkshire won by an innings and
52 runs

191   *run out*   25

74   0*ct*
65   0*ct*

79   Yorkshire *v* **Worcestershire**
at Leeds   *May 15, 17, 18*
Drawn

227   *lbw* Flavell   11

122   0*ct*
70–2   0*ct*   9–6–9–1
(Headley   *ct* Nicholson)

80   Yorkshire *v* **Hampshire**
at Middlesbrough   *May 19, 20*
Hampshire won by 10 wickets

121   *b* Shackleton   0
23   *lbw* White   5

125   0*ct*   5–2–5–0
20–0   0*ct*

81   ENGLAND *v* **NEW
ZEALAND**
1st Test at Birmingham
May 27, 28, 29, 31, June 1
England won by 9 wickets

435   *ct* Dick   *b* Motz   23
96–1   *not out*   44

116   0*ct*
413   0*ct*

82   Yorkshire *v* **New Zealand**
at Bradford   *June 2, 3, 4*
Yorkshire won by an innings and
77 runs

419   *ct* Reid   *b* Taylor   4

134   1*ct* (Taylor   *b* Close)
0·1–0–0–1 (Motz   *ct* Close)
208   1*ct* (Jarvis   *b* Close)

83   Yorkshire *v* **Lancashire**
at Manchester   *June 5, 7, 8*
Drawn

262   *b* Howard   53
111–5   *b* Howard   40

218   0*ct*   3–0–6–0
187   2 *ct* (Sullivan   *b* Wilson,
Higgs   *b* Illingworth)

84   Yorkshire *v* **Glamorgan**
at Swansea   *June 9, 10*
Glamorgan won by 31 runs

96   *ct* A. R. Lewis   *b* Pressdee   18
134   *ct* Walker   *b* Pressdee   21

140   1*ct* (Shepherd   *b* Close)
121   0*ct*

85   Yorkshire *v* **Nottinghamshire**
at Sheffield   *June 12, 14, 15*
Drawn

212   *ct* Millman   *b* Forbes   37
216–9d   *ct* Moore   *b* Corran   2

136   0*ct*
15–2   0*ct*

86   ENGLAND *v* **NEW
ZEALAND**
2nd Test at Lord's   *June 17, 18,
19, 21, 22*
England won by 7 wickets

307   *ct* Dick   *b* Motz   14
218–3   *lbw* Motz   76

175   0ct
347   0ct

87   Yorkshire v Nottinghamshire
at Nottingham   *June 26, 28, 29*
Yorkshire won by 207 runs

320   *lbw* Forbes   30
153–7d   *ct* M. Hill   *b* Moore   59

122   0ct   8–3–15–1 (M. Hill *st*
Binks)
144   0ct

88   Yorkshire v South Africa
at Sheffield   *June 30, July 1, 2*
Drawn

197   *run out*   4
55–3   *run out*   22

266–7d   0ct   4–1–18–0
140–2   0ct   8–2–13–0

89   Yorkshire v Kent
at Gillingham   *July 17, 19, 20*
Yorkshire won by 82 runs

295   *lbw* Dixon   55
173–7d   *ct* Cowdrey
b Dixon   30

204   0ct
182   0ct

90   ENGLAND v SOUTH AFRICA
1st Test at Lord's   *July 22, 23, 24, 26, 27*
Drawn

338   *ct* Barlow   *b* Botten   31
145–7   *ct-b* Dumbrill   28

280   0ct
248   0ct

91   Yorkshire v Gloucestershire
at Lydney   *July 28, 29, 30*
Drawn

160   *ct-b* A. S. Brown   1

87   0ct   6–5–3–0
80–2   0ct

92   Yorkshire v Lancashire
at Sheffield   *July 31, August 2, 3*
Yorkshire won by 7 wickets

194–3d   *ct* Goodwin   *b* Lever   8
56–3   *not out*   31

175   0ct
74   0ct

93   ENGLAND v SOUTH AFRICA
2nd Test at Nottingham
August 5, 6, 7, 9
South Africa won by 94 runs

240   *ct* Lance   *b* P. Pollock   0
224   *b* McKinnon   16

269   0ct
289   0ct   26–10–60–0

94   Yorkshire v Leicestershire
at Leeds   *August 11, 12, 13*
Yorkshire won by 148 runs

300   *b* Spencer   11
192   *ct* Jayasinghe
b Barratt   84

165   0ct
179   1ct (Cotton   *b* Trueman)

95   Yorkshire v Surrey
at The Oval   *August 14, 16, 17*
Drawn

251–5d   *ct* Sydenham
b Barrington   92
175–7   *ct-b* Harman   47

248   2ct (W. Smith   *b* Wilson,
Storey   *b* Wilson)
223–7d   0ct

96   Yorkshire v Essex
at Leyton   *August 18, 19, 20*
Yorkshire won by 7 wickets

228   *ct* Taylor   *b* Edmeades   28
112–3   *ct* Taylor   *b* Knight   28

141   0ct
195   1ct (Fletcher   *b* Trueman)

97 Yorkshire *v* **Middlesex**
at Lord's *August 21, 23, 24*
Drawn

248 *b* Herman 1

154–6 0*ct*

98 Yorkshire *v* **Somerset**
at Taunton *August 25, 26*
Yorkshire won by an innings and
61 runs

240 *run out* 23

89 0*ct*
90 1*ct* (Groves *b* Nicholson)

99 Yorkshire *v* **Somerset**
at Hull *August 28, 30, 31*
Yorkshire won by 142 runs

156 *b* Alley 43
203 *ct-b* Robinson 95

123 0*ct*
94 0*ct*

100 Yorkshire *v* **Derbyshire**
at Scarborough *September 1, 2, 3*
Drawn

307 *ct* Harvey *b* Jackson 64

112 0*ct*

101 Yorkshire *v* **MCC**
at Scarborough *September 11,
13, 14*
Yorkshire won by 7 wickets

312–7d *b* Rumsey 8
184–3 *not out* 88

277 2*ct* (Titmus *b* Illingworth,
Hobbs *b* Illingworth)
214 1*ct* (Titmus *b* Wilson)

1965–66 MCC Tour of Australia and New Zealand

This was the first of four tours to Australia for Boycott. He started
with a splendid 94 against South Australia, a team which he was
always to perform well against. In the first Test against Australia
at Brisbane Boycott scored steadily in both innings, 45 and 63 not
out. In the return match with South Australia he again produced a
score of over fifty, another half century came in the second Test
which was followed by 84 in the Third, in which he shared a first
wicket partnership of 234 with Bob Barber. This was the third
highest partnership by an English first wicket pair against
Australia. His only century of the tour came against a Combined
X I when he scored 156, which included 19 fours in just over four
hours. Boycott only had moderate scores in the final two Tests and
was dismissed by McKenzie on three occasions. His total for the
Test series was 300 runs, which included three fifties.

From Australia the MCC team moved on to New Zealand,
where Boycott did not score many runs, especially in the Test
matches. The four-match tour began with a game against a President's X I at Wellington, where he struck 51. Then followed two
disastrous Tests where scores of 4, 4 and 5 were recorded, a total
of thirteen from three innings. He was dropped for the third Test.

40

102 MCC *v* **South Australia**
at Adelaide *November 12, 13, 15, 16*
MCC won by 6 wickets

310 *ct* Robins *b* Sincock 94
158–4 *did not bat*

103 0*ct*
364 0*ct*

103 MCC *v* **Queensland**
at Brisbane *December 3, 4, 6, 7*
Drawn

452–5d *ct* Allan *b* Veivers 30
123–2d *ct* Grout *b* Allan 0

222 0*ct* 1–1–0–0
315–8 0*ct* 1–1–0–0

104 ENGLAND *v* **AUSTRALIA**
1st Test at Brisbane
December 10, 11, 13, 14, 15
Drawn

280 *b* Philpott 45
186–3 *not out* 63

443–6d 0*ct* 4–0–16–0

105 MCC *v* **South Australia**
at Adelaide *December 23, 24, 27, 28*
MCC won by 6 wickets

444 *ct* Chappell *b* Frost 0
270–4 *b* Sincock 58

459–7d 0*ct* 5–0–21–0
253–4d 1*ct* (Dansie
b Parfitt) 4–0–28–0

106 ENGLAND *v* **AUSTRALIA**
2nd Test at Melbourne
December 30, 31, January 1, 3, 4
Drawn

558 *ct* McKenzie
b Walters 51
5–0 *not out* 5

358 0*ct*
426 0*ct* 9–0–32–2 (Burge
ct Edrich, Veivers *st* Parks)

107 ENGLAND *v* **AUSTRALIA**
3rd Test at Sydney *January 7, 8, 10, 11, 12*
England won by an innings and 93 runs

488 *ct-b* Philpott 84

221 0*ct* 3–1–8–0
174 1*ct* (Cowper *b* Titmus)

108 MCC *v* **Combined XI**
at Hobart *January 22, 24, 25*
Drawn

471–9d *ct* Farrell
b Walters 156

199 0*ct*
273–1 0*ct* 7–0–39–0

109 ENGLAND *v* **AUSTRALIA**
4th Test at Adelaide
January 28, 29, 31, February 1
Australia won by an innings and 9 runs

241 *ct* Chappell *b* Hawke 22
266 *lbw* McKenzie 12

516 0*ct* 7–3–33–0

110 MCC *v* **New South Wales**
at Sydney *February 4, 5, 7, 8*
Drawn

329 *ct* Booth *b* Renneberg 5
472–6 *ct* Thomas *b* Simpson 77

488 1*ct* (Martin
b Allen) 4–0–37–1 (Thomas
bowled)

111 ENGLAND *v* **AUSTRALIA**
5th Test at Melbourne
February 11, 12, 14, 15, 16
Drawn

485–9d *ct* Stackpole
b McKenzie 17
69–3 *lbw* McKenzie 1

543–8d 0*ct*

In New Zealand

112 MCC v President's XI
at Wellington *February 19, 21, 22*
Drawn

359–6d *ct* Sinclair *b* Yuile 51

237 0ct 11–7–14–0
188–7 1ct (Sinclair
b Russell) 16–6–27–1 (Bilby
bowled)

113 ENGLAND v NEW ZEALAND
1st Test at Christchurch
February 25, 26, 28, March 1

Drawn

342 *ct* Petrie *b* Motz 4
201–5d *run out* 4

347 0ct 12–6–30–0
48–8 0ct

114 ENGLAND v NEW ZEALAND
2nd Test at Dunedin *March 4, 5, 7, 8* Drawn

254–8d *b* Bartlett 5

192 2ct (Shrimpton *b* Higgs, Cunis *b* Allen)
147–9 0ct

1966

Due to some deplorable weather throughout the summer, seven of the county matches that Boycott was involved in had to be restricted to 65 overs in the first innings, thus not giving him a chance to reach 2,000 runs.

He started the season in great style, scoring 123 against an MCC side which included d'Oliveira, Hobbs, Mortimore and Cottam, all Test bowlers. His next century did not come until June when Warwickshire were the victims. Variable form all season seemed to plague him but he did manage to score 1,850 runs.

Nottinghamshire provided Boycott with his first instance of scoring a hundred in each innings, but he was dropped several times in the second. This was the last time a Yorkshire player scored a century in each innings for the county. At the Scarborough festival match, T. N. Pearce's XI v West Indies, Boycott scored 20 in an over, the highest amount of runs he has scored in one over. The sequence went 4,6,4,4,2 and he was stumped from the last ball of the over. Rohan Kanhai, not a regular bowler, was the bowler, Boycott's final score being 131, which included one six and 12 fours. His only other century of the year was against Sussex. His 164 was his highest score of the season and also the highest he has scored against the county. In the Roses match with Lancashire he was out for a duck, caught second ball off Peter Lever, the third of his four ducks in the season.

The home Test series with the West Indies did not prove to be one of his best.

115 Yorkshire v MCC
at Lord's *April 30, May 2, 3*
Drawn

281–6d *ct* Smedley
b d'Oliveira 123
254–4d *ct* Mortimore
b Hobbs 68

282–4d 1*ct* (Edrich
b Wilson) 7–3–21–0
206–9 1*ct* (Taylor *b* Nicholson)

116 Yorkshire v Gloucestershire
at Middlesbrough *May 7, 9*
Yorkshire won by 7 wickets

171 *ct* Meyer *b* Windows 23
34–3 *ct* Nicholls
b Mortimore 3

135 0*ct* 5–2–4–0
69 1*ct* (Shepherd *b* Illingworth)

117 Yorkshire v Cambridge University
at Cambridge *May 18, 19, 20*
Yorkshire won by 8 wickets

235–9d *ct* Murray
b Russell 11
96–2 *b* Russell 8

81 1*ct* (Murray *b* Waring)
247 1*ct* (Roopnaraine
b Illingworth)

118 Yorkshire v West Indies
at Bradford *May 25, 26, 27*
Drawn

177–6d *ct* Allan *b* Griffith 40
64–3 *ct* Sobers *b* Hall 14

168 0*ct*

119 Yorkshire v Lancashire
at Leeds *May 28, 30*
Yorkshire won by 10 wickets
(65-over match)

196–9 *b* Higgs 6
6–0 *did not bat*

57 0*ct*
144 1*ct* (D. Lloyd *b* Wilson)

120 Yorkshire v Leicestershire
at Leicester *June 1, 2, 3*
Yorkshire won by 7 wickets

300 *ct* Inman
b Birkenshaw 34
54–3 *b* Savage 10

253 0*ct*
100 0*ct*

121 Yorkshire v Middlesex
at Lord's *June 4, 6, 7*
Drawn (65-over match)

175 *ct* Parfitt *b* Stewart 56
195–6 *ct* Hooker *b* Price 35

190 0*ct*
234–7d 0*ct*

122 Yorkshire v Warwickshire
at Birmingham *June 8, 9, 10*
Yorkshire won by 8 wickets
(65-over match)

242–2 *not out* 136
130–2 *b* Brown 0

223–6 1*ct* (Ibadulla *b* Close)
148 0*ct*

123 Yorkshire v Derbyshire
at Chesterfield *June 11, 13*
Yorkshire won by an innings and
15 runs (65-over match)

258–6 *b* T. Eyre 63

89 0*ct*
154 0*ct*

124 ENGLAND v WEST INDIES
2nd Test at Lord's *June 16, 17,
18, 20, 21* Drawn

355 *ct* Griffith *b* Gibbs 60
197–4 *ct* Allan *b* Griffith 25

269 0*ct*
369–5d 0*ct*

125 Yorkshire v Derbyshire
at Sheffield *June 25, 27, 28*
Yorkshire won by 10 wickets

149 *ct* Page *b* Rhodes 5
2–0 *not out* 0

85 0*ct*
65 0*ct*

126 ENGLAND v WEST INDIES
3rd Test at Nottingham *June 30, July 1, 2, 4, 5*
West Indies won by 139 runs

325 *lbw* Sobers 0
253 *ct* Sobers *b* Griffith 71

235 0*ct*
482–5d 0*ct*

127 Yorkshire v Essex
at Bradford *July 6, 7, 8*
Yorkshire won by 139 runs
(65-over match)

263–8 *lbw* Knight 28
123–3 *ct* Hobbs *b* Bailey 23

125 0*ct*
122 0*ct*

128 Yorkshire v Sussex
at Hove *July 9, 11, 12* Drawn

383–8d *ct* Parks *b* A. Buss 164
276–9d 1*ct* (M. Buss *b* Wilson)
223–4 0*ct*

129 Yorkshire v Northamptonshire
at Leeds *July 13, 14, 15*
Northamptonshire won by 66 runs

175 *b* Crump 2
123 *ct* Watts *b* Crump 6

174 0*ct*
190 0*ct*

130 Yorkshire v Nottinghamshire
at Sheffield *July 16, 18, 19*
Yorkshire won by 229 runs
(65-over match)

234–9 *run out* 103
243–4d *ct* Murray *b* Taylor 105

163–8 0*ct*
85 0*ct*

131 Yorkshire v Middlesex
at Sheffield *July 23, 25, 26*
Yorkshire won by 120 runs

214 *ct* Clifton *b* Price 4
240 *run out* 53

220 1*ct* (Latchman *b* Nicholson)
114 0*ct*

132 Yorkshire v Nottinghamshire
at Worksop *July 27, 28, 29*
Yorkshire won by 10 wickets

332–8d *ct* Swetman *b* Forbes 25
9–0 *did not bat*

204 0*ct*
134 0*ct*

133 Yorkshire v Lancashire
at Manchester *July 30, August 1, 2*
Yorkshire won by 12 runs
(one-innings match)

146–7d *ct* Worsley *b* Lever 0
1–0 0*ct*
133 0*ct*

134 ENGLAND v WEST INDIES
4th Test at Leeds *August 4, 5, 6, 8*
West Indies won by an innings and 55 runs

240 *ct* Holford *b* Hall 12
205 *ct* Hendricks *b* Lashley 14

500–9d 0*ct*

135 Yorkshire v Surrey
at Bradford *August 13, 15, 16*
Surrey won by 21 runs (65-over match)

115 *ct* Stewart *b* Jefferson 11
151 *ct* Edwards *b* Jefferson 5

189–9   1*ct* (Smith   *b* Illingworth)
98   1*ct* (Smith   *b* Close)

136   ENGLAND *v* WEST INDIES
5th Test at The Oval   *August 18, 19, 20, 22*
England won by an innings and 34 runs

527   *b* Hall   4

268   0*ct*
225   0*ct*

137   Yorkshire *v* Warwickshire
at Hull   *August 24, 25, 26*
Warwickshire won by 3 wickets

197   *ct* Allan   *b* Bannister   12
101   *b* Cartwright   52

193   0*ct*
109–7   0*ct*

138   Yorkshire *v* Surrey
at The Oval   *August 27, 29, 30*
Drawn

143   *ct* Edwards   *b* Arnold   0
108–5   *not out*   44

150   0*ct*

139   Yorkshire *v* Kent
at Harrogate   *August 31, September 1, 2*
Yorkshire won by 24 runs

210   *ct* Ealham   *b* Brown   80
109   *ct* Knott   *b* Underwood   9

119   0*ct*
176   0*ct*

140   T. N. Pearce's XI *v* West Indies
at Scarborough   *September 3, 5, 6*
T. N. Pearce's XI won by 2 wickets

300–5d   *st* Hendricks   *b* Kanhai   131
277–8   *b* Hall   65

234   0*ct*
342–8d   0*ct*

141   An England XI *v* Rest of the World XI
at Scarborough   *September 7, 8, 9*
England XI won by 5 wickets

257   *ct* Thomas   *b* Mushtaq Mohammed   33
301–5   *b* Nadkarni   51

289–6d   0*ct*
266–8d   0*ct*

142   Yorkshire *v* MCC
at Scarborough   *September 10, 12, 13*
MCC won by 83 runs

117   *ct* Griffith   *b* Underwood   17
159   *b* Palmer   10

252–9d   0*ct*
107–2   0*ct*

1967

1967 saw Boycott at his best, even if administrators and spectators did not always agree. In the first Test against India at Headingley, his home ground, he produced a mammoth innings which brought him his highest test score of 246 not out, the top score in an England–India rubber. He hit 29 fours and one six off 555 balls in 573 minutes. The first hundred took him 300 minutes. He shared in three different hundred partnerships, with Barrington, Graveney and d'Oliveira, the highest being 252 with d'Oliveira for the fourth wicket. It was a long innings that the selectors considered unnecessarily slow. The selectors had called for a positive approach, and reacted strongly by dropping Boycott as a disciplinary measure. Over the whole Test series he topped the averages with 138·50.

In the county matches Boycott scored well, but did suffer the only 'pair' in his first-class career against Kent at Bradford, where Norman Graham claimed his wicket in both innings. In the second innings he was out first ball. He opened both the batting and bowling against Nottinghamshire and Derbyshire, although the reasons for him bowling were (against Nottinghamshire) to give away quick runs for a declaration, and (against Derbyshire) to help bowl out time for a draw.

During the season Boycott scored a second double hundred – 220 not out against Northamptonshire. His only other century of the season was 102 against Glamorgan, which included 16 fours.

143   Yorkshire v MCC
at Lord's   *April 29, May 1, 2*
Yorkshire won by 157 runs

302–9d   *ct* Steele
b Mortimore   45
201–5d   *ct* Johnson
b I. Jones   9

157   0*ct*
187   0*ct*   4–0–15–0

144   Yorkshire v Glamorgan
at Harrogate   *May 3, 4, 5*
Drawn

217–5d   *ct* Rees
b Shepherd   102

130   0*ct*
41–2   0*ct*

145   Yorkshire v Kent
at Bradford   *May 6, 8, 9*   Drawn

40   *b* Graham   0
13–2   *ct* Knott   *b* Graham   0
94–4d   0*ct*

146   Yorkshire v Worcestershire
at Hull   *May 10, 11, 12*
Yorkshire won by 5 wickets

225   *lbw* Flavell   6
37–5   *ct* Headley   *b* Flavell   4

187   0*ct*
74   0*ct*

147   Yorkshire v Nottinghamshire
at Bradford   *May 20, 22, 23*
Yorkshire won by 5 wickets

62–3d   *ct* Swetman   *b* Forbes   0
150–5   *ct* Hassan   *b* Taylor   24

159–9d   0*ct*
52–0d   0*ct*   6–0–25–0

148   Yorkshire *v* Worcestershire
at Kidderminster   *May 31, June 1, 2*
Yorkshire won by an innings and 2 runs

318–4d   lbw D'Oliveira   60

119   1*ct* (Coldwell   *b* Trueman)
197   0*ct*

149   Yorkshire *v* Middlesex
at Lord's   *June 3, 5, 6*
Middlesex won by an innings and 58 runs

163   *b* Titmus   24
146   *b* Latchman   6

367–7d   0*ct*

150   ENGLAND *v* INDIA
1st Test at Leeds   *June 8, 9, 10, 12, 13*
England won by 6 wickets

550–4d   *not out*   246
126–4   *did not bat*

164   0*ct*
510   0*ct*

151   Yorkshire *v* Gloucestershire
at Bristol   *June 17, 19, 20*
Yorkshire won by 9 wickets

227–7d   *lbw* Allen   20
193–1   *not out*   98

356–8d   1*ct* (Mortimore   *b* Illingworth)
63–1d   0*ct*

152   Yorkshire *v* Northamptonshire
at Sheffield   *June 21, 22, 23*
Yorkshire won by an innings and 116 runs

388–5d   *not out*   220

173   0*ct*
99   0*ct*

153   Yorkshire *v* Leicestershire
at Leicester   *July 5, 6*
Yorkshire won by an innings and 123 runs

380   *ct* Lock   *b* Matthews   59

161   0*ct*
96   0*ct*

154   Yorkshire *v* Derbyshire
at Chesterfield   *July 8, 10, 11*
Drawn

310   *lbw* Jackson   57

346–7d   0*ct*
125–5   1*ct* (D. Smith   *b* Old)
4–1–10–1 (Taylor   *ct* Close)

155   ENGLAND *v* INDIA
3rd Test at Birmingham
July 13, 14, 15
England won by 132 runs

298   *st* Engineer   *b* Bedi   25
203   *b* Subramanya   6

92   0*ct*
277   2*ct* (Wadekar
b Illingworth, Chandrasekhar
b Close)

156   Yorkshire *v* Surrey
at The Oval   *July 22, 24, 25*
Surrey won by an innings and 8 runs

178   *ct* Barrington   *b* Storey   34
209   *ct* Stewart   *b* Pocock   74

395–8d   1*ct* (W. Smith
b Illingworth)

157   Yorkshire *v* Hampshire
at Bournemouth   *July 29, August 1*
Hampshire won by 6 wickets

179   *lbw* Sainsbury   90
39–4d   *b* Shackleton   10

90–5d   0*ct*
129–4   0*ct*

158 Yorkshire *v* **Pakistan**
at Leeds   *August 2, 3, 4*
Drawn

414–3d   *b* Intikhab   128

150   1*ct* (Nasim-ul-Ghani
b Hutton)
38–0   0*ct*

159 Yorkshire *v* **Lancashire**
at Sheffield   *August 5, 7, 8*
Drawn

207   *lbw* Statham   0
75–4   *ct* Pullar   *b* Lloyd   54

183   0*ct*
206–6d   0*ct*

160 Yorkshire *v* **Warwickshire**
at Birmingham   *August 16, 17, 18*
Drawn

238   *b* Cartwright   57
145   *ct* A. Smith   *b* Cook   14

242   0*ct*
133–5   0*ct*

161 Yorkshire *v* **Essex**
at Scarborough   *August 19, 21, 22*
Essex won by 9 runs

214   *ct* Boyce   *b* Hobbs   83
109   *b* Boyce   3

87   0*ct*
245   1*ct* (Taylor   *b* Illingworth)

162 ENGLAND *v* **PAKISTAN**
2nd Test at Nottingham
August 10, 11, 12, 14, 15
England won by 10 wickets

252–8d   *b* Asif   15
3–0   *not out*   1

140   0*ct*
114   0*ct*

163 Yorkshire *v* **Warwickshire**
at Middlesbrough   *August 30, 31,*
September 1
Yorkshire won by 229 runs

250   *ct* Amiss   *b* Cartwright   1
197–5d   *st* A. Smith
b Ibadulla   86

148   0*ct*
70   0*ct*

164 T. N. Pearce's XI *v* **Pakistan**
at Scarborough   *September 2, 4, 5*
Drawn

310–7d   *b* Salahuddin   58
144–6   *ct* Niaz   *b* Butt   29

365–7d   0*ct*   8–2–27–1 (Burki
bowled)
141–9d   0*ct*

165 Yorkshire *v* **Gloucestershire**
at Harrogate   *September 6, 7*
Yorkshire won by an innings and
76 runs

309   *b* Bissex   74

134   0*ct*
99   0*ct*

166 Yorkshire *v* **MCC**
at Scarborough   *September 9, 11, 12*
Yorkshire won by 39 runs

145   *ct* Prideaux   *b* Rumsey   2
221   *lbw* Hobbs   86

132   0*ct*
195   0*ct*

1967–68 MCC Tour of the West Indies

The West Indies seemed to suit Geoff Boycott. In a successful tour he scored 1,154 runs, averaging 82·42 from sixteen innings, and was England's top run getter. Ten of the sixteen innings were scores of fifty or more, including four hundreds. The tour started with a score of 135 against the President's XI at Bridgetown, in which Boycott shared in a second wicket partnership of 249 with Colin Cowdrey. The first Test produced a high scoring match in which Boycott got 68. The second Test proved his worst match of the whole tour, with 17 and 0. After this he had an amazing run of 165, 243 and 90. His highest score of the tour was 243 against Barbados, the most successful Island in the West Indies, who had such Test bowlers as Sobers, Holder, Holford and Shepherd. The innings contained one six and 38 fours, and there were three hundred partnerships, with Edrich, Milburn and d'Oliveira. In the fourth Test at Port-of-Spain. Boycott scored two half centuries, 62 and 80 not out, helping England to an easy win. Against Guyana he knocked up scores of 60 and 50 not out, and in the final match of the tour, the fifth Test, he scored his only Test century, 116. The total of Test runs scored was 463, averaging 66·14 and in his last six innings he totalled 398 from four completed innings. MCC went through the tour undefeated.

167   MCC v President's XI
at Bridgetown   *January 3, 4, 5, 6*
Drawn

365   *run out*   135
94–2   *did not bat*

435–9d   1ct (Fredericks
b Barrington)
116–1d   0ct

168   MCC v Trinidad
at Port of Spain   *January 9, 10, 11, 12*   Drawn

207   ct Smart   *b* Rodriguez   22
188–6   *did not bat*

321   0ct   8–3–9–1
(Rodriguez   *ct* Milburn)
204–3d   0ct   3·3–0–18–1
(Davis *lbw*)

169   ENGLAND v WEST INDIES
1st Test at Port of Spain
January 19, 20, 22, 23, 24
Drawn

568   *lbw* Holford   68
363   0ct
243–8   0ct

170   ENGLAND v WEST INDIES
2nd Test at Kingston
February 8, 9, 10, 12, 13
Drawn

376   *b* Hall   17
68–8   *b* Sobers   0
143   0ct
391–9d   0ct

171　MCC *v* **Leeward Islands**
at Antigua　*February 15, 16, 17*
Drawn

362–4d　*ct* Hector
b L. Thomas　165
8–0　*did not bat*

144　0*ct*
323–8d　0*ct*

172　MCC *v* **Barbados**
at Bridgetown　*February 22, 23, 24, 26*
Drawn

578–5d　*ct* Sobers
b Edwards　243

276　0*ct*
161–5　0*ct*　2–2–0–0

173　ENGLAND *v* **WEST INDIES**
3rd Test at Bridgetown
February 29, March 1, 2, 4, 5
Drawn

449　*lbw* Sobers　90

349　0*ct*
284–6　0*ct*

174　MCC *v* **Windward Islands**
at St. Lucia　*March 8, 9, 11*
Drawn

215　*ct* Findlay
b Charlemagne　4
34–3　*ct* Findlay　*b* Laurent　12

165　0*ct*

175　ENGLAND *v* **WEST INDIES**
4th Test at Port of Spain
March 14, 15, 16, 18, 19
England won by 7 wickets

414　*ct* Nurse　*b* Rodriguez　62
215–3　*not out*　80

526–7d　0*ct*
92–2d　0*ct*

176　MCC *v* **Guyana**
at Georgetown　*March 21, 22, 23*
MCC won by 10 wickets

207　*run out*　60
119–0　*not out*　50

163　0*ct*
160　0*ct*

177　ENGLAND *v* **WEST INDIES**
5th Test at Georgetown
March 28, 29, 30, April 1, 2, 3
Drawn

371　*ct* Murray　*b* Hall　116
206–9　*b* Gibbs　30

414　0*ct*
264　1*ct* (Murray　*b* Pocock)

1968

A back injury reduced the season for Boycott but he did score 1,487 runs at an average of 64·65 even though it rained for the first part of May. It was the first time that he topped the national averages. He also carried his bat for Yorkshire against Leicestershire, another first for him, his score of 114 being from a Yorkshire total of 297.

Seven centuries were scored during the season, against Sussex, Leicestershire twice, Warwickshire, Gloucestershire, MCC and for an England XI against a Rest of the World XI, in which he missed a century in each innings by only seven runs when he gave a return catch to bowler Clive Lloyd. The highest score was 180 not out against Warwickshire, which included 3 sixes, one five and 17 fours. He shared a fifth wicket partnership of 142 with Brian Close. This was followed in the next match by 125 against Gloucestershire, including 10 fours, and for whom Mike Procter got his wicket in each innings.

On the Test scene, Boycott again did not score a hundred in the series, scoring only 162 runs from five innings. His best batting display of the summer was for Yorkshire against MCC at the Scarborough festival, where he scored a flawless 102 not out, which included one six and 15 fours.

With Boycott's contribution Yorkshire won the County Championship for the third consecutive season.

178 Yorkshire v MCC
at Lord's   *April 27, 29, 30*
Drawn

did not bat

309–6d   0ct

179 Yorkshire v Cambridge University
at Cambridge   *May 1, 2, 3*
Yorkshire won by an innings and 66 runs

268   *ct* Ponniah   *b* Cottrell   17

100   1ct (Taylor   *b* Nicholson)
102   0ct

180 Yorkshire v Hampshire
at Harrogate   *May 4, 5, 6*
Drawn

41–2   *ct* White   *b* Cottam   5

122   0ct   1–0–5–0

181 Yorkshire v Somerset
at Taunton   *May 9, 10*
Drawn

0–0d   *not out*   0
2–0   *not out*   2

67–3d   0ct
107–4d   0ct

182 Yorkshire v Sussex
at Bradford   *May 11, 13, 14*
Drawn

242–5d   *ct* Graves   *b* Greig   100

96–7   0ct

183 Yorkshire v Leicestershire
at Leicester   *May 15, 16, 17*
Yorkshire won by an innings and 14 runs

288–8d   *ct* Norman
b Marner   132

128   1ct (Knight   *b* Wilson)
146   0ct

184 MCC v Australians
at Lord's   *May 18, 20, 21*
Drawn

142   *ct* Redpath   *b* Connolly   13
56–1   *lbw* Connolly   6

246–9d   0ct

185 Yorkshire v Warwickshire
at Middlesbrough   *May 22, 23, 24*
Yorkshire won by an innings and 42 runs

308–4d   *not out*   180

129   0ct
137   0ct   1–0–5–0

186   Yorkshire v Gloucestershire
at Bristol   *May 29, 30, 31*
Drawn

266   *b* Procter   125
93–9   *lbw* Procter   13

163   0*ct*
238   0*ct*

187   Yorkshire v Lancashire
at Leeds   *June 1, 3, 4*
Yorkshire won by an innings and
56 runs

348   *lbw* Statham   36

176   0*ct*
116   0*ct*

188   ENGLAND v AUSTRALIA
1st Test at Manchester   *June 6, 7,
8, 10, 11*
Australia won by 159 runs

165   *ct* Jarman   *b* Cowper   35
253   *ct* Redpath   *b* McKenzie   11

357   1*ct* (Lawry   *b* Barber)
220   0*ct*

189   Yorkshire v Leicestershire
at Sheffield   *June 15, 17, 18*
Yorkshire won by 143 runs

297   *not out*   114
228–5d   *ct* Tolchard   *b* Knight   5

239   0*ct*
143   1*ct* (Booth   *b* Trueman)

190   ENGLAND v AUSTRALIA
2nd Test at Lord's
June 20, 21, 22, 24, 25
Drawn

351–7d   *ct* Sheahan
b McKenzie   49

78   0*ct*
127–4   0*ct*

191   Yorkshire v Gloucestershire
at Bradford   *June 26, 27, 28*
Drawn

219   *ct* Meyer   *b* Procter   2
1–0   *not out*   0

143   1*ct* (Meyer   *b* Illingworth)

192   Yorkshire v Australians
at Sheffield   *June 29, July 1, 2*
Yorkshire won by an innings and
69 runs

355–9d   *ct* Taber   *b* Chappell   86

148   0*ct*
138   0*ct*   1–1–0–0

193   Yorkshire v Glamorgan
at Sheffield   *July 6, 8, 9*
Glamorgan won by 103 runs

95–5d   *b* Wheatley   60
101   *ct* E. Jones   *b* Wheatley   0

244   1*ct* (R. Davis   *b* Illingworth)
55–5d   0*ct*

194   ENGLAND v AUSTRALIA
3rd Test at Birmingham
July 11, 12, 13, 15, 16
Drawn

409   *lbw* Gleeson   36
142–3d   *ct* Taber   *b* Connolly   31

222   0*ct*
68–1   0*ct*

195   Yorkshire v MCC
at Scarborough   *September 11,
12, 13*
Drawn

199   *ct* Prideaux   *b* Buss   25
329–4d   *not out*   102

322–9d   0*ct*
158–9   1*ct* (Buss   *b* Wilson)

**196   An England XI v Rest of the
World XI**
at Scarborough   *September 4, 5, 6*
England won by 133 runs

274–8d   *ct-b* Lloyd   93
204–5d   *not out*   115

174   1*ct* (Nurse   *b* Close)
171   2*ct* (Barlow   *b* Trueman,
Nurse   *b* Hobbs)

197 An England XI _v_ An England Under 25 XI
at Scarborough _September 7, 9, 10_ Tied

312–8d _b_ Underwood 63
190–3d _ct_ Pocock _b_ Fletcher 31

320–9d 0_ct_
182 0_ct_

1969

With the tour to South Africa during the winter of 1968–69 being cancelled Boycott took the opportunity to rest a back injury and to change from spectacles to contact lenses, with which he began the 1969 season.

He had only moderate success, scoring 1,283 runs from 39 innings and averaging 38·87, the last time he was to average under fifty for eleven seasons. He carried his bat for the second time in his career against Warwickshire at Bradford, scoring 53 out of 119 in a close game where Yorkshire were dismissed for a mere 115 in the second innings, needing only six more runs to win. His fifty came in 182 minutes and included 5 fours. For the third time he opened both the batting and bowling against Northamptonshire.

During the season he collected five noughts, the highest number he ever got in a single season. Three of these were in Test matches, two versus New Zealand and one against the West Indies.

Boycott performed well during the Test series, although he did play another slow innings in the Lord's Test, scoring 106. Many thought that he might be disciplined again as in 1967, but no action was taken, possibly allowing him time to change from spectacles to contact lenses. There were two other hundreds in 1969, another against the West Indies, of 128, his highest score of the season, and 105 not out against Somerset, which included fourteen fours and took nearly four hours.

198 Yorkshire _v_ MCC
at Lords _April 26, 28, 29_
MCC won by 7 wickets

250–5d _ct_ Amiss _b_ Higgs 6
132–8d _lbw_ Ward 0

195–5d 1_ct_ (Amiss _b_ Wilson)
188–3 1_ct_ (Milburn _b_ Close)

199 Yorkshire _v_ Oxford University
at Oxford _April 30, May 1_
Yorkshire won by 10 wickets

227 _st_ S. Westley _b_ Walsh 52
16–0 _did not bat_

90 0_ct_
152 0_ct_ 2–1–4–0

200   Yorkshire *v* **Glamorgan**
at Swansea   *May 3, 5, 6*   Drawn

265   *ct* E. Jones   *b* Williams   68
127–5d   *ct* Shepherd
b Majid Khan   5

225–9d   0*ct*
109–9   0*ct*

201   Yorkshire *v* **Warwickshire**
at Bradford   *May 17, 19, 20*
Warwickshire won by 5 runs

119   *not out*   53
115   *ct* Amiss   *b* Blenkiron   5

167   1*ct* (Cartwright   *b* Wilson)
72   0*ct*

202   Yorkshire *v* **Nottinghamshire**
at Nottingham   *May 21, 22, 23*
Drawn

159–8d   *ct* Frost   *b* White   42
119–2d   *not out*   37

72–9d   0*ct*
83–3   0*ct*   2–1–1–0

203   Yorkshire *v* **Lancashire**
at Manchester   *May 24, 26, 27*
Drawn

did not bat

243–9d   0*ct*

204   Yorkshire *v* **West Indies**
at Sheffield   *May 28, 29, 30*
Drawn

181–4d   *b* Holder   0

25–0   0*ct*

205   MCC *v* **West Indies**
at Lord's   *May 31, June 2, 3*
Drawn

200   *ct* Fredericks   *b* Holder   20
127–0   *retired hurt*   49

285   0*ct*

206   ENGLAND *v* **WEST INDIES**
1st Test at Manchester   *June 12, 13, 14, 16, 17*
England won by 10 wickets

413   *lbw* Shepherd   128
12–0   *not out*   1

147   0*ct*
275   0*ct*

207   Yorkshire *v* **Gloucestershire**
at Middlesbrough   *June 18, 19*
Yorkshire won by an innings and 53 runs

202   *ct-b* Bissex   84

41   0*ct*
108   0*ct*

208   Yorkshire *v* **Essex**
at Sheffield   *June 21, 23, 24*
Drawn

288–6d   *ct* Irvine   *b* East   49
56–3   *b* Hobbs   27

139   0*ct*

209   ENGLAND *v* **WEST INDIES**
2nd Test at Lord's   *June 26, 27, 28, 30, July 1*
Drawn

344   *ct* Findlay   *b* Shepherd   23
295–7   *ct* Butcher
b Shillingford   106

380   0*ct*
295–9d   0*ct*

210   Yorkshire *v* **Hampshire**
at Bournemouth   *July 5, 7, 8*
Drawn

179   *ct* Richards   *b* Cottam   12
89–4   *ct* Sainsbury   *b* Cottam   1

151   0*ct*
230–7d   0*ct*

211 ENGLAND v WEST INDIES
3rd Test at Leeds   *July 10, 11, 12, 14, 15*
England won by 30 runs

223   *lbw* Sobers   12
240   *ct* Findlay   *b* Sobers   0

161   0*ct*
272   0*ct*

212 Yorkshire v Derbyshire
at Chesterfield   *July 19, 21, 22*
Drawn

214   *ct* Taylor   *b* Eyre   35
170–6   *lbw* E. Smith   8

344   1*ct* (Taylor   *b* Wilson)

213 ENGLAND v NEW ZEALAND
1st Test at Lord's   *July 24, 25, 26, 28*
England won by 230 runs

190   *ct* Congdon   *b* Motz   0
340   *ct* Turner   *b* Pollard   47

169   0*ct*
131   0*ct*

214 Yorkshire v Lancashire
at Sheffield   *August 2, 4, 5*
Drawn

290–8d   *lbw* Lever   80
64–6   *ct-b* Higgs   17

171   1*ct* (D. Lloyd   *b* Wilson)
183   1*ct* (C. Lloyd   *b* Wilson)

215 ENGLAND v NEW ZEALAND
2nd Test at Nottingham
August 7, 8, 9, 11, 12
Drawn

451–8d   *b* Motz   0

294   0*ct*
66–1   0*ct*

216 Yorkshire v Somerset
at Leeds   *August 16, 18, 19*
Drawn

140   *lbw* Palmer   11
233–6d   *not out*   105

139   1*ct* (Galley   *b* Hutton)
141–7   0*ct*

217 ENGLAND v NEW ZEALAND
3rd Test at The Oval
August 21, 22, 23, 25, 26
England won by 8 wickets

242   *b* Cunis   46
138–2   *b* Cunis   8

150   0*ct*
229   0*ct*

218 Yorkshire v Leicestershire
at Leicester   *August 27, 28, 29*
Yorkshire won by 4 wickets

225   *ct* Norman   *b* Barratt   49
127–6   *b* McKenzie   56

203–7d   0*ct*
148   2*ct* (Marner   *b* Wilson, Birkenshaw   *b* Wilson)

219 Yorkshire v Northamptonshire
at Hull   *August 30, September 1, 2*
Northamptonshire won by 10 wickets

200   *ct* Johnson   *b* Crump   18
130   *ct* Willey   *b* Breakwell   20

326–7d   0*ct*
8–0   0*ct*   0·3–0–8–0

220 Yorkshire v Sussex
at Hove   *September 3, 4, 5*
Sussex won by 6 wickets

188   *retired hurt*   3
180   *absent hurt*

195   0*ct*
174–4   0*ct*

1969–70 MCC Tour of Ceylon

As there was no full tour abroad, MCC visited Ceylon to play some one day games and one first-class match against the national side. It was a very undistinguished game for Boycott, who scored only seven runs from two innings, with one duck.

221   MCC v **Ceylon**
at Colombo Oval   *February 20, 21, 22, 23*
MCC won by 173 runs

132   *b* Kehelgamuwa   0
302–7d   *ct* Heyn   *b* Fuard   7

134   0*ct*   3–1–5–0
127   0*ct*

1970

There was a big improvement in Boycott's play compared with the previous season. He scored 2,051 runs, averaging over 50, with a top score of 260 not out against Essex at Colchester, which was his highest score in England. It contained 27 fours in 428 minutes, and during it Boycott shared in two partnerships of over a hundred, 144 with Sharpe and 212 with Hampshire. During the season Boycott hit four centuries and two nineties, including his first 99, against Derbyshire at Chesterfield.

As South Africa had been banned from playing Test cricket, their proposed tour was cancelled and a Rest of the World XI took their place. It contained World-class players from all seven countries, including South Africa. Boycott played in two of the five tests, scoring 260 runs with a top score of 157 at The Oval, against such bowlers as Procter, McKenzie, Sobers, Intikhab and Barlow.

In the two Roses matches Boycott scored well, although being dismissed first ball by Peter Lever in the second match. In the first innings he was out for 98, caught behind by Farokh Engineer.

The Scarborough Festival provided him with plenty of runs, including a fine century for an England eleven versus an England under 25 eleven. He scored 147 not out, sharing in a third wicket partnership of 157 with Keith Fletcher.

Boycott was an automatic choice when the selectors picked the party to tour Australia and New Zealand at the end of the season.

222 Yorkshire v Derbyshire
at Bradford   *May 2, 4*
Yorkshire won by an innings and
20 runs

238   *lbw* Ward   13

107   1*ct* (Buxton   *b* Wilson)
111   0*ct*

**223 Yorkshire v Cambridge
University**
at Cambridge   *May 6, 7, 8*
Yorkshire won by 170 runs

295–7d   *b* Wilkin   50
153–1d   *ct* Carling   *b* Wilkin   18

149   0*ct*
129   0*ct*

224 Yorkshire v Surrey
at The Oval   *May 9, 11, 12*
Drawn

186   *ct* Edwards   *b* Roope   31

306–7d   0*ct*

225 Yorkshire v Glamorgan
at Middlesbrough   *May 16, 18, 19*
Glamorgan won by 5 wickets

124   *ct* E. Jones   *b* Nash   11
159   *st* E. Jones   *b* R. Davis   68

161   0*ct*
124–5   0*ct*

226 Yorkshire v Lancashire
at Leeds   *May 23, 25, 26*
Lancashire won by 10 wickets

121   *ct* Engineer
b Shuttleworth   4
281   *ct* Engineer   *b* Lever   71

381   0*ct*
25–0   0*ct*

227 Yorkshire v Gloucestershire
at Bradford   *June 3, 4, 5*
Gloucestershire won by 9 wickets

267   *b* Procter   0
152   *ct* Meyer   *b* Bissex   45

304   0*ct*
116–1   0*ct*

228 Yorkshire v Hampshire
at Sheffield   *June 6, 8, 9*
Yorkshire won by an innings and 5
runs

288–9d   *ct* Livingstone
b Cottam   16

144   0*ct*
139   1*ct* (Sainsbury   *b* Wilson)

229 Yorkshire v Warwickshire
at Birmingham   *June 20, 22, 23*
Yorkshire won by 3 wickets

203   *ct* Ibadulla   *b* Brown   5
181–7   *lbw* Brown   3

120   1*ct* (Abberley   *b* Wilson)
263   0*ct*

230 Yorkshire v Nottinghamshire
at Sheffield   *June 24, 25, 26*
Drawn

252   *ct* Bolus   *b* Sobers   16
189–7d   *ct* Smedley   *b* Sobers   2

106   1*ct* (Smedley   *b* Wilson)
259–6   0*ct*

231 Yorkshire v Leicestershire
at Sheffield   *July 1, 2, 3*   Drawn

131   *ct* Steele   *b* Marner   44
187–2   *not out*   82

184   0*ct*
265–3d   0*ct*

232 Yorkshire v Derbyshire
at Chesterfield   *July 4, 6, 7*
Yorkshire won by 4 wickets

246–6d   *ct* E. Smith
b Wilkins   99
266–6   *ct* Hall
b Swarbrook   27

307–7d   0*ct*
201–4d   0*ct*

233 Yorkshire v Sussex
at Leeds   *July 11, 13, 14*   Drawn

307–8d   *ct* Parks   *b* Snow   62

175   0*ct*
216–4   0*ct*

234 Yorkshire v Leicestershire
at Leicester   *July 15, 16, 17*
Yorkshire won by 17 runs

242   *ct* R. Tolchard
b McKenzie   11
208   *ct* Steele   *b* Birkenshaw   22

321–9d   0*ct*
112   0*ct*

235 Yorkshire v Kent
at Sheffield   *July 18, 20, 21*
Drawn

349   *ct* Nicholls   *b* Shepherd   148

132   0*ct*
292   0*ct*

236 Yorkshire v Essex
at Colchester   *July 25, 27, 28*
Yorkshire won by an innings and
101 runs

450–4d   *not out*   260

226   1*ct* (Baker   *b* Hutton)
123   0*ct*

**237 ENGLAND v REST OF
THE WORLD**
4th Test at Leeds
July 30, 31, August 1, 3, 4
Rest of the World won by 2 wickets

222   *ct* Murray   *b* Barlow   15
376   *ct* G. Pollock   *b* Barlow   64

376–9d   1*ct* (Barlow   *b* Greig)
226–8   0*ct*

238 Yorkshire v Surrey
at Bradford   *August 8, 10, 11*
Yorkshire won by 5 wickets

244   *run out*   77
122–5   *lbw* Jackman   5

193   1*ct* (Jackman   *b* Cope)
171   0*ct*

**239 ENGLAND v REST OF
THE WORLD**
5th Test at The Oval
August 13, 14, 15, 17, 18
Rest of the World won by 4 wickets

294   *ct* Sobers   *b* Intikhab   24
344   *ct* Barlow   *b* Lloyd   157

355   2*ct* (Procter   *b* Lever,
Intikhab   *b* Lever)
287–6   0*ct*

240 Yorkshire v Middlesex
at Scarborough   *August 19, 20, 21*
Drawn

304–7d   *st* Murray   *b* Jones   64

183–7   0*ct*

241 Yorkshire v Gloucestershire
at Bristol   *August 22, 24, 25*
Drawn

132–3d   *b* Smith   21
62–3   *not out*   52

226–7d   1*ct* (Shepherd   *b* Old)
96–3d   0*ct*

242 Yorkshire v Somerset
at Taunton   *August 26, 27, 28*
Somerset won by 6 wickets

309   *lbw* Cartwright   49
197–8d   *ct-b* Langford   19

303–9d   1*ct* (Clarkson   *b* Cope)
204–4   1*ct* (Virgin   *b* Old)

243 Yorkshire v Lancashire
at Manchester
August 29, 31, September 1
Drawn

282–3d   *ct* Engineer   *b* Lever   98
45–1   *lbw* Lever   0

430–7d   0*ct*
61–1d   0*ct*

244   An England XI v An England Under 25 XI
at Scarborough   *September 2, 3, 4*
England XI won by 7 wickets

156–5d   *ct* Tolchard
b Graves   30
275–3   *not out*   147

240–7d   0ct
189–4d   0ct

245   T. N. Pearce's XI v A Rest of the World XI
at Scarborough
September 5, 7, 8   Drawn

229   *ct* Murray   *b* Ibadulla   22
74–3   *ct* Saeed   *b* Sarfraz   34

253   0ct
321–5d   0ct

246   Yorkshire v MCC
at Scarborough   *September 9, 10, 11*
Yorkshire won by 7 wickets

316–6d   *retired hurt*   65
138–3   *did not bat*

247   0ct
206   0ct

1970–71 MCC Tour of Australia

In Australia in 1970–71 Boycott was at his brilliant best. He started the tour with 173 against South Australia in 330 minutes, which included 19 fours. This was followed by 129 not out against New South Wales, in which he shared in an opening stand of 228 with Brian Luckhurst. In the match against Queensland he scored 124 before retiring hurt, the innings including one six and 14 fours, and recorded another double century stand, this time with John Edrich, totalling 242. Western Australia provided him with another century, 126, and a share in a first-wicket partnership of 215 with Luckhurst. This was his third 200 partnership of the tour. The only state side he did not score a century against was Victoria. Boycott would surely have broken Wally Hammond's record tour aggregate of 1,553 runs had he not fractured his wrist. He was eighteen runs short of Hammond's total at the end of the tour, finishing top of the averages for both the Tests and the tour.

In the Tests he scored 657 runs at an average of 93·85 and topped fifty in seven out of ten innings. His top score was 142 not out at Sydney, which included 12 fours in six hours fifty minutes batting. This innings helped England to a large score and gave captain Ray Illingworth over nine hours to bowl out Australia to win the match. But it was his 77 in the first innings which won him high acclaim. He showed a full range of shots all round the wicket and hit eleven fours before being out to a long hop which he hooked to fielder Gleeson. In the sixth Test at Adelaide Boycott shared in a century partnership in both innings with John Edrich.

They were only the third English pair to achieve this feat, the others being Hobbs and Sutcliffe in 1924 and Hutton and Washbrook in 1947. By the end of the tour, Geoff Boycott was voted by the press as the best batsman in the world.

247 MCC v South Australia
at Adelaide
October 30, 31, November 1, 2
Drawn

451–9d *ct* Blundell
b McCarthy   173
235–4 *ct* Woodcock
b Jenner   29

649–9d   0*ct*

248 MCC v Victoria
at Melbourne
November 6, 7, 8, 9
Victoria won by 6 wickets

142 *ct* Redpath *b* Thomson   4
341 *ct* Jordan *b* Thomson   40

304–8d   0*ct*
180–4   0*ct*   0.4–0–1–0

249 MCC v New South Wales
at Sydney
November 13, 14, 15, 16
Drawn

204 *ct* Taber *b* O'Keefe   36
325–1 *not out*   129

410–5d   0*ct*

250 MCC v Queensland
at Brisbane
November 21, 22, 23, 24
Drawn

418–4 *retired hurt*   124

360 1*ct* (Parker *b* Underwood)

251 ENGLAND v AUSTRALIA
1st Test at Brisbane *November 27, 28, 29, December 1, 2* Drawn

464 *ct* Marsh *b* Gleeson   37
39–1 *ct-b* Jenner   16

433 1*ct* (Jenner *b* Shuttleworth)
214   0*ct*

252 MCC v Western Australia
at Perth
December 5, 6, 7, 8
Drawn

258–3d *ct* Chadwick
b Lock   126
256–6 *ct* Marsh *b* Lillee   9

257–5d   0*ct*
285 1*ct* (Inverarity *b* Fletcher)
3–0–23–1 (Chadwick *st* Taylor)

253 ENGLAND v AUSTRALIA
2nd Test at Perth
December 11, 12, 13, 15, 16
Drawn

397 *ct* McKenzie *b* Gleeson   70
287–6d *st* Marsh *b* Gleeson   50

440   0*ct*   1–0–7–0
100–3   0*ct*

254 MCC v South Australia
at Adelaide
December 18, 19, 20, 21
Drawn

238 *not out*   42
336–8 *ct* Cunningham
b Mallett   92

297–2d   0*ct*
338–7d   0*ct*

255 MCC v Combined XI
at Launceston
December 27, 28, 29
Drawn

184–4 *ct* Miller
b Patterson   74

256 ENGLAND v AUSTRALIA
4th Test at Sydney

January 9, 10, 12, 13, 14
England won by 299 runs

332 *ct* Gleeson *b* Connolly 77
319–5d *not out* 142

236 1ct (Stackpole
b Underwood)
116 0ct

257 ENGLAND v AUSTRALIA
5th Test at Melbourne
January 21, 22, 23, 25, 26
Drawn

392 *ct* Redpath *b* Thomson 12
161–0 *not out* 76

493–9d 0ct
169–4d 0ct

258 ENGLAND v AUSTRALIA
6th Test at Adelaide
January 29, 30, February 1, 2, 3
Drawn

470 *run out* 58
233–4d *not out* 119

235 2ct (Gleeson *b* Willis,
Lillee *b* Lever)
328–3 0ct

1971

This was the best-ever season for Geoff Boycott, his form being outstanding and consistent. He scored a total of 2,503 runs, 400 runs more than in any other season and his average was 100·12. This was the first time an Englishman had achieved an average of over 100 in an English season. He was to do it again in 1979. Thirteen hundreds were scored, five fewer than the record eighteen by Denis Compton in 1947.

The first two matches of the season were missed because of the injury sustained in Australia. This was the season that Boycott took over the county captaincy from Brian Close, who moved to Somerset after a dispute with Yorkshire. Thus Boycott fulfilled one of his greatest ambitions, and in his first match he scored a century against Warwickshire, the innings of 110 including 2 sixes, one five and 16 fours. His hundred took him exactly 100 minutes. For the second successive season he made his top score against Essex at Colchester, this time scoring 233 in 6 hours, taking 341 minutes with 14 fours. This meant that in two innings at Colchester he had totalled 493 runs for once out.

During the season he shared in fourteen century partnerships, the highest being 240 with Sharpe against Essex for the first wicket.

In the Test series he performed well against Pakistan, scoring two centuries. Against India he played in only one Test, missing the other two because of a pulled hamstring sustained in the John Player League match with Lancashire.

The final nine innings produced five centuries and two fifties. In the last two matches he scored 138 not out, 84 and 124 not out. During the first of these innings Boycott carried his bat in a 270-minute stay against Warwickshire. The side's score was 232 and his percentage of the Yorkshire total was 59·48. Boycott's score included 18 fours and 2 sixes. In the four innings of the 1971 season against Warwickshire, he scored 379, only being dismissed twice.

Boycott was the last Yorkshire player to score 2,000 runs in a season.

259 Yorkshire *v* Warwickshire
at Middlesbrough   *May 8, 10, 11*
Yorkshire won by 3 wickets

269   *b* Gibbs   61
267–7   *ct* Gibbs
b Jameson   110

303–8d   0*ct*
232–6d   0*ct*

260   Yorkshire *v* Sussex
at Hove   *May 15, 17, 18*   Drawn

378–8d   *ct* Greenidge
b Greig   30

197   0*ct*
107–4   0*ct*

261   Yorkshire *v* Derbyshire
at Chesterfield
May 22, 24, 25
Drawn

344–5d   *ct* Gibbs
b Swarbrook   75

82–5d   0*ct*
28–1   0*ct*

262   Yorkshire *v* Middlesex
at Leeds   *May 26, 27, 28*
Yorkshire won by 8 wickets

200   *run out*   88
213–2   *not out*   112

258   0*ct*
153–7d   1*ct* (Brearley
b Leadbeater)

263   Yorkshire *v* Lancashire
at Manchester
May 29, 31, June 1   Drawn

79   *run out*   9
103–6   *did not bat*

168   0*ct*
75   0*ct*

264   Yorkshire *v* Nottinghamshire
at Leeds   *June 5, 7, 8*
Yorkshire won by an innings and
131 runs

375–5d   *ct* Hassan
b W. Taylor   169

142   0*ct*
102   1*ct* (Sobers   *b* Hampshire)

265   Yorkshire *v* Pakistan
at Bradford   *June 9, 10, 11*   Drawn

422–9d   *b* Intikhab   24

140–5   0*ct*

266   ENGLAND *v* PAKISTAN
2nd Test at Lord's
June 17, 18, 19, 21, 22
Drawn

241–2d   *not out*   121
117–0   *did not bat*

148   0*ct*

267   Yorkshire *v* Essex
at Colchester   *June 23, 24, 25*
Drawn

421–4d *lbw* Hobbs 233

217 0*ct*
230–7 0*ct*

268 Yorkshire *v* **Surrey**
at Sheffield *June 26, 28, 29*
Drawn

209 *b* Pocock 58
83–0 *did not bat*

167 0*ct*
213–6d 1*ct* (Younis
b Nicholson)

269 Yorkshire *v* **Middlesex**
at Lord's *July 3, 5, 6* Drawn

320 *not out* 182
157 *b* Titmus 6

304–5d 0*ct*
22–1 0*ct*

270 ENGLAND *v* **PAKISTAN**
3rd Test at Leeds *July 8, 9, 10,*
12, 13 England won by 25 runs

316 *ct* Wasim Bari
b Intikhab 112
264 *ct* Mushtaq Mohammed
b Asif Masood 13

350 0*ct*
205 0*ct*

271 Yorkshire *v* **Derbyshire**
at Scarborough *July 14, 15, 16*
Drawn

349–7d *ct* Gibbs *b* Russell 133

159 0*ct*
268–8 1*ct* (Wilkins *b* Cope)

272 Yorkshire *v* **Gloucestershire**
at Sheffield *July 17, 19, 20*
Gloucestershire won by 4 wickets

225 *ct-b* Brown 34
251–5d *ct* Mortimore
b Procter 0

276–9d 1*ct* (Meyer *b* Bore)
201–6 0*ct*

273 ENGLAND *v* **INDIA**
1st Test at Lord's
July 22, 23, 24, 26, 27
Drawn

304 *ct* Engineer *b* Abid Ali 3
191 *ct* Wadekar *b*
Venkataraghavan 33

313 0*ct*
145–8 1*ct* (Wadekar *b* Price)

274 Yorkshire *v* **Lancashire**
at Sheffield *July 31, August 1, 2*
Drawn

320–5d *ct* Bond *b* Wood 169
54–0 *did not bat*

277 0*ct*

275 Yorkshire *v* **Leicestershire**
at Bradford *August 21, 23, 24*
Drawn

325–6d *ct* R. Tolchard
b Davison 151

204 0*ct*
53–2 0*ct*

276 Yorkshire *v* **Hampshire**
at Bournemouth
August 25, 26, 27
Hampshire won by 8 wickets

96 *ct* Richards *b* Jesty 40
233 *ct* Gilliat *b* White 111

299 0*ct*
33–2 0*ct*

277 Yorkshire *v* **Surrey**
at The Oval *August 28, 30, 31*
Surrey won by an innings and 12
runs

118 *b* Pocock 14
251 *st* Long *b* Intikhab 66

381 0*ct*

278 Yorkshire v Warwickshire
at Birmingham *September 1, 2, 3*
Warwickshire won by 22 runs

232 *not out* 138
261 *ct* Ibadulla *b* Tidy 84

354–8d 0ct
161 0ct

279 Yorkshire v Northamptonshire
at Harrogate *September 11, 13*
Yorkshire won by an innings and
99 runs

266–2d *not out* 124

61 0ct
106 0ct

1971–72

In 1971–72 Boycott went to South Africa to coach, as there was
no MCC tour. Because of injuries Northern Transvaal invited
Boycott to play and he obliged by scoring a century on his debut. It
took three hours and was reached by hitting two successive sixes.
He became the fourth player to score a century on his debut in
South Africa, having played first-class cricket elsewhere. He is
also the only batsman to score a century on his only appearance in
domestic cricket in South Africa. Northern Transvaal's was also
the lowest innings total to include a century in South Africa.

280 Northern Transvaal v Rhodesia
at Pretoria *February 3, 4, 5*
Rhodesia won by 176 runs

172 *lbw* Kaschula 107
204 *b* Kaschula 41

356–9d 2ct (Procter *b* Lance,
Mitchell *b* Robinson)
196–4d 0ct

1972

Boycott played in only twenty-two innings during the season, and
scored 1,230 runs, averaging 72·35, for the second successive year
being top of the national averages. Ten of the twenty-two innings
were over fifty, and for the first time since joining Yorkshire he
was not dismissed for a duck during the season.

A split middle finger of his right hand caused him to miss most
of July and August. He was struck by Bob Willis in a Gillette Cup
match with Warwickshire at Leeds, and the wound needed ten
stitches. This meant that Boycott played in only two Tests against
Australia, in which his record was poor. He scored only 72 runs in

four innings, being dismissed by spinner Gleeson in the first Test, and in the famous Test at Lord's being one of Robert Massie's sixteen wickets.

Boycott looked like getting a century in each innings against Nottinghamshire, but the weather interfered leaving him 75 not out after a splendid 100 in the first innings, which included three sixes and 13 fours in 160 minutes. Lancashire again suffered during an innings of 105, which included 12 fours. He was dismissed in both innings by pace bowler Ken Shuttleworth. The season finished in fine style for Boycott, who scored an undefeated 204 against Leicestershire, which included 27 fours and took five and a half hours. There were two other centuries, against Essex and Hampshire, the last five innings producing 528 runs.

At times during the season Boycott was very dour and scored slowly. Many thought the pressure of captaincy was proving to be a heavy burden. Yorkshire had a very inexperienced side so there was enormous pressure on Boycott to perform well which he did for most of the season, but Yorkshire still could finish only tenth in the Championship.

281 Yorkshire v Gloucestershire
at Middlesbrough *May 10, 11, 12*
Yorkshire won by 126 runs

185 *ct* Swetman *b* Procter 47
173 *ct* Sub (Bore) *b* Procter 68

135 0*ct*
97 0*ct*

282 MCC v Australians
at Lord's *May 20, 22, 23*
Australia won by 3 wickets

208 *lbw* Lillee 2
178–4d *did not bat*

195–6d 0*ct*
195–6 0*ct*

283 Yorkshire v Somerset
at Taunton *May 24, 25, 26*
Drawn

226–4d *not out* 122

242 0*ct*
109–2 1*ct* (Virgin *b* Wilson)

284 Yorkshire v Lancashire
at Leeds *May 27, 29, 30* Drawn

253–8d *b* Shuttleworth 105
95–9d *ct* Wood
b Shuttleworth 4

190 0*ct*
36–2 0*ct*

285 Yorkshire v Glamorgan
at Scarborough *May 21, June 1, 2*
Yorkshire won by an innings and 124 runs

345–8d *ct* Fredericks
b Williams 9

86 0*ct*
135 1*ct* (Shepherd *b* Nicholson)

286 ENGLAND v AUSTRALIA
1st Test at Manchester
June 8, 9, 10, 12, 13
England won by 89 runs

249 *ct* Stackpole *b* Gleeson 8
234 *lbw* Gleeson 47

142 0*ct*
252 0*ct*

287 Yorkshire v **Derbyshire**
at Chesterfield *June 17, 19, 20*
Drawn

276 *run out* 21
110–1d *not out* 54

136 0ct
150–8 0ct

288 ENGLAND v **AUSTRALIA**
2nd Test at Lord's
June 22, 23, 24, 26
Australia won by 8 wickets

272 *b* Massie 11
116 *b* Lillee 6

308 0ct
81–2 0ct

289 Yorkshire v **Nottinghamshire**
at Worksop *July 1, 3, 4* Drawn

228 *ct-b* Plummer 100
155–2 *not out* 75

270 0ct

290 Yorkshire v **Surrey**
at Scarborough *August 9, 10, 11*
Yorkshire won by 9 wickets

296 *ct* Long *b* Jackman 4
41–1 *not out* 19

206 0ct
130 0ct

291 Yorkshire v **Leicestershire**
at Leicester *August 12, 14, 15*
Drawn

310–7d *not out* 204
146–6d *lbw* Matthews 12

231 0ct
141–4 0ct

292 Yorkshire v **Essex**
at Chelmsford *August 19, 21, 22*
Essex won by 6 wickets

285–6d *b* Turner 121
239–5d *ct* Taylor *b* Lever 86

282–7d 1*ct* (Turner *b* Clifford)
246–4 1*ct* (Ward *b* Bore)

293 Yorkshire v **Hampshire**
at Southampton
September 9, 11, 12 Drawn

255–3d *b* Rice 105

147 1*ct* (Greenidge *b* Wilson)
224–3 0ct

1973

The season started with a bang with Boycott scoring 141 not out against Cambridge University, which included 15 fours, then 86 versus Warwickshire and 73 versus Hampshire. Again he scored a century (101) against Lancashire. In the second Test against New Zealand he narrowly missed a century by 8 runs, being caught and bowled trying to drive Hedley Howarth, in an otherwise perfect innings.

In his next two matches he took his toll on both the touring sides. Playing for Derrick Robins XI v West Indies, he scored 114 and 74 not out in a match which the home team won by ten wickets. The next match was the Test versus New Zealand, and Boycott scored his eleventh Test century, hitting 115 in three hours twenty minutes.

As well as striking five centuries during the summer he had three nineties, all against the touring sides; 97 in the Test against the West Indies before he edged a Bernard Julien outswinger, 93 for Yorkshire against the West Indies before being caught behind and 92 in the second Test against New Zealand.

The only instance of Boycott sharing a hundred partnership for the tenth wicket occurred when he batted with Michael Bore against Nottinghamshire at Bradford. Boycott was eventually run out trying to keep the bowling.

The season was a bad one for Yorkshire, who finished fourteenth, the lowest County Championship position in their history. One of the reasons was doubtless that Boycott played in only eight of the twenty Championship matches because of injury and Test selection.

294   Yorkshire v **Cambridge University**
at Cambridge   *April 28, 30, May 1*
Drawn

247–1d   *not out*   141
132–3d   *did not bat*

122   0*ct*
15–1   0*ct*

295   Yorkshire v **Warwickshire**
at Birmingham   *May 2, 3, 4*
Drawn

245–9   *ct* Smith   *b* Brown   86

302   0*ct*

296   Yorkshire v **Hampshire**
at Leeds   *May 16, 17, 18*
Hampshire won by 7 wickets

168   *ct* Stephenson
b Taylor   73
259   *b* Mottram   30

341   0*ct*
87–3   0*ct*

297   Yorkshire v **Glamorgan**
at Cardiff   *May 23, 24, 25*
Glamorgan won by 65 runs

13–0d   *not out*   6
98   *ct* A. Jones   *b* Solanky   30

79–2d   0*ct*
97   0*ct*

298   Yorkshire v **Lancashire**
at Manchester   *May 26, 28, 29*
Drawn

286–7d   *lbw* Shuttleworth   101
69   *ct* Simmons   *b* Lever   16

284–9d   0*ct*
4–0   0*ct*

299   The Rest v **MCC Tour XI**
at Hove, Test Trial
May 30, 31, June 1
The Rest won by 4 wickets

246   *ct* Knott   *b* Greig   22
170–6   *retired hurt*   22

187   0*ct*
228–2d   0*ct*

300   ENGLAND v **NEW ZEALAND**
1st Test at Nottingham
June 7, 8, 9, 11, 12
England won by 38 runs

250   *lbw* Taylor   51
325–8d   *run out*   1

97   0*ct*
440   0*ct*

301 Yorkshire *v* **Derbyshire**
at Chesterfield   *June 16, 18, 19*
Drawn

315   *ct* Bolus   *b* Ward   4

311   0*ct*
72–2   0*ct*

302 ENGLAND *v* **NEW
ZEALAND**
2nd Test at Lord's
June 21, 22, 23, 25, 26
Drawn

253   *ct* Parker   *b* Collinge   61
463–9   *ct-b* Howarth   92

551–9d   0*ct*

303 Derrick Robins' XI *v* **West
Indies**
at Eastbourne   *June 27, 28, 29*
Derrick Robins' XI won by 10
wickets

316–8d   *st* Murray
b Julien   114
172–0   *not out*   74

328   2*ct* (Boyce   *b* Mushtaq
Mohammed, Julien   *b* Bedi)
159   0*ct*

304 ENGLAND *v* **NEW
ZEALAND**
3rd Test at Leeds
July 5, 6, 7, 9, 10
England won by an innings and 1
run

419   *ct* Parker   *b* Congdon   115

276   1*ct* (Pollard   *b* Old)
142   0*ct*

305 Yorkshire *v* **Surrey**
at The Oval   *July 14, 16*
Surrey won by an innings and 165
runs

60   *ct* Roope   *b* Arnold   8
43   *ct* Roope   *b* Arnold   9

268–9d   0*ct*

306 Yorkshire *v* **Nottinghamshire**
at Bradford   *July 21, 23, 24*
Drawn

219   *run out*   129
59–1   *did not bat*

248–9d   1*ct* (Smedley   *b* Carrick)
126–3d   0*ct*

307 ENGLAND *v* **WEST
INDIES**
1st Test at The Oval
July 26, 27, 28, 30, 31
West Indies won by 158 runs

257   *ct* Murray   *b* Julien   97
255   *ct-b* Gibbs   30

415   1*ct* (Inshan Ali
b Underwood)
255   0*ct*

308 Yorkshire *v* **Lancashire**
at Sheffield   *August 4, 6, 7*
Drawn

99   *ct* Engineer   *b* Lee   9
114–2   *ct* Hughes   *b* Lee   6

111–8d   0*ct*

309 ENGLAND *v* **WEST
INDIES**
2nd Test at Birmingham
August 9, 10, 11, 13, 14   Drawn

305   *not out*   56
182–2   *did not bat*

327   1*ct* (Holder   *b* Underwood)
302   0*ct*

310 Yorkshire *v* **West Indies**
at Scarborough
August 18, 20, 21   Drawn

312–5d   *ct* D. A. Murray
b Inshan Ali   93
71–0   *not out*   32

307   0*ct*

311 ENGLAND v WEST INDIES
3rd Test at Lord's
August 23, 24, 25, 27
West Indies won by an innings and 226 runs

233   *ct* Kanhai   *b* Holder   4
193   *ct* Kallicharran
b Boyce   15

652–8d   0*ct*

1973–74 MCC Tour of the West Indies

Boycott was disappointed in not getting the England captaincy for the 1973–74 tour, Denness being preferred. One view is that perhaps the selectors thought Boycott too unadventurous to be an international captain.

This was another successful tour for him, which opened with 261 not out, his highest score in first-class cricket, against the West Indies Board of Control President's XI at Bridgetown, where Boycott occupied the crease for nine hours twenty-five minutes, hitting one six, one five and 29 fours. He faced bowling from Andy Roberts, Michael Holding and Albert Padmore, all of whom became Test bowlers. His score is the fourth highest by an Englishman in the West Indies, behind Andrew Sandham's 325 versus West Indies, 1930, Walter Hammond's 281 not out versus Barbados, 1935, and Dennis Amiss's 262 not out versus West Indies, 1974.

In the first Test Boycott was dismissed for 93, the first of his two nineties in the series. He hit another hundred against Guyana retiring ill with his score on 133. In the final match of the tour, the fifth Test at Port-of-Spain, Boycott missed getting a century in each innings by only one run. Had he scored this run he would have been the first Englishman to achieve this feat in England–West Indies Tests, and still remains the closest Englishman to it. His scores were 99 and 112 and he shared in a first wicket partnership of 209 with Dennis Amiss, the second highest opening stand against West Indies, the highest being 212 by Washbrook and Simpson in 1950.

312 MCC v West Indies Board of Control President's XI
at Bridgetown
January 23, 24, 25, 26   Drawn

511–4d   *not out*   261
131–5d   *did not bat*

164   0ct
368–9   0ct

313 MCC v Trinidad
at Port-of-Spain
January 28, 29, 30, 31   Drawn

293   *b* Julien   9
387–6   *ct* Gabriel
b Imtiaz Ali   45

312   0ct

314 ENGLAND v WEST INDIES
1st Test at Port-of-Spain
February 2, 3, 5, 6, 7
West Indies won by 7 wickets

131   *ct* Julien   *b* Boyce   6
392   *ct* Fredericks   *b* Gibbs   93

392   1ct (Boyce   *b* Pocock)
132–3   0ct

315 MCC v Jamaica
at Kingston   *February 9, 10, 12, 13*
Drawn

402   *retired hurt*   83

178   1ct (Chang   *b* Arnold)
204–4   0ct   8–1–25–1
(Morgan   *ct* Greig)

316 ENGLAND v WEST INDIES
2nd Test at Kingston
February 16, 17, 19, 20, 21
Drawn

353   *ct* Kanhai   *b* Sobers   68
432–9   *ct* Murray   *b* Boyce   5

583–9d   0ct

317 MCC v Barbados
at Bridgetown
February 28, March 1, 2, 3
Barbados won by 10 wickets

270   *ct* Greenidge   *b* Selman   2
199   *ct* Greenidge   *b* Selman   6

462–8d   0ct   1–0–8–0
11–0   0ct

318 ENGLAND v WEST INDIES
3rd Test at Bridgetown
March 6, 7, 9, 10, 11   Drawn

395   *ct* Murray   *b* Julien   10
277–7   *ct* Kanhai   *b* Sobers   13

596   0ct

319 MCC v Guyana
at Georgetown
March 14, 15, 16, 17   Drawn

326–3d   *retired ill*   133
139–1   *did not bat*

393   0ct
202–9d   0ct

320 ENGLAND v WEST INDIES
4th Test at Georgetown
March 22, 23, 24, 26, 27
Drawn

448   *b* Julien   15

198–4   0ct

321 ENGLAND v WEST INDIES
5th Test at Port-of-Spain
March 30, 31, April 2, 3, 4, 5
England won by 26 runs

267   *ct* Murray   *b* Julien   99
263   *b* Gibbs   112

305   1ct (Rowe   *b* Greig)
199   0ct

1974

For the second consecutive season Boycott opened with a century against Cambridge University, 140 which included 15 fours, then scored 89 versus Oxford, which is his highest against this University, one of the few first-class teams in England against whom he has not scored a century. He played in the first Test against India, and did not make many runs, being dismissed for 10 and 6 by Abid Ali and Solkar in a match in which England made two declarations and won easily. This Test was to be his last for three years as he began his self-imposed exile from Test cricket.

Boycott scored a century in each innings for the second time in the Test trial at Worcester against the bowling of John Snow, John Lever and Jack Birkenshaw. His scores were 160 not out and 116, 276 runs out of the side's two-innings total of 500, which was 55·2% of his team's runs.

By 1974 Boycott had found a steady opening partner for Yorkshire in Richard Lumb and they shared in four hundred partnerships including a century stand in both innings for the first time against Sussex, scoring 104 in each innings.

Boycott was in fine form by the end of the season, finishing with a flawless 142 not out against Surrey at Bradford, which included 16 fours and took 343 minutes.

This was Boycott's benefit season, and his benefit raised £20,639, at the time a Yorkshire record.

322 Yorkshire v Cambridge University
at Cambridge   *May 1, 2, 3*
Yorkshire won by 9 wickets

300–6d   *ct* Coverdale
b Field   140

110   0*ct*
194   0*ct*

323 Yorkshire v Northamptonshire
at Northampton   *May 8, 9, 10*
Northamptonshire won by 2 wickets

265–8   *ct* Steele   *b* Sarfraz   1
105   *ct* Sharp   *b* Sarfraz   17

250–8   1*ct* (Sharp   *b* Carrick)
122–8   0*ct*

324 Yorkshire v India
at Bradford
May 11, 12, 13   Drawn

206   *lbw* Abid Ali   15
170–3d   *lbw* Solkar   14

102   0*ct*
144–5   0*ct*

325 Yorkshire v Oxford University
at Oxford   *May 15, 16, 17*
Yorkshire won by an innings and 169 runs

342–9d   *b* Imran Khan   89

106   1*ct* (M. Lloyd   *b* Hutton)
67   1*ct* (T. Lamb   *b* Cope)

326 MCC v India
at Lord's *May 18, 20, 21* Drawn

305–8d *ct* Gavaskar
b Solkar 12
173–2d *ct* Gavaskar *b* Solkar 1

231 0*ct*
136–3 0*ct*

327 Yorkshire v Warwickshire
at Sheffield *May 22, 23, 24*
Drawn

43–1 *b* Willis 15

309 1*ct* (Hemmings *b* Nicholson)

328 Yorkshire v Lancashire
at Leeds *May 25, 27, 28*
Drawn

220–9 *b* Shuttleworth 41
124–3 *not out* 79

250 0*ct*
213–7d 0*ct*

329 England v The Rest
at Worcester Test Trial
May 29, 30, 31 Drawn

281–6d *not out* 160
219–3d *ct* Taylor *b* East 116

267–8d 0*ct*
142–3 0*ct*

330 ENGLAND v INDIA
1st Test at Manchester
June 6, 7, 8, 10, 11
England won by 113 runs

328–9d *lbw* Abid Ali 10
213–3d *ct* Engineer *b* Solkar 6

246 0*ct*
182 1*ct* (Abid Ali *b* Greig)

331 Yorkshire v Derbyshire
at Sheffield *June 19, 20, 21*
Drawn

251–4d *not out* 149
199–5d *lbw* Russell 8

152 0*ct*
260–7 1*ct* (Harvey-Walker
b Cope)

332 Yorkshire v Middlesex
at Middlesbrough *June 22, 24*
Middlesex won by 8 wickets

116 *ct* Edmonds *b* Titmus 24
144 *lbw* Titmus 63

204 0*ct*
60–2 0*ct*

333 Yorkshire v Leicestershire
at Leicester *June 29, July 1, 2*
Leicester won by 7 wickets

108 *b* Illingworth 8
174 *retired hurt* 10

220 1*ct* (Norman *b* Wilson)
63–3 0*ct*

334 Yorkshire v Nottinghamshire
at Worksop *July 13, 15, 16*
Yorkshire won by an innings and
69 runs

250–7d *ct* Harris *b* Sobers 35

94 0*ct*
87 0*ct*

335 Yorkshire v Gloucestershire
at Harrogate *July 17, 18*
Yorkshire won by an innings and
165 runs

406–8d *b* Knight 23

71 0*ct*
170 0*ct*

336 Yorkshire v Middlesex
at Lord's *July 27, 29, 30*
Middlesex won by 104 runs

227–6 *b* Titmus 8
187 *ct* Edmonds *b* Price 71

303–3 0*ct*
215–5d 0*ct*

337 Yorkshire v Lancashire
at Manchester *August 3, 5, 6*
Drawn

263–6   *ct* D. Lloyd
b Shuttleworth   60
170–9d   *ct* Simmons
b Lever   17

216–9   0*ct*
169–5   0*ct*

338   Yorkshire *v* Essex
at Leyton   *August 7, 8, 9*
Essex won by an innings and 19
runs

131   *ct* East   *b* Boyce   68
163   *ct-b* East   25

313   0*ct*

339   Yorkshire *v* Sussex
at Leeds   *August 10, 12, 13*
Drawn

253–3   *ct* Mansell
b Phillipson   117
122–2d   *not out*   49

150–8d   0*ct*
74–5   0*ct*

340   Yorkshire *v* Derbyshire
at Chesterfield   *August 17, 19, 20*
Yorkshire won by 124 runs

254–8   *ct* Rowe
b Venkataraghavan   69
211   *ct-b* Miller   66

199   0*ct*
142   0*ct*

341   Yorkshire *v* Kent
at Scarborough
August 21, 22, 23   Drawn

257–7   *ct* Ealham
b Woolmer   31
158–3   *ct* Nicholls
b Woolmer   24

279–8   0*ct*
238–5d   0*ct*

342   Yorkshire *v* Surrey
at Bradford   *August 24, 26, 27*
Yorkshire won by an innings and
2 runs

343–5d   *not out*   142

204   0*ct*
137   0*ct*

1975

In the first year in which Boycott devoted his services to Yorkshire
County Cricket Club only, he scored 1,915 runs at an average of
73·65. He had stunned the selectors and general public at the end
of the 1974 season by not accepting the invitation to tour
Australia and New Zealand in the winter, because of 'very per-
sonal reasons'.

During the season he helped Yorkshire to their highest position
in the County Championship since they finished top in 1968. They
finished second, which was also to be the highest place they would
reach under Boycott's reign as captain. His first century of the
summer was 152 not out against Worcestershire, hitting two sixes
and 12 fours. It was his first hundred against this county, and
completed for him a hundred against all sixteen first class counties. It took him fourteen years, and he was the twenty-fifth
batsman to achieve the feat. Boycott was the quickest, it taking
him 315 innings, but Viv Richards did it quicker in 1981.

Boycott struck six hundreds and eight fifties in the season, which included two nineties: 92 versus Lancashire and 92 versus Essex. His highest score for 1975 was 201 not out against Middlesex, hitting 17 fours in 297 minutes. He had mixed fortunes in the home match with Lancashire, in the first innings being caught in the slips off Peter Lever for nought, and in the next innings scoring 105 not out, in nearly four hours with 13 fours. Boycott shared in seven hundred partnerships with Richard Lumb, the highest being 228 against Gloucestershire.

343 Yorkshire v Surrey
at Leeds *April 30, May 1, 2*
Drawn

288–7 *b* Butcher 23
31–0 *not out* 24

203–7 1*ct* (Skinner *b* Carrick)

344 Yorkshire v Kent
at Dartford *May 6, 7, 8* Drawn

181 *ct* Johnson
b Underwood 50
132 *ct* Cowdrey *b* Julien 4

168 0*ct*
55–6 0*ct*

345 Yorkshire v Worcestershire
at Worcester *May 14, 15, 16*
Drawn

278–8 *not out* 152
171–3d *ct* Ormrod
b Hemsley 47

177–6d 0*ct*
40–0 0*ct*

346 Yorkshire v Lancashire
at Manchester *May 24, 26, 27*
Drawn

157 *b* Shuttleworth 19
285–7d *ct* Engineer *b* Lee 92

199 0*ct*
103–3 0*ct*

347 Yorkshire v Leicestershire
at Bradford *May 31, June 2, 3*
Drawn

303–6 *ct* Tolchard
b McVicker 35
23–0 *not out* 23

201–8d 0*ct*

348 Yorkshire v Gloucestershire
at Bristol *June 11, 12, 13*
Yorkshire won by an innings and 122 runs

446–2d *ct* Knight
b Nicholls 141

131 0*ct*
193 0*ct*

349 Yorkshire v Middlesex
at Scarborough *June 14, 16, 17*
Middlesex won by 20 runs

328–5 *not out* 175
176 *ct* Edmonds *b* Selvey 16

351–7 0*ct*
173 1*ct* (Lamb *b* Cooper)

350 Yorkshire v Warwickshire
at Birmingham *June 18, 19, 20*
Yorkshire won by 9 wickets

256–9 *ct* Abberley
b Brown 66
183–1 *lbw* Lewington 64

158 2*ct* (Whitehouse *b*
Robinson, Brown *b* Carrick)
280 0*ct*

351 Yorkshire v Hampshire
at Sheffield *June 25, 26, 27*
Yorkshire won by 9 wickets

278   *ct* Rice   *b* Jesty   61
109–1   *did not bat*

174   0*ct*
212   0*ct*

352   Yorkshire v Somerset
at Harrogate   *June 28, 30, July 1*
Drawn

387–9   *ct* Taylor   *b* Burgess   25
335–7d   *ct* Taylor
b Botham   14

423–7   0*ct*
116–9   2*ct* (Slocombe   *b* Cope,
Burgess   *b* Cope)

353   Yorkshire v Nottinghamshire
at Sheffield   *July 23, 24, 25*
Yorkshire won by 172 runs

312–4   *lbw* Wilkinson   139
137–1d   *ct* Smedley   *b* White   21

211–4   0*ct*
66   2*ct* (Wilkinson   *b* Carrick,
Stead   *b* Cope)

354   Yorkshire v Surrey
at The Oval   *July 26, 28, 29*
Yorkshire won by 35 runs

383   *ct* Jackman   *b* Roope   25
251–8d   *lbw* Arnold   78

368–9   0*ct*
231   0*ct*

355   Yorkshire v Derbyshire
at Scarborough   *August 9, 11, 12*
Yorkshire won by 8 wickets

255   *ct* Morris   *b* Russell   21
143–2d   *not out*   49

169   0*ct*
228   2*ct* (Taylor   *b* Cope,
Hendrick   *b* Carrick)

356   Yorkshire v Middlesex
at Lord's   *August 13, 14, 15*
Yorkshire won by 5 runs

376–4   *not out*   201
106   *ct* Emburey   *b* Lamb   0

325–8   1*ct* (Featherstone
b Cope)
152   0*ct*

357   Yorkshire v Glamorgan
at Cardiff   *August 16, 18, 19*
Drawn

287   *lbw* Nash   23

192   0*ct*
78–1   0*ct*

358   Yorkshire v Lancashire
at Leeds   *August 23, 25, 26*
Drawn

201–8d   *ct* Simmons   *b* Lever   0
219–1   *not out*   105

340–5   0*ct*
191–3d   0*ct*

359   Yorkshire v Northamptonshire
at Bradford
August 30, September 1, 2
Yorkshire won by 78 runs

178   *lbw* Sarfraz   6
192   *ct-b* Mushtaq Mohammed   71

190   0*ct*
102   0*ct*

360   Yorkshire v International XI
at Scarborough
September 10, 11, 12
Yorkshire won by 7 wickets

280   *retired hurt*   24
56–3   *did not bat*

247   2*ct* (V. Richards   *b* Cooper,
Sarfraz   *b* Nicholson)
85   0*ct*

361   Yorkshire v Essex
at Middlesbrough
September 13, 15, 17
Yorkshire won by 59 runs

286   *ct* Hobbs   *b* Turner   92
210–6d   *hit wicket*   *b* Lever   29

170   1*ct* (Edmeades   *b* Old)
267   0*ct*

1976

For Geoff Boycott, 1976 proved to be a season of injuries. He suffered from a broken bone in his right hand and had disc trouble. This was the reason why he played only twelve matches, from which he scored 1,288 runs at a high average of 67·78.

In the opening match versus Gloucestershire he scored 161 not out, with one six and 21 fours, a fine batting display, sharing an opening partnership of 264 with Richard Lumb. He equalled the Yorkshire record of four centuries against Gloucestershire, the other record holders being George Hirst, Herbert Sutcliffe and John Hampshire. He scored heavily against Cambridge University, scoring 207 not out, which included 26 fours in five hours, the highest score against the University by a Yorkshire player. Of the 420 runs that Yorkshire scored he had 248 of them, which is 59·04 per cent. In Boycott's two previous innings he scored 141 not out and 140, a total of 529 runs in four innings for once out. His fifth and final century of the 1976 season was against the old enemy Lancashire at Old Trafford, 103 not out in 247 minutes with 13 fours.

Boycott's other centuries were 141 against Nottinghamshire and 156 versus Glamorgan. The one match in which he performed miserably was against Essex, where he scored 9 and 2, being out to John Lever in both innings.

362   Yorkshire v Gloucestershire
at Leeds   *April 28, 29, 30*
Drawn

344–3d	*ct* Zaheer *b* Procter	30
321–2d	*not out* 161	
321–6	0*ct*	
235–4	0*ct*	

363   Yorkshire v Essex
at Ilford   *May 5, 6, 7*
Essex won by 9 wickets

113	*ct* Fletcher *b* Lever	9
228	*ct* Smith *b* Lever	2
324	0*ct*	
18–1	0*ct*	

364   Yorkshire v Cambridge University
at Cambridge   *May 12, 13, 14*
Yorkshire won by 9 wickets

313–3d	*not out* 207	
107–1	*not out* 41	
146	0*ct*	
273	0*ct*	

365   Yorkshire v Somerset
at Taunton   *July 17, 19, 20*
Yorkshire won by 5 wickets

290	*lbw* Gurr	49
165–5	*ct* Slocombe *b* Breakwell	46
259	0*ct*	
193	2*ct* (Roebuck *b* Robinson, Botham *b* Carrick)	

366 Yorkshire v Warwickshire
at Birmingham *July 21, 22, 23*
Warwickshire won by 7 wickets

318 *ct* Humpage *b* Rouse 71
212 *ct* Humpage *b* Brown 7

393–3 0*ct*
139–3 0*ct*

367 Yorkshire v Worcestershire
at Scarborough *July 28, 29, 30*
Drawn

290–9 *ct* Wilcock
b Inchmore 36
253–8d *b* Inchmore 4

258 1*ct* (Inchmore *b* Carrick)
172–5 0*ct*

368 Yorkshire v Derbyshire
at Chesterfield *July 31,
August 2, 3* Drawn

251 *lbw* Ward 7
175–4 *ct* Stevenson
b Miller 73

325–5 1*ct* (Sharpe *b* Cope)
196–6d 0*ct*

369 Yorkshire v Nottinghamshire
at Bradford *August 7, 9, 10*
Yorkshire won by 95 runs

415–7 *ct* Todd *b* Stead 141
210–8d *run out* 7

349–6 0*ct*
181 0*ct*

370 Yorkshire v Leicestershire
at Leicester, *August 14, 16, 17*
Leicestershire won by 152 runs

85 *lbw* Booth 8
227 *ct* Birkenshaw *b* Clift 26

242–8 0*ct*
222–6d 0*ct*

371 Yorkshire v Glamorgan
at Middlesbrough
August 21, 23, 24
Yorkshire won by 7 wickets

352–8 *lbw* Cordle 30
318–3 *not out* 156

349–7 0*ct*
320–3d 0*ct*

372 Yorkshire v Lancashire
at Manchester *August 28, 30, 31*
Yorkshire won by 109 runs

260 *ct* Engineer *b* Lee 34
174–6d *not out* 103

167 0*ct*
158 0*ct*

**373 Yorkshire v
Northamptonshire**
at Scarborough *September 8, 9, 10*
Northamptonshire won by 198 runs

200 *run out* 17
134 *ct* Virgin *b* Bedi 23

323 3*ct* (Mushtaq Mohammed
b Cope, Larkins *b* Cope,
Dye *b* Carrick)
209–7d 0*ct*

1977

This was one of Boycott's best seasons, in which he created records, returned to the England Test team and scored his hundredth hundred.

He announced during the season that he would be available to play for England again, but was not selected for the first two Tests. Rain affected the opening part of the season and Boycott's scores were moderate by his standards. By the end of the season he had hit a high proportion of hundreds, scoring centuries against Somerset, Middlesex, Nottinghamshire, Warwickshire and Australia three times. A total of 1,701 runs were scored at an average of 68·04. In the tour match with Australia Boycott started with a duck, then followed it with a century, which included 16 fours. This was his second hundred for Yorkshire against an Australian touring side, equalling Denton's Yorkshire record. It helped pave the way for his return to Test cricket.

When Boycott had scored 36 in the match against Northamptonshire he had completed 30,000 first-class runs, the forty-seventh batsman to do so. In three matches at the beginning of July he scored a century in each match: 103 versus Australia, 117 versus Middlesex and 154 versus Nottinghamshire. Again at the end of the month and early August he scored hundreds in three matches: 107 against Australia, 104 against Warwickshire and 191 against Australia. The first was his Test comeback match. The innings took seven hours and included 11 fours, and he shared in a sixth wicket stand with Alan Knott of 215, which equalled the record partnership against Australia by L. Hutton and J. Hardstaff Jr. at the Oval in 1938 for this wicket. Boycott batted on all five days of the Test and was on the field for all but one and three quarter hours. Only two other batsmen have batted on all five days of a Test: M. Jaisimha for India against Australia in 1960 at Calcutta, and K. Hughes for Australia against England in 1980 at Lord's, although this was a rain affected game. The 104 against Warwickshire in his next match was Boycott's ninety-ninth hundred, and the 191 against Australia in the fourth Test was his hundredth. He hit one five and 23 fours and became the eighteenth cricketer to complete a hundred hundreds and the only player to do it in a Test match. It was the highest score in an England–Australia Test at Headingley by an Englishman, passing F. S. Jackson's score of 144 not out in 1905. Boycott became only the third batsman to score his ninety-ninth and hundredth hundred in consecutive innings, the others being D. Bradman and C. Cowdrey.

At the end of the Test series Boycott's average of 147·33 bettered Don Bradman's England–Australia record of 139·14 in 1930.

374   Yorkshire *v* **Cambridge University**
at Cambridge   *April 27, 28, 29*
Yorkshire won by an innings and 166 runs

381   *b* Bannister   59

164   0ct
51   1 *ct* (Roebuck   *b* Robinson)

375   Yorkshire *v* **Derbyshire**
at Chesterfield   *May 7, 9, 10*
Drawn

did not bat

82–2   0ct

376   Yorkshire *v* **Northamptonshire**
at Northampton   *May 11, 12, 13*
Drawn

113–6   *lbw* Sarfraz   0

235   1*ct* (Sarfraz   *b* Robinson)

377   Yorkshire *v* **Surrey**
at Sheffield   *May 18, 19, 20*
Yorkshire won by an innings and 8 runs

279   *ct* Edrich   *b* Jackman   16

171   0ct
100   0ct

378   Yorkshire *v* **Northamptonshire**
at Bradford   *May 25, 26, 27*
Yorkshire won by 6 wickets

277   *lbw* Dye   70
213–4   *st* Sharp   *b* Bedi   74

186   1*ct* (Mushtaq Mohammed *b* Robinson)
303–6d   0ct

379   Yorkshire *v* **Glamorgan**
at Cardiff   *May 28, 30, 31*
Yorkshire won by 10 wickets

293   *lbw* Cartwright   39
32–0   *not out*   24

149   0ct
172   0ct   3–2–1–0

380   Yorkshire *v* **Lancashire**
at Manchester   *June 4, 6, 7*
Drawn

65–6d   *b* Croft   0

270–4   0ct

381   Yorkshire *v* **Nottinghamshire**
at Leeds   *June 11, 13, 14*
Drawn

52–0   *not out*   32

232–5d   0ct   1–0–5–0

382   Yorkshire *v* **Somerset**
at Harrogate   *June 18, 20, 21*
Yorkshire won by 4 wickets

275–7d   *not out*   139
152–6   *ct* Slocombe
b Breakwell   60

280–9   0ct
143   0ct

383   Yorkshire *v* **Warwickshire**
at Bradford   *June 25, 27, 28*
Drawn

28–3   *ct* Humpage   *b* Rouse   14

330–5   0ct

384   Yorkshire *v* **Australians**
at Scarborough   *July 2, 3, 4*
Drawn

75   *lbw* Walker   0
233–5   *lbw* Bright   103

186   0ct
215–7d   1*ct* (Chappell
b Robinson)

385   Yorkshire *v* **Middlesex**
at Lord's   *July 6, 7, 8*   Drawn

244–4   *ct* Gould
b Edmonds   117
219–7   *ct* Gatting
b Emburey   54

256   0ct
269–6d   2 *ct* (Smith   *b* Bore,
Butcher   *b* Stevenson)

386 Yorkshire v Nottinghamshire
at Nottingham *July 9, 11, 12*
Yorkshire won by 5 wickets

200 *ct* French *b* Rice 13
323–5 *run out* 154

279–8 0ct
243–1d 1 *ct* (Coote *b* Carrick)

387 Yorkshire v Kent
at Folkestone *July 23, 25, 26*
Kent won by 6 wickets

236 *ct* Clinton *b* Shepherd 9
127 *ct* Knott *b* Underwood 61

268 0ct
96–4 0ct

388 ENGLAND v AUSTRALIA
3rd Test at Nottingham
July 28, 29, 30, August 1, 2
England won by 7 wickets

364 *ct* McCosker
b Thomson 107
189–3 *not out* 80

243 0ct
309 0ct

389 Yorkshire v Warwickshire
at Birmingham *August 6, 8, 9*
Drawn

353–5 *b* Perryman 104
188–4d *did not bat*

204–3d 0ct
74–2 0ct 6–2–10–1
(Savage *ct* Leadbeater)

390 ENGLAND v AUSTRALIA
4th Test at Leeds
August 11, 12, 13, 15
England won by an innings and 85 runs

436 *ct* Chappell *b* Pascoe 191

103 0ct
248 0ct

391 Yorkshire v Lancashire
at Bradford *August 20, 22, 23*
Yorkshire won by 5 wickets

234–9d *b* Arrowsmith 47
177–5 *ct* Wood *b* Hogg 35

302–4d 0ct
108 1ct (Lyon *b* Carrick)

392 ENGLAND v AUSTRALIA
5th Test at The Oval
August 25, 26, 27, 29, 30
Drawn

214 *ct* McCosker *b* Walker 39
57–2 *not out* 25

385 0ct

393 Yorkshire v Derbyshire
at Scarborough *September 7, 8, 9*
Drawn

261 *ct* Barlow *b* Swarbrook 18
219–7d *ct-b* Swarbrook 17

205 0ct
184–3 0ct

1977–78 England tour to Pakistan and New Zealand

This was Boycott's first tour for four years, his last being to the West Indies in 1973–74. He had never been to Pakistan (or India) before, declining the invitation for the 1972–73 Indian tour by declaring himself unavailable. In the opening match against BCCP Patrons XI Boycott scored only 2 and 8 on a wet, difficult pitch. In the second and third matches of the tour he scored two undefeated centuries, 123 and 115. Then came the Test matches, where his lowest score in the five innings was 31, and he exceeded fifty in the other four. In the second Test he had scores of 79 and 100 not out. With Mike Brearley breaking his arm in a one-day match, Boycott realised one of his greatest ambitions by becoming Captain of England. Because of the dead pitches the series with Pakistan ended in a draw with only the batsmen winning.

In New Zealand Boycott did not perform particularly well. New Zealand and its pitches did not seem to suit his style of play and very rarely did he get large scores.

The tour was noted for New Zealand winning their very first Test match against England after forty-eight attempts. The series was levelled by some excellent work by Ian Botham.

For the whole tour Boycott finished top of both the Test and tour averages.

England tour of Pakistan

394 England v BCCP Patrons XI
at Rawalpindi *November 30, December 1, 2* Drawn

64–9d b Liaqat 2
32–1 *ct* Mudassar *b* Qasim 8

151 1*ct* (Mohsin Khan *b* Willis)
118–6d 0*ct*

395 England v United XI
at Faisalabad *December 4, 5, 6*
Drawn

284–1d *not out* 123
165–3d *did not bat*

210–4d 0*ct* 1–0–1–0
58–2 0*ct*

396 England v N.W. Frontier Governor's XI
at Peshawar *December 8, 9, 10*
England won by 212 runs

285–3d *not out* 115
122–3d *did not bat*

127 0*ct*
68 0*ct*

397 ENGLAND v PAKISTAN
1st Test at Lahore *December 14, 15, 16, 18, 19* Drawn

288 *b* Qasim 63

407–9d 0*ct* 3–0–4–0
106–3 0*ct*

398 ENGLAND v PAKISTAN
2nd Test at Hyderabad
January 2, 3, 4, 6, 7 Drawn

191 *run out* 79
186–1 *not out* 100

275 0*ct*
259–4d 0*ct*

399 ENGLAND v PAKISTAN
3rd Test at Karachi
January 18, 19, 20, 22, 23
Drawn

266 *b* Qasim 31
222–5 *ct* Miandad
b Sikander 56

281 0*ct*

England Tour to New Zealand

400 England v Auckland
at Auckland *January 27, 28, 29*
Drawn

210 *ct* Snedden *b* Cushen 32
208–3d *ct* Stott *b* Snedden 25

182–4d 0*ct*
114–3 0*ct*

401 England v Canterbury
at Christchurch *February 5, 6, 7*
Drawn

173 *ct* Boock *b* D. Hadlee 11
230–4d *did not bat*

144 1*ct* (McEwan *b* Botham)
142–5 0*ct*

402 ENGLAND v NEW ZEALAND
1st Test at Wellington
February 10, 11, 12, 14, 15
New Zealand won by 72 runs

215 *ct* Congdon *b* Collinge 77
64 *b* Collinge 1

228 0*ct*
123 2*ct* (Burgess *b* Botham,
Hadlee *b* Willis)

403 England v Otago
at Dunedin *February 17, 18, 19*
England won by 6 wickets

195 *ct* Lees *b* McKechnie 37
82–4 *ct* Lees *b* Thomson 14

130 0*ct*
146 0*ct*

404 England v Young New Zealand
at Temuka *February 20, 21, 22*
England won by an innings and 23 runs

310 *ct* D. Bracewell
b Snedden 5

139 0*ct*
148 0*ct*

405 ENGLAND v NEW ZEALAND
2nd Test at Christchurch
February 24, 25, 26, 28
England won by 174 runs

418 *lbw* Collinge 8
96–4d *run out* 26

235 0*ct*
105 0*ct*

406 ENGLAND v NEW ZEALAND
3rd Test at Auckland
March 4, 5, 6, 8, 9, 10
Drawn

429 *ct* Burgess *b* Collinge 54

315 0*ct*
382–8 0*ct*

1978

Boycott started the season in good form by scoring 61 against Kent, in a one innings match restricted by rain, followed by 115 versus Warwickshire, where he became Russell Flower's first wicket in first class cricket. But in the University match against Oxford he only managed 0 and 3, further proof of his dislike of The Parks pitches, if not the ground, which he likes.

Boycott missed the whole of the Pakistan tour and the first Test versus New Zealand because of injury. In fact injury limited his appearances to twenty-five innings. When picked again for the second Test, he scored a fine 131, after being dropped when 2. The innings helped pave the way for an England victory.

It took Boycott a few innings to get back in the scoring mood after injury, but when he did, he struck three consecutive hundreds: 113 versus Northamptonshire, 103 not out for Yorkshire against New Zealand and 118 versus Glamorgan. His other century came at the end of the summer against Nottinghamshire at Scarborough, when he hit 129 before being run out.

The last match of the season was reduced to a one innings game which Yorkshire won by two wickets. This was to be Boycott's last match as Yorkshire captain. During the summer, when Boycott played for Yorkshire they won five matches and lost only one, to Warwickshire.

For the first time, apart from his first season, Boycott did not top the Yorkshire batting averages, breaking a sequence of fifteen consecutive years at the top.

407   Yorkshire *v* **Kent**
at Leeds   *May 3, 4, 5*   Drawn

222–8   *ct* Shepherd
b Johnson   61

408   Yorkshire *v* **Warwickshire**
at Birmingham   *May 10, 11, 12*
Warwickshire won by 34 runs

302–6   *ct* Willis   *b* Flower   115
110   *lbw* Willis   4

307   0*ct*
139   0*ct*

409   Yorkshire *v* **Oxford University**
at Oxford   *May 17, 18, 19*
Drawn

468–6d   *ct-b* Wookey   0
205–5d   *ct* Moulding   *b* Marie   3

125   0*ct*   8–5–10–0
156   0*ct*   4–1–3–0

410   Yorkshire *v* **Somerset**
at Taunton   *June 24, 26, 27*
Drawn

345–7   *b* Jennings   48
217–3d   *run out*   38

253   0*ct*
157–8   0*ct*

411   Yorkshire *v* **Essex**
at Chelmsford   *July 1, 3, 4*
Drawn

260–9   *b* East   49
186–3   *ct* Phillip   *b* Acfield   59

382–8   0*ct*

412   Yorkshire *v* **Warwickshire**
at Bradford   *July 8, 10, 11*
Yorkshire won by 63 runs

227   *ct* Abberley
b Perryman   17
185–3d   *ct* Kallicharran
b Perryman   55

85   0*ct*
264   0*ct*

413   Yorkshire *v* **Surrey**
at The Oval   *July 12, 13, 14*
Yorkshire won by 5 wickets

165   *ct* Richards   *b* Jackman   19
155–5   *ct* Jackman   *b* Knight   5

164   0*ct*
155   1*ct* (Intikhab   *b* Athey)

414   Yorkshire *v* **Northamptonshire**
at Northampton   *July 15, 17, 18*
Drawn

278–3   *ct* Steele   *b* Griffiths   113
100–2   *did not bat*

280–7   0*ct*
287–5d   0*ct*

415   Yorkshire *v* **New Zealand**
at Leeds   *July 22, 24, 25*   Drawn

281–5d   *not out*   103
75–2   *did not bat*

263–4d   0*ct*
249–9d   1*ct* (Howarth
   b Whiteley)

416   Yorkshire *v* **Glamorgan**
at Sheffield   *July 26, 27, 28*
Yorkshire won by an innings and
99 runs

318–6   *ct* Hopkins   *b* Lloyd   118

122   1*ct* (Nash   *b* Whiteley)
97   0*ct*

417   Yorkshire *v* **Derbyshire**
at Chesterfield   *July 29, 31,*
August 1   Drawn

183–4   *b* Hendrick   33

261–9   0*ct*

418   Yorkshire *v* **Hampshire**
at Southampton   *August 5, 7, 8*
Drawn

253–8d   *ct* Stephenson
b Rice   29
98–7   *ct* Rice   *b* Tremlett   20

269   0*ct*
115   0*ct*

419   ENGLAND *v* **NEW
ZEALAND**
2nd Test at Trent Bridge
August 10, 11, 12, 14
England won by an innings and
119 runs

429   *ct-b* Hadlee   131

120   0*ct*
190   0*ct*

420   Yorkshire *v* **Nottinghamshire**
at Scarborough   *August 19, 21, 22*
Yorkshire won by 8 wickets

325–8   *run out*   129
147–2   *b* White   33

294–2   0*ct*
176   0*ct*

421   ENGLAND *v* **NEW
ZEALAND**
3rd Test at Lord's   *August 24, 25,
26, 28*
England won by 7 wickets

289   *ct* Hadlee   *b* Bracewell   24
118–3   *b* Hadlee   4

339   0*ct*
67   0*ct*

422   Yorkshire *v* **Gloucestershire**
at Scarborough   *September 6, 7, 8*
Yorkshire won by 2 wickets (one
innings match)

162–8   *st* Brassington
b Graveney   23

161   0*ct*

1978–79 England Tour of Australia

This proved to be Boycott's poorest tour. The death of his mother, his losing the Yorkshire captaincy, and not being selected as England's vice-captain, all came within a couple of days of each other at the end of the 1978 season. He never really came to terms with it all, and it affected his play on the field. He batted slowly and often struggled to get even a boundary. When facing the faster bowlers he had the habit of stepping in front of his stumps and he was dismissed several times leg before wicket, especially to Rodney Hogg who claimed his wicket this way on five occasions.

Boycott's highest score of the tour was 90 not out against Tasmania. This was the only time he did not score a century during a tour abroad. His top Test score of 77 at Perth took 454 minutes and 337 balls with one four, all run. In the next match, Brearley, the England captain, put Boycott in at number eleven in the second innings because he wanted to give other batsmen a chance to bat. In the fourth Test at Sydney Boycott was out first ball to a loosener from Hogg, the only time he was ever out first ball in a Test match. It was his first Test duck for sixty-seven innings, the last being back in 1969 against the West Indies. During the six Tests he received 1,163 balls in 1,448 minutes and hit six fours, averaging a run every four balls, a four every one hundred and ninety-three balls and a run every five and a half minutes. His total runs in Tests was 263, averaging 21·91.

423 England v South Australia
at Adelaide   *November 3, 4, 5, 6*
South Australia won by 32 runs

232	*lbw* Hogg	62
196	*lbw* Hogg	6
311	0*ct*	
149	0*ct*	

424 England v New South Wales
at Sydney   *November 17, 18, 19, 20*
England won by 10 wickets

374   *ct* Border   *b* Lawson   14
4–0   *not out*   4

165   2*ct* (Dyson   *b* Miller, Watson   *b* Emburey)
210   0*ct*

425 England v Queensland
at Brisbane   *November 24, 25, 26, 27*
England won by 6 wickets

254   *ct* Cosier   *b* Brabon   6
208–4   *ct* Maclean   *b* Balcam   60

172   1*ct* (Maclean   *b* Botham)
289   0*ct*

426 ENGLAND v AUSTRALIA
1st Test at Brisbane   *December 1, 2, 3, 5, 6*
England won by 7 wickets

286   *ct* Hughes   *b* Hogg   13
170–3   *run out*   16

116   0*ct*
339   0*ct*

427 England v Western Australia
at Perth *December 9, 10, 11*
England won by 140 runs

144 *lbw* Clark 4
126 *ct* Marsh *b* Yardley 13

52 0*ct*
78 0*ct*

428 ENGLAND v AUSTRALIA
2nd Test at Perth *December 15,*
16, 17, 19, 20
England won by 166 runs

309 *lbw* Hurst 77
208 *lbw* Hogg 23

190 0*ct*
161 1*ct* (Darling *b* Lever)

429 England v South Australia
at Adelaide *December 22, 23, 24*
Drawn, scores level

234–5d *ct* Gentle *b* Sincock 4
238–9 *not out* 7

241–7d 0*ct*
231–6d 0*ct* 1–0–1–0

430 ENGLAND v AUSTRALIA
3rd Test at Melbourne
December 29, 30, January 1, 2, 3
Australia won by 103 runs

143 *b* Hogg 1
179 *lbw* Hurst 38

258 0*ct*
167 0*ct*

431 ENGLAND v AUSTRALIA
4th Test at Sydney *January 6, 7,*
8, 10, 11
England won by 93 runs

152 *ct* Border *b* Hurst 8
346 *lbw* Hogg 0

294 0*ct*
111 0*ct*

432 England v Tasmania
at Hobart *January 19, 20, 21*
Drawn

210–5d *not out* 90

105 0*ct*
118–4 0*ct* 1–0–4–0

433 ENGLAND v AUSTRALIA
5th Test at Adelaide *January 27,*
28, 29, 31, February 1
England won by 205 runs

169 *ct* Wright *b* Hurst 6
360 *ct* Hughes *b* Hurst 49

164 0*ct*
160 0*ct*

434 ENGLAND v AUSTRALIA
6th Test at Sydney *February 10,*
11, 12, 14
England won by 9 wickets

308 *ct* Hilditch *b* Hurst 19
35–1 *ct* Hughes *b* Higgs 13

198 0*ct*
143 1*ct* (Wright
b Miller) 1–0–6–0

1979

Boycott had a point to make in the 1979 season, as he had just lost
the Yorkshire captaincy and had a poor winter in Australia. He
proved it by having a successful season, averaging over a hundred
for the second time, the only person ever to do so, and, of course,
finishing top of the national averages. In the County Championship he had an amazing average of 116. He finished top of
both the Yorkshire batting and bowling averages for the first time,
the only other Yorkshireman to do so being George Hirst in 1910.

If Boycott had qualified for the national bowling averages by getting another wicket he would have been top. He recorded the best bowling performance of his career, 4–14 against Lancashire.

During the season Boycott scored 1,538 runs, including six centuries and seven fifties, which meant that of the twenty innings he played thirteen were over fifty. Four of his six hundreds were over 150. Again Boycott missed most of June because of injury, and played fewer innings than in any but his first season. He scored his tenth century against Nottinghamshire, a record for Yorkshire, and during this innings he carried his bat in scoring 175 out of a Yorkshire score of 360. This was his highest score for the 1979 season.

Boycott's highest partnership ever was achieved in this season when he put on 288 for the first wicket with Richard Lumb against Somerset. Boycott's contribution was 130, and this was the tenth highest first wicket partnership for Yorkshire.

435 Yorkshire v Northamptonshire
at Middlesbrough   *May 2, 3, 4*   Drawn

322–8   *ct* Sharp   *b* T. Lamb   53
18–1   *not out*   5

251–9   1*ct* (Sharp   *b* Stevenson)

436 Yorkshire v Derbyshire
at Leeds   *May 9, 10, 11*   Drawn

299–7   *not out*   151

200–6d   1*ct* (Steele
b Carrick)   4–1–15–1
(Kirsten   *ct* Oldham)

437 Yorkshire v Glamorgan
at Cardiff   *May 16, 17, 18*   Drawn

200–8d   *lbw* Cordle   58

87–6   0*ct*

438 Yorkshire v Lancashire
at Manchester   *May 26, 28, 29*   Drawn

did not bat

29–0   0*ct*

439 Yorkshire v Surrey
at Bradford   *June 2, 4, 5*   Drawn

162   *ct* Thomas   *b* Clarke   52
191–6d   *st* Richards   *b* Roope   34

161   0*ct*   7–4–16–2 (Jackman
bowled, Thomas bowled)
181–5   0*ct*   5–0–18–0

440 Yorkshire v Somerset
at Harrogate   *June 30, July 1, 2*   Drawn

305–1d   *not out*   130
230–5   *did not bat*

313   0*ct*
308–6d   0*ct*

441 Yorkshire v Derbyshire
at Chesterfield   *July 7, 9, 10*   Yorkshire won by 9 wickets

366–7d   *b* Tunnicliffe   167
113–1   *not out*   57

203   0*ct*   8–2–17–1
(Tunnicliffe   *ct* Carrick)
272   0*ct*   4–3–1–1 (Borrington
lbw)

442 ENGLAND v INDIA
1st Test at Birmingham   *July 12, 13, 14, 16*
England won by an innings and 83 runs

633–5d   *lbw* Kapil Dev   155

297   0ct   5–1–8–0
253   0ct

443 Yorkshire v Nottinghamshire
at Worksop   *July 25, 26, 27*
Nottinghamshire won by 8 wickets

159   *ct* Harris   *b* Watson   2
360   *not out*   175

371–6d   0ct
149–2   0ct

444 Yorkshire v Middlesex
at Scarborough   *July 28, 30, 31*
Yorkshire won by 6 wickets

202–9d   *ct* Gould   *b* Selvey   76
217–4   *ct* Brearley
b Edmonds   11

307–9d   1*ct* (Emburey
b Sidebottom)
111–6d   0ct

445 ENGLAND v INDIA
2nd Test at Lord's   *August 2, 3, 4, 6, 7*   Drawn

419–9d   *ct* Gavaskar
b Ghavri   32

96   0ct
318–4   1*ct* (Vengsarkar
b Edmonds)

446 Yorkshire v Gloucestershire
at Cheltenham   *August 11, 13, 14*
Drawn

303–8d   *lbw* Childs   95

288–8   0ct

447 ENGLAND v INDIA
3rd Test at Leeds   *August 16, 17, 18, 20, 21*   Drawn

270   *ct* Viswanath   *b* Kapil
Dev   31

233–6   0ct   2–2–0–0

448 Yorkshire v Lancashire
at Leeds   *August 25, 27, 28*
Yorkshire won by 6 wickets

322   *ct* Lyon   *b* Ratcliffe   94
104–4   *did not bat*

155   0ct   14·2–9–14–4
(Wood bowled, Simmons *lbw*,
Lyon bowled, Ratcliffe bowled)
270   0ct   3–1–3–0

449 ENGLAND v INDIA
4th Test at The Oval
August 30, 31, September 1, 3, 4
Drawn

305   *lbw* Kapil Dev   35
334–8d   *b* Ghavri   125

202   0ct
429–8   0ct

1979–80 England Tour of Australia and India

This was the second consecutive tour to Australia and the first since the Kerry Packer affair. To attract the falling crowds, Australia invited both England and the West Indies to compete in a triangular tournament. It was not a full tour and the Ashes were not at stake. Boycott started the tour well, scoring 101 not out against Tasmania, then 110 and 63 not out versus South Australia. In the opening Test match he fell to his old enemy Dennis Lillee leg before, and in the second innings he made 99 not out, in the process carrying his bat. He thus became only the third Englishman to bat through an innings against Australia, the others being R. Abel in 1892 and L. Hutton in 1951. It was his second Test match 99 equalling M. J. K. Smith's record. Another distinction about this innings was that it made him the only batsman ever to be left not out on 99 in a Test. But Boycott did confess later that he would rather have scored a century.

In the remaining four matches he did not even score a fifty, but he did have a tour average of 53·40. He scored 534 runs from thirteen innings whereas in the 1978–79 tour he scored 533 from twenty-three.

From Australia the England team went to India to play in the Jubilee Test match to celebrate nearly fifty years of Test cricket between the countries. It was a match of record breaking performances from R. Taylor and I. Botham. Boycott was making his first visit to India, as he did not tour in 1972–73. He made 22 before being caught behind in the first innings, and in the second innings, with Gooch, saw England through to an easy ten wicket victory.

450   England *v* **Queensland**
at Brisbane   *November 12, 13, 14*
Drawn

176   *ct* Chappell   *b* Schuller   11
226–5d   *ct* Madders
b Schuller   20

219–9d   0*ct*   4–0–19–0
97–1   0*ct*

451   England *v* **Tasmania**
at Hobart   *November 30,*
December 1, 2
England won by 100 runs

214–3d   *not out*   101
135–1d   *did not bat*

71–3d   0*ct*
178   0*ct*

452   England *v* **South Australia**
at Adelaide   *December 4, 5, 6*
Drawn

252–2d   *ct-b* Sleep   110
227–7d   *not out*   63

226–4d   1*ct* (Sleep   *b* Stevenson)
181–3   0*ct*

453   ENGLAND *v* **AUSTRALIA**
1st Test at Perth   *December 14,*
15, 16, 18, 19
Australia won by 138 runs

228   *lbw* Lillee   0
215   *not out*   99

244   1*ct* (G. Chappell   *b* Botham)
337   0*ct*

454   ENGLAND *v* **AUSTRALIA**
2nd Test at Sydney
January 4, 5, 6, 8
Australia won by 6 wickets

123   *b* Dymock   8
237   *ct* McCosker   *b* Pascoe   18

145   0*ct*
219–4   0*ct*

455　England v New South Wales
at Canberra　*January 27, 28, 29*
England won by 8 wickets

203　*ct* Rixon　*b* Lawson　2
254–2　*ct* Toohey　*b* Beard　51

212–7d　0*ct*
243–2d　0*ct*

456　ENGLAND v AUSTRALIA
3rd Test at Melbourne
February 1, 2, 3, 5, 6
Australia won by 8 wickets

306　*ct* Mallett　*b* Dymock　44
273　*b* Lillee　7

477　0*ct*
103–2　1*ct* (Laird　*b* Underwood)

England Tour of India

JUBILEE TEST

457　ENGLAND v INDIA
at Bombay
February 15, 17, 18, 19
England won by 10 wickets

296　*ct* Kirmani　*b* Binny　22
98–0　*not out*　43

242　0*ct*
149　0*ct*

1980

The 1980 season built up slowly for Boycott. It took him twenty-four innings to score his first century. He then scored three in three matches, including 128 not out in the Centenary Test against Australia at Lord's which included 12 fours. This was a flawless innings of 252 balls, which lasted 316 minutes and made sure the game was safe for England. In the two innings his total was 190 runs. Boycott's other centuries were 135 against Lancashire, which was his ninth hundred against the county, equalling Herbert Sutcliffe's Yorkshire record and 154 not out against Derbyshire, his highest score of the season and including 18 fours.

Boycott scored 1,264 runs at an average of 52·66 which meant that he had averaged 50 or over on eleven consecutive seasons, beating Jack Hobbs' record of ten. At one time it looked like Boycott would not make 1,000 runs in the season, as with five innings left he had totalled just 782 runs. In the remaining innings he scored 482 runs.

Boycott started the season well by scoring 57 not out against Leicestershire, followed by 77 versus Oxford University, also bowling economically 10 overs for 10 runs with two wickets. Nine times he got between 50 and 100, twice getting into the eighties before being dismissed leg before wicket.

In the Test series with the West Indies Boycott fared better than most of the other England batsmen, scoring three fifties with a top score of 86.

458 Yorkshire v **Leicestershire**
at Leicester   *April 30, May 1, 2*
Drawn

158–5d   *ct* Tolchard   *b* Cook   31
111–0   *not out*   57

257–5d   0*ct*
169–6d   0*ct*

459 Yorkshire v **Oxford
University**
at Oxford   *May 3, 5, 6*
Yorkshire won by an innings and
71 runs

268–6d   *ct* Ezekowitz
b Sutcliffe   77

81   3*ct* (Rawlinson   *b* Stevenson,
Marsden   *b* Stevenson,
Ross   *b* Sidebottom)
10–4–10–2 (Rodgers *lbw*,
Sutcliffe   *ct* Athey)
116   1*ct* (MacPherson
b Sidebottom)   1–1–0–0

460 Yorkshire v **Nottinghamshire**
at Nottingham   *May 7, 8, 9*
Yorkshire won by an innings and
47 runs

332   *b* Bore   24

162   3*ct* (Todd   *b* Stevenson,
Rice   *b* Sidebottom, Bore
b Stevenson)   4–1–3–0
123   1*ct* (Curzon   *b* Old)
2–1–4–1 (Cooper   *ct* Carrick)

461 Yorkshire v **Lancashire**
at Leeds   *May 24, 26, 27*
Drawn

257   *ct* Scott   *b* Hogg   12

234   1*ct* (Cockbain   *b* Stevenson)
9–3–17–1 (Hayes   *ct* Hampshire)
182–8   0*ct*

462 Yorkshire v **Sussex**
at Middlesbrough   *May 31, June
2, 3*   Drawn

216–5d   *lbw* Wells   85
241–7d   *ct* Phillipson   *b* Imran   3

208–7d   0*ct*
146–4   1*ct* (Mendis   *b* Carrick)

463 ENGLAND v **WEST
INDIES**
1st Test at Nottingham   *June 5, 6,
7, 9, 10*
West Indies won by 2 wickets

263   *ct* Murray   *b* Garner   36
252   *b* Roberts   75

308   0*ct*
209–8   0*ct*

464 ENGLAND v **WEST
INDIES**
2nd Test at Lord's   *June 19, 20,
21, 23, 24*   Drawn

269   *ct* Murray   *b* Holding   8
133–2   *not out*   49

518   0*ct*   7–2–11–0

465 Yorkshire v **Hampshire**
at Southampton   *June 30,
July 1, 2*   Drawn

263–6d   *lbw* Graf   4

166–8d   1*ct* (Turner   *b* Cope)

466 Yorkshire v **Glamorgan**
at Bradford   *July 5, 7, 8*   Drawn

317–3d   *ct* E. Jones   *b* Hobbs   11
213–5d   *ct* Lloyd   *b* A. A.
Jones   24

231   1*ct* (A. Jones   *b* Stevenson)
11–2–25–0
57–1   0*ct*

467 ENGLAND v **WEST
INDIES**
3rd Test at Manchester   *July 10,
11, 12, 14, 15*   Drawn

150   *ct* Garner   *b* Roberts   5
391–7   *lbw* Holding   86

260   0*ct*

468 Yorkshire v West Indies
at Leeds *July 19, 20, 21*
West Indies won by 58 runs

194–5d *b* Parry 53
209 *ct* Bacchus *b* Holding 4

342–3d 0*ct* 5–1–6–0
119–1d 0*ct*

469 ENGLAND v WEST INDIES
4th Test at The Oval *July 24, 25, 26, 28, 29* Drawn

370 *run out* 53
209–9d *ct* Murray *b* Croft 5

265 0*ct*

470 Yorkshire v Derbyshire
at Chesterfield *August 2, 4, 5*
Drawn

223 *run out* 29

147 0*ct*
314–8d 0*ct* 2–0–6–0

471 ENGLAND v WEST INDIES
5th Test at Leeds *August 7, 8, 9, 11, 12* Drawn

143 *ct* Kallicharran
b Holding 4
227–6 *ct* Kallicharran
b Croft 47

245 0*ct*

472 Yorkshire v Lancashire
at Manchester *August 23, 25, 26*
Lancashire won by 3 wickets

346–7 *ct-b* D. Lloyd 135
265–5d *ct* D. Lloyd *b* Hogg 3

310–5 1*ct* (Kennedy
b Carrick)
305–7 1*ct* (Kennedy *b* Old)

473 ENGLAND v AUSTRALIA
Centenary Test at Lord's
August 28, 29, 30, September 1, 2
Drawn

205 *ct* Marsh *b* Lillee 62
244–3 *not out* 128

385–5d 0*ct*
189–4d 0*ct*

474 Yorkshire v Derbyshire
at Scarborough *September 3, 4, 5*
Drawn

338–6 *not out* 154

136 0*ct*
180–7 0*ct*

1980–81 England Tour of the West Indies

In 1980–81 Boycott became the first Englishman to make three tours to the West Indies. It proved to be an ill-fated tour for many reasons, including the sad death of Ken Barrington. There was bad weather to start with, then a political upheaval concerning Robin Jackman and his relationship with South Africa, which resulted in the cancellation of the Guyana Test and almost the tour. This was the reason why there were only four Tests instead of the normal five. It is ironic that six other England players had played in South Africa and Boycott had been in South Africa only the previous October. When England toured the West Indies in 1974 the Guyana government said nothing about Tony Greig who was born in South Africa!

On the playing front it proved to be another successful tour for Boycott. He scored the most runs, 818, of any of the batsmen. In the first match he scored 87 in both innings. It was the first time he had got this score, and each time was bowled by off spinner Harper.

In the Test matches Boycott, Gooch and Willey were the only English batsmen whose technique and application resisted the West Indies battery of fast bowlers.

During the Test series he received several unplayable balls, especially from Holding. Trying to save the first Test Boycott batted five and a half hours for 70 before being out to Holding. Holding was most effective in the Bridgetown Test when Boycott was dismissed for 0 and 1. It was the closest Boycott had come to a Test match 'pair'. Some of the overs Boycott faced were perhaps the fastest in the history of cricket. The only hundred of the tour was in the Antigua Test, the 52nd Test venue to be used, where Boycott batted all the last day to give England a draw.

475 England v President's Young West Indies XI
at Point-a-Pierre *January 24, 25, 26, 27*
England won by 190 runs

483–8d *b* Harper 87
208–5d *b* Harper 87

320 0*ct*
181 0*ct*

476 England v Trinidad and Tobago
at Port-of-Spain *February 7, 8, 9, 10* Drawn

355 *b* Joseph 70

392 0*ct*

477 ENGLAND v WEST INDIES
1st Test at Port-of-Spain
February 13, 14, 16, 17, 18
West Indies won by an innings and 79 runs

178 *ct* Richards *b* Croft 30
169 *ct* Haynes *b* Holding 70

426–9d 0*ct*

478 England v Barbados
at Bridgetown *March 7, 8, 9, 10* Drawn

298 *ct* Trotman *b* Padmore 77
220–6 *ct* King *b* Clarke 13

334 0*ct*

479 ENGLAND v WEST INDIES
3rd Test at Bridgetown
March 13, 14, 15, 17, 18
West Indies won by 298 runs

122 *b* Holding 0
224 *ct* Garner *b* Holding 1

265 0*ct*
379–7d 1*ct* (Croft *b* Jackman)

480   England v Leeward Islands
at Montserrat   *March 21, 22, 23, 24*
England won by 5 wickets

251   *run out*   72
174–5   *lbw* Guishard   15

161   0*ct*
263   0*ct*

481   ENGLAND v WEST INDIES
4th Test at Antigua   *March 27, 28, 29, 31, April 1*   Drawn

271   *ct* Murray   *b* Croft   38
234–3   *not out*   104

468–9d   1*ct* (Murray   *b* Botham)
3–2–5–0

482   England v Jamaica
at Kingston   *April 4, 5, 6, 7*
Drawn

413   *ct* Mattis   *b* Malcolm   98
294–8d   *not out*   4

368   0*ct*

483   ENGLAND v WEST INDIES
5th Test at Kingston   *April 10, 11, 12, 14, 15*   Drawn

285   *ct* Murray   *b* Garner   40
302–6   *ct* Garner   *b* Croft   12

442   0*ct*

1981

The 1981 season was a poor one for Boycott, and a controversial one. By the end of the summer his future with Yorkshire was in some doubt, as Boycott had said in a public announcement that he was 'not getting a fair deal' from the manager Ray Illingworth and 'wanted to have it out with him at the end of the season'. The remarks arose when he was not picked for the John Player League, Fenner Trophy games or the tour match with Barbados, although Boycott had made himself available to play. Illingworth suspended Boycott for the rest of the season because of these comments.

Boycott created some new records in Tests, beating Colin Cowdrey's total of 7,624 Test runs. The record came just before 12 noon on 13 August at Old Trafford, when Boycott clipped pace bowler Terry Alderman for four, thus becoming the top English run-getter in Test matches. By the end of the series he had scored 7,802, leaving him only 230 runs behind Gary Sobers' record of 8,032, a record Boycott was later to break during the winter tour to India.

His 1981 total of 1,009 runs was his lowest aggregate for one season, apart from 1962, and the average of 38·80 was the poorest for sixteen years, it being the first time since 1969 that he had not averaged fifty.

Boycott's first hundred was against Nottinghamshire who were to become the County Champions of 1981. The match celebrated one hundred years of cricket at Park Avenue, Bradford. Boycott batted well, especially against Richard Hadlee and Clive Rice, the best opening pair of bowlers in 1981. His next century came against Derbyshire, with 122 not out. It was his sixth century against the county, beating Percy Holmes' Yorkshire record of five. The three hundreds scored in the season took him on to 124, overtaking both Tom Graveney and Denis Compton, and leaving him equal eighth on the list of hundred scorers.

The Test series between England and Australia proved to be a very low scoring one. As the pitches seemed to suit the pace bowlers and not the batsmen, England had only two century makers, Boycott and Botham. During the first few Tests some cricket reporters tried to write off Boycott, saying he was too old and not quick enough to play the fast bowlers. In each of the first five Tests Boycott managed to get into double figures but then got dismissed. In the last Test he scored a century, his twenty-first Test century, equalling the total of Neil Harvey, and leaving him eight behind Don Bradman. His innings of 137 contained 7 fours, lasted 441 minutes and came from 321 balls. This was the sixty-first time that Boycott had passed fifty in Tests, beating Colin Cowdrey's record of sixty. In the second innings he was out fourth ball, leg before to Dennis Lillee for nought.

The Lord's Test was Boycott's hundredth. He was the second player to reach this number, Colin Cowdrey having done so in 1968. It took Boycott seventeen years to complete.

At the end of the Test series Boycott had scored 2,945 runs against Australia, which makes him the second highest run-getter for England against Australia, behind Jack Hobbs.

484 Yorkshire v Oxford University
at Oxford   *May 2, 4, 5*   Drawn

278–6d   *ct* Ellis   *b* Curtis   51

120   1*ct* (Orders   *b* Carrick)
123–6   1*ct* (Ellis   *b* Sidebottom)

485 Yorkshire v Warwickshire
at Birmingham   *May 6, 7, 8*
Drawn

396   *ct* Amiss   *b* Lethbridge   24
112–1   *not out*   51

260   0*ct*   5–2–11–0

486 Yorkshire v Middlesex
at Lord's   *May 13, 14, 15*
Middlesex won by 81 runs

207   *ct* Emburey   *b* Selvey   22
183   *lbw* Daniel   29

329–4d   1*ct* (Brearley
b Sidebottom)   4–2–6–0
142–9d   0*ct*   2–1–1–0

487 Yorkshire v Lancashire
at Manchester *May 23, 25, 26*
Drawn

348–9d *ct* Scott *b* Allott 35

310–8d 0ct

488 Yorkshire v Kent
at Dartford *May 27, 28, 29*
Drawn

164–5d *ct* Knott *b* Jarvis 5
112–5 *b* Johnson 33

200–6d 0ct
191–6d 0ct

489 Yorkshire v Nottinghamshire
at Bradford *June 13, 15, 16*
Drawn

78 *ct* Todd *b* Rice 18
355–7 *ct* Hadlee *b* Bore 124

322–8d 0ct

490 ENGLAND v AUSTRALIA
1st Test at Nottingham
June 18, 19, 20, 21, 22
Australia won by 4 wickets

185 *ct* Border *b* Alderman 27
125 *ct* Marsh *b* Alderman 4

179 2ct (Marsh *b* Willis,
Hogg *b* Dilley)
132–6 0ct

491 Yorkshire v Worcestershire
at Worcester *June 27, 29, 30*
Worcestershire won by 3 wickets

319–7d *b* Pridgeon 8
251 *ct* Humphries
b Pridgeon 3

303–3d 0ct
271–7 0ct

492 ENGLAND v AUSTRALIA
2nd Test at Lord's *July 2, 3, 4,
6, 7* Drawn

311 *ct* Alderman
b Lawson 17
265–8d *ct* Marsh *b* Lillee 60

345 0ct
90–4 0ct

493 ENGLAND v AUSTRALIA
3rd Test at Leeds *July 16, 17,
18, 20, 21*
England won by 18 runs

174 *b* Lawson 12
356 *lbw* Alderman 46

401–9d 0ct 3–2–2–0
111 0ct

494 Yorkshire v Sri Lanka
at Sheffield *July 22, 23, 24*
Drawn

275–5d *b* de Silva 43

495 ENGLAND v AUSTRALIA
4th Test at Birmingham
July 30, 31, August 1, 2
England won by 29 runs

189 *ct* Marsh *b* Alderman 13
219 *ct* Marsh *b* Bright 29

258 0ct
121 0ct

496 Yorkshire v Hampshire
at Middlesbrough
August 8, 10, 11 Drawn

205–6d *ct* Greenidge
b Stevenson 10
208–3d *run out* 39

150–0d 0ct
130–7 1ct (Parks *b* Stevenson)

497 ENGLAND v AUSTRALIA
5th Test at Manchester
August 13, 14, 15, 16, 17
England won by 103 runs

231 *ct* Marsh *b* Alderman 10
404 *lbw b* Alderman 37

130 0ct
402 0ct

498   Yorkshire *v* **Derbyshire**
at Derby   *August 22, 24, 25*
Yorkshire won by 6 wickets

252–4d   *not out*   122
300–4   *did not bat*

400–8d   0ct
151–3d   0ct

499   ENGLAND *v* **AUSTRALIA**
6th Test at The Oval   *August 27,
28, 29, 31, September 1*   Drawn

314   *ct* Yallop   *b* Lillee   137
261–7   *lbw* Lillee   0

352   0ct
344–9d   0ct

1981–82 England Tour of India

For the second successive winter, the England tour abroad was threatened by the selection of players with South African 'connections', namely Boycott and Cook, and it was in doubt until the last minute.

Boycott had a good winter, scoring 701 runs. Had he not returned home early he might well have scored 1,000 runs.

The Delhi Test Match produced his most important record, when at 4.22 pm on 23 December he clipped a ball from Doshi to the mid-wicket boundary for four, thus bringing his Test aggregate past Sobers' record of 8,032. Boycott said: 'I've been playing so long these records are bound to come my way. My supporters make me very much aware of them, so it's nice to get this one out of the way.'

In this innings, when Boycott reached 11, he completed 40,000 runs in a career, the 13th player to do so, and reached 1,000 runs against India in Tests. He went on to complete his 126th first-class hundred and 22nd Test century, his fourth against India, a record for England.

Boycott was unwell during the Calcutta Test, and did not field on the last day. He had a temperature of 102°, a chest infection and stomach complaint, and a tour committee meeting decided he 'should go home to get well'. He therefore left India on 7 January 1982. He finished the tour with 40,152 runs, the 12th highest aggregate of all time, and the second highest for a Yorkshire player after Herbert Sutcliffe.

500   England *v* **India Under 22 XI**
at Pune   *November 13, 14, 15*
England won by 6 wickets

219–1d   *not out*   101
303–4   *did not bat*

339–7d   0*ct*
180–2d   0*ct*

501   England *v* **West Zone**
at Baroda   *November 21, 22, 23*
Drawn

278–4d   *ct* Mankad   *b* Joshi   66
171–2d   *not out*   73

179   1*ct* (Bhalekar
b Willis)
197–4   0*ct*

502   ENGLAND *v* **INDIA**
1st Test at Bombay
November 27, 28, 29, December 1
India won by 136 runs

166   *ct* Srikkanth
b Kirti Azad   60
102   *lbw* Madan Lal   3

179   1*ct* (Viswanath   *b* Botham)
227   0*ct*

503   England *v* **South Zone**
at Hyderabad   *December 4, 5, 6*
Drawn

186–0d   *not out*   55
223–4   *did not bat*

247–9d   0*ct*
241–7d   0*ct*

504   ENGLAND *v* **INDIA**
2nd Test at Bangalore
December 9, 10, 12, 13, 14
Drawn

400   *ct* Gavaskar   *b* Kapil Dev   36
174–3   *b* Doshi   50

428   1*ct* (Doshi   *b* Underwood)

505   England *v* **North Zone**
at Jammu   *December 16, 17, 18*
Drawn

154   *lbw* Amarnath   35
127–0   *not out*   59

167   0*ct*
200–5d   0*ct*

506   ENGLAND *v* **INDIA**
3rd Test at Delhi
December 23, 24, 26, 27, 28
Drawn

476–9d   *ct* Madan Lal
b Doshi   105
68–0   *not out*   34

487   0*ct*

507   ENGLAND *v* **INDIA**
4th Test at Calcutta
January 1, 2, 3, 5, 6   Drawn

248   *ct* Kirmani   *b* Kapil Dev   18
265–5d   *lbw* Madan Lal   6

208   0*ct*
170–3   0*ct*

Boycott's Innings in First-class Matches Season by Season

Season	Matches	Innings	Not Outs	Runs	Highest Score	Average	Hundreds	Fifties	Catches	Ducks
1962	5	9	2	150	47	21·42	0	0	4	1
1963	28	43	7	1,628	165*	45·22	3	11	12	3
1964	27	44	4	2,110	177	52·75	6	11	6	1
1964–65 S A	15	25	5	1,135	193*	56·75	4	6	7	1
1965	26	44	3	1,447	95	35·29	0	10	14	2
1965–66 A	10	17	2	720	156	48·00	1	6	3	2
1965–66 NZ	3	4	0	64	51	16·00	0	1	3	0
1966	28	50	3	1,854	164	39·44	6	10	11	4
1967	24	40	4	1,910	246*	53·05	4	13	8	4
1967–68 WI	11	16	2	1,154	243	82·42	4	6	2	1
1968	20	30	7	1,487	180*	64·65	7	4	10	1
1969	23	39	6	1,283	128	38·87	3	6	9	5
1969–70 C	1	2	0	7	7	3·50	0	0	0	1
1970	25	42	5	2,051	260*	55·43	4	12	12	2
1970–71 A	12	22	6	1,535	173	95·93	6	7	6	0
1971	21	30	5	2,503	233	100·12	13	6	6	1
1971–72 S A	1	2	0	148	107	74·00	1	0	2	0
1972	13	22	5	1,230	204*	72·35	6	4	5	0
1973	18	30	6	1,527	141*	63·62	5	9	6	0
1973–74 WI	10	16	3	960	261*	73·84	3	4	3	0
1974	21	36	6	1,783	160*	59·43	6	8	7	0
1975	19	34	8	1,915	201*	73·65	6	8	14	2
1976	12	24	5	1,288	207*	67·78	5	2	7	0
1977	20	30	5	1,701	191	68·04	7	7	8	3
1977–78 P	6	9	3	577	123*	96·16	3	3	1	0
1977–78 NZ	7	11	0	290	77	26·36	0	2	3	0
1978	16	25	1	1,233	131	51·37	6	3	3	1
1978–79 A	12	23	3	533	90*	26·65	0	4	5	0
1979	15	20	5	1,538	175*	102·53	6	7	4	0
1979–80 A	7	13	3	534	110	53·40	2	3	3	1
1980 I	1	2	1	65	43*	65·00	0	0	0	0
1980	17	28	4	1,264	154*	52·66	3	8	14	0
1980–81 WI	9	17	2	818	104*	54·53	1	7	2	1
1981	16	28	2	1,009	137	38·80	3	3	6	1
1981–82 I	8	14	5	701	105	77·88	2	6	3	0
TOTALS	507	841	128	40,152	261*	56·31	126	197	209	38

Boycott's Bowling in All First-class Matches Season by Season

Season	Overs	Maidens	Runs	Wickets	Average	Best Bowling
1962		*did not bowl*				
1963	2	0	20	0	—	—
1964	17	4	55	0	—	—
1964–65 S A	94	24	262	8	32·75	3–47
1965	72·1	30	134	4	33·50	1–0
1965–66 A	45	6	214	3	71·33	2–32
1965–66 N Z	39	19	71	1	71·00	1–27
1966	12	5	25	0	—	—
1967	22	3	77	2	38·50	1–10
1967–68 W I	13·3	5	27	2	13·50	1–9
1968	3	1	10	0	—	—
1969	4·3	2	13	0	—	—
1969–70 C	3	1	5	0	—	—
1970		*did not bowl*				
1970–71 A	4·4	0	31	1	31·00	1–23
1971		*did not bowl*				
1971–72 S A		*did not bowl*				
1972		*did not bowl*				
1973		*did not bowl*				
1973–74 W I	9	1	33	1	33·00	1–25
1974		*did not bowl*				
1975		*did not bowl*				
1976		*did not bowl*				
1977	10	4	16	1	16·00	1–10
1977–78 P	4	0	5	0	—	—
1977–78 N Z		*did not bowl*				
1978	12	6	13	0	—	—
1978–79 A	3	0	11	0	—	—
1979	52·2	23	92	9	10·22	4–14
1979–80 A	4	0	19	0	—	—
1980 I		*did not bowl*				
1980	51	15	82	4	20·50	2–10
1980–81 W I	3	2	5	0	—	—
1981	14	7	20	0	—	—
1981–82 I		*did not bowl*				
TOTALS	494·1 (3,085 balls)	158	1,240	36	34·44	4–14

100

Boycott's First-class Innings on Each Ground in the UK

Ground	Matches	Innings	Not Outs	Runs	Highest Score	Average	Hundreds	Fifties	Catches	Ducks
Birmingham	16	28	5	1,447	155	62·91	5	8	7	1
Bournemouth	3	6	0	264	111	44·00	1	1	0	0
Bradford	35	60	7	2,208	151	41·66	7	10	18	4
Bristol	6	9	3	696	177	116·00	3	2	2	0
Cambridge	9	12	3	787	207*	87·44	3	3	7	0
Cardiff	5	7	2	260	80	52·00	0	2	1	0
Chelmsford	2	4	0	315	121	78·75	1	2	2	0
Cheltenham	1	1	0	95	95	95·00	0	1	0	0
Chesterfield	16	22	3	1,052	167	55·36	1	9	3	0
Clacton	1	2	0	5	4	2·50	0	0	0	0
Colchester	2	2	1	493	260*	493·00	2	0	1	0
Dartford	2	4	0	92	50	23·00	0	1	0	0
Derby	1	1	1	122	122*	–	1	0	0	0
Eastbourne	1	2	1	188	114	188·00	1	1	2	0
Folkestone	1	2	0	70	61	35·00	0	1	0	0
Gillingham	1	2	0	85	55	42·50	0	1	0	0
Gravesend	1	2	1	48	27	48·00	0	0	2	0
Harrogate	12	16	4	930	139*	77·50	4	4	4	0
Hove	4	5	2	241	164	80·33	1	0	1	0
Hull	5	10	0	346	95	34·60	0	3	1	0
Ilford	1	2	0	11	9	5·50	0	0	0	0
Kidderminster	1	1	0	60	60	60·00	0	1	1	0
Leeds	41	64	12	3,562	246*	68·50	15	12	12	3
Leicester	11	19	4	982	204*	65·46	3	4	4	0
Leyton	2	4	0	149	68	37·25	0	1	1	0
Lord's	39	68	6	2,729	201*	44·01	7	13	10	3
Lydney	1	1	0	1	1	1·00	0	0	0	0
Manchester	22	35	2	1,567	131	47·48	6	6	6	3
Middlesbrough	15	28	3	1,354	180*	54·16	3	9	6	2
Northampton	5	7	1	166	113	27·66	1	0	3	1
Nottingham	15	25	3	1,043	154	47·40	3	5	7	3
Oxford	5	6	0	272	89	45·33	0	4	8	1
Scarborough	35	61	12	3,206	175*	65·42	10	16	23	1
Sheffield	36	56	6	2,568	220*	51·36	10	9	17	6
Southampton	3	4	0	158	105	39·50	1	0	2	0
Swansea	3	6	0	204	83	34·00	0	2	2	0

Ground	Matches	Innings	Not Outs	Runs	Highest Score	Average	Hundreds	Fifties	Catches	Ducks
Taunton	7	12	3	525	122*	58·33	1	2	6	0
The Oval	19	36	4	1,636	157	51·12	4	8	7	2
Worcester	5	10	2	562	160*	70·25	3	0	0	1
Worksop	4	6	2	412	175*	103·00	2	1	0	0
TOTALS	394	648	93	30,911	260*	55·69	99	142	166	31

Boycott's First-class Innings on Yorkshire Grounds Only

Ground	Matches	Innings	Not Outs	Runs	Highest Score	Average	Hundreds	Fifties	Catches	Ducks
Bradford	35	60	7	2,208	151	41·66	7	10	18	4
Harrogate	12	16	4	930	139*	77·50	4	4	4	0
Hull	5	10	0	346	95	34·60	0	3	1	0
Leeds	41	64	12	3,562	246*	68·50	15	12	12	3
Middlesbrough	15	28	3	1,354	180*	54·16	3	9	6	2
Scarborough	35	61	12	3,206	175*	65·42	10	16	23	1
Sheffield	36	56	6	2,568	220*	51·36	10	9	17	6
TOTALS	179	295	44	14,174	246*	56·47	49	63	81	16

Boycott's Modes of Dismissal Season by Season

Season	Bowled	Caught	Hit Wicket	LBW	Run Out	Stumped
1962	2	3	0	2	0	0
1963	10	19	0	7	0	0
1964	8	26	0	5	1	0
1964–65 SA	2	15	0	3	0	0
1965	8	23	0	6	4	0
1965–66 A	2	11	0	2	0	0
1965–66 NZ	1	2	0	0	1	0
1966	11	31	0	2	2	1
1967	11	16	0	7	0	2
1967–68 WI	3	7	0	2	2	0
1968	3	16	0	4	0	0

Season	Bowled	Caught	Hit Wicket	L B W	Run Out	Stumped
1969	6	21	0	6	0	0
1969–70 C	1	1	0	0	0	0
1970	3	26	0	5	1	2
1970–71 A	0	14	0	0	1	1
1971	5	16	0	1	2	1
1971–72 S A	1	0	0	1	0	0
1972	5	8	0	3	1	0
1973	1	18	0	2	2	1
1973–74 W I	3	10	0	0	0	0
1974	6	19	0	5	0	0
1975	2	18	1	5	0	0
1976	1	12	0	4	2	0
1977	4	14	0	5	1	1
1977–78 P	3	2	0	0	1	0
1977–78 N Z	1	8	0	1	1	0
1978	5	15	0	1	2	1
1978–79 A	1	11	0	7	1	0
1979	2	8	0	4	0	1
1979–80 A	2	7	0	1	0	0
1980 I	0	1	0	0	0	0
1980	3	16	0	3	2	0
1980–81 W I	4	9	0	1	1	0
1981	4	17	0	4	1	0
1981–82 I	1	5	0	3	0	0
TOTALS	125	445	1	102	29	11
In England	100	342	1	81	21	10
Abroad	25	103	0	21	8	1

Boycott's Bowling on Each Ground in the UK

Ground	Overs	Maidens	Runs	Wickets	Average	Best Bowling
Birmingham	16	5	29	1	29·00	1–10
Bradford	29·1	6	84	3	28·00	2–16
Cardiff	3	2	1	0	—	—
Chesterfield	19	6	35	3	11·66	1–1
Harrogate	14	3	52	0	—	—
Hull	0·3	0	8	0	—	—
Leeds	50·2	25	71	7	10·14	4–14
Lord's	27	9	59	1	59·00	1–5
Lydney	6	5	3	0	—	—
Manchester	4	0	9	0	—	—
Middlesbrough	11	4	14	0	—	—
Nottingham	42	16	83	2	41·50	1–4
Oxford	25	12	27	2	13·50	2–10
Scarborough	10	3	31	1	31·00	1–27
Sheffield	15	4	51	0	—	—
TOTALS	272	100	557	20	27·85	4–14

Boycott's Modes of Dismissal for Bowling

Season	Bowled	Caught	LBW	Stumped
1964–65 SA	3	5	0	0
1965	1	2	0	1
1965–66 A	1	1	0	1
1965–66 NZ	1	0	0	0
1967	1	1	0	0
1967–68 WI	0	1	1	0
1970–71 A	0	0	0	1
1973–74 WI	0	1	0	0
1977	0	1	0	0
1979	5	2	2	0
1980	0	3	1	0
TOTALS	12	17	4	3

Boycott's Innings in County Championship Matches, Season by Season

Season	Matches	Innings	Not Outs	Runs	Highest Score	Average	Hundreds	Fifties	Catches	Ducks
1962	4	7	2	142	47	28·40	0	0	3	1
1963	25	38	7	1,446	165	46·64	3	9	10	3
1964	17	28	4	1,427	177	59·45	4	7	4	1
1965	17	28	1	942	95	34·88	0	7	8	1
1966	18	31	3	1,097	164	39·17	4	5	7	3
1967	17	28	2	1,260	220*	48·46	2	11	5	4
1968	10	15	5	774	180*	77·40	5	1	4	1
1969	13	22	4	785	105*	43·61	1	5	7	0
1970	19	31	3	1,425	260*	50·89	2	9	9	2
1971	17	24	4	2,197	233	109·85	11	6	5	1
1972	10	17	5	1,156	204*	96·33	6	4	5	0
1973	8	13	1	507	129	42·25	2	2	1	0
1974	15	26	5	1,220	149*	58·09	3	7	4	0
1975	18	33	7	1,891	201*	72·73	6	8	12	2
1976	11	22	3	1,040	161*	54·73	4	2	7	0
1977	15	22	3	1,097	154	57·73	4	5	6	2
1978	12	19	0	968	129	50·94	4	3	2	0
1979	11	15	5	1,160	175*	116·00	4	7	3	0
1980	9	13	2	572	154*	52·00	2	2	10	0
1981	8	14	2	523	124	43·58	2	1	2	0
TOTALS	274	446	68	21,629	260*	57·21	69	101	114	21

Boycott's Innings Against Each Team for Yorkshire

Team	Matches	Innings	Not Outs	Runs	Highest Score	Average	Hundreds	Fifties	Catches	Ducks
Australia	3	5	0	365	122	73·00	2	2	3	1
Cambridge University	9	12	3	787	207*	87·44	3	3	6	0
Derbyshire	27	38	9	1,968	167*	67·86	6	10	9	1
Essex	14	25	1	1,423	260*	59·29	3	6	9	0

Team	Matches	Innings	Not Outs	Runs	Highest Score	Average	Hundreds	Fifties	Catches	Ducks
Glamorgan	17	26	3	1,060	156*	46·08	3	6	7	2
Gloucestershire	21	30	5	1,471	177	58·84	4	6	5	2
Hampshire	12	19	0	661	111	34·78	2	3	4	1
India	1	2	0	29	15	14·50	0	0	0	0
International XI	1	1	1	24	24*	—	0	0	2	0
Kent	12	22	2	749	148	37·45	1	6	5	3
Lancashire	31	47	5	2,345	169	55·83	9	10	9	5
Leicestershire	17	29	8	1,696	204*	80·76	6	6	6	0
MCC	12	20	3	840	123	49·41	2	5	8	1
Middlesex	17	31	5	1,836	201*	70·61	6	10	8	1
New Zealand	2	2	1	107	103*	107·00	1	0	3	0
Northamptonshire	14	23	4	924	220*	48·63	3	4	8	1
Nottinghamshire	22	37	5	2,131	175*	66·59	11	3	11	1
Oxford University	5	6	0	272	89	45·33	0	4	8	1
Pakistan	3	4	0	160	128	40·00	1	0	1	0
Somerset	13	22	6	1,184	139*	74·00	4	4	11	0
South Africa	1	2	0	26	22	13·00	0	0	0	0
Sri Lanka	1	1	0	43	43	43·00	0	0	0	0
Surrey	20	36	5	1,241	142*	40·03	1	9	10	2
Sussex	8	11	3	620	164	77·50	3	2	2	0
Warwickshire	20	35	6	1,863	180*	64·24	6	14	8	1
West Indies	5	9	1	320	93	40·00	0	3	0	1
Worcestershire	9	15	1	457	152*	32·64	1	2	2	1
TOTALS	317	510	77	24,602	260*	56·81	78	118	145	25

Boycott's Bowling for Yorkshire in the County Championship

Season	Overs	Maidens	Runs	Wickets	Average	Best Bowling
1962		did not bowl				
1963	2	0	20	0	—	—
1964	16	4	52	0	—	—
1965	31	16	38	2	19·00	1–9
1966	5	2	4	0	—	—
1967	10	1	35	1	35·00	1–10

Season	Overs	Maidens	Runs	Wickets	Average	Best Bowling
1968	2	0	10	0	—	—
1969	2·3	1	9	0	—	—
1970						
1971						
1972						
1973		did not bowl				
1974						
1975						
1976						
1977	10	4	16	1	16·00	1–10
1978		did not bowl				
1979	45·2	20	84	9	9·33	4–14
1980	28	7	55	2	27·50	1–4
1981	11	5	18	0	—	—
TOTALS	162·5	60	341	15	22·73	4–14
	(977 balls)					

Boycott's Bowling Against Each Team (First-class)

Team	Overs	Maidens	Runs	Wickets	Average	Best Bowling
Australia	1	1	0	0	—	—
Derbyshire	23	7	50	4	12·50	1–1
Glamorgan	14	4	26	0	—	—
Gloucestershire	11	7	7	0	—	—
Hampshire	6	2	10	0	—	—
Lancashire	29·2	13	40	5	8·00	4–14
MCC	14	4	41	1	41·00	1–5
Middlesex	6	3	7	0	—	—
New Zealand	0·1	0	0	1	—	1–0
Northamptonshire	0·3	0	8	0	—	—
Nottinghamshire	25	7	57	2	28·50	1–4
Oxford University	25	12	27	2	13·50	2–10
South Africa	12	3	31	0	—	—
Surrey	14	4	54	2	27·00	2–16
Warwickshire	25	7	73	1	73·00	1–10
West Indies	5	1	6	0	—	—
Worcestershire	9	6	9	1	9·00	1–9
TOTALS	220	81	446	19	23·47	4–14

Boycott's Innings in Other Matches in England (First-class)

Team	Matches	Innings	Not Outs	Runs	Highest Score	Average	Hundreds	Fifties	Catches	Ducks
An England XI v An England Under 25 XI	2	4	1	271	147*	90·33	1	1	0	0
An England XI v Rest of the World XI	2	4	1	292	115*	97·33	1	2	3	0
An England XI v Sir Frank Worrell XI	1	1	0	13	13	13·00	0	0	0	0
Derrick Robins' XI v West Indies	1	2	1	188	114	188·00	1	1	2	0
England v The Rest	1	2	1	276	160*	276·00	2	0	0	0
England v Rest of the World	2	4	0	260	157	65·00	1	1	3	0
MCC v Australia	3	5	0	101	63	20·20	0	1	0	0
MCC v India	1	2	0	13	12	6·50	0	0	0	0
MCC v Surrey	1	2	0	11	7	5·50	0	0	0	0
MCC v West Indies	1	2	1	69	49*	69·00	0	0	0	0
President of MCC XI v Australia	1	2	0	76	53	38·00	0	1	0	0
T. N. Pearce's XI v Pakistan	1	2	0	87	58	43·50	0	1	0	0
T. N. Pearce's XI v Rest of the World XI	1	2	0	56	34	28·00	0	0	0	0
T. N. Pearce's XI v West Indies	1	2	0	196	131	98·00	1	1	0	0
The Rest v MCC Tour XI	1	2	1	44	22	44·00	0	0	0	0
TOTALS	20	38	6	1,953	160*	61·03	7	9	8	0

Boycott's Innings in Other Matches Overseas (First-class)

Team	Matches	Innings	Not Outs	Runs	Highest Score	Average	Hundreds	Fifties	Catches	Ducks
Northern Transvaal *v* Rhodesia at Pretoria	1	2	0	148	107	74·00	1	0	2	0
MCC *v* Ceylon at Colombo Oval	1	2	0	7	7	3·50	0	0	0	1
TOTALS	2	4	0	155	107	38·75	1	0	2	1

Boycott's Bowling in Other Matches (First-class)

Team	Overs	Maidens	Runs	Wickets	Average	Best Bowling
MCC *v* Ceylon at Colombo Oval	3	1	5	0	—	—
T. N. Pearce's XI *v* Pakistan at Scarborough	8	2	27	1	27·00	1–27
TOTALS	11	3	32	1	32·00	1–27

Bowlers Who Have Dismissed Boycott the Most in All First-class Matches

G. McKenzie	11	L. Gibbs	6
G. Sobers	10	J. Gleeson	6
P. Lever	9	R. Hogg	6
D. Lillee	9	A. Hurst	6
M. Procter	8	D. Motz	6
K. Shuttleworth	8	D. Underwood	6
T. Cartwright	7	G. Arnold	5
W. Hall	7	K. Boyce	5
R. Hobbs	7	R. Collinge	5
M. Holding	7	C. Croft	5
B. Julien	7	Kapil Dev	5
T. Alderman	6	Intikhab Alam	5
D. Brown	6	Sarfraz Narwaz	5
G. Forbes	6	F. Titmus	5

Boycott's Position in the Batting Averages, Season by Season

Season	National Averages	Yorkshire Averages (County Championship)
1962	149	6
1963	2	1
1964	5	1
1965	15	1
1966	9	1
1967	3	1
1968	1	1
1969	17	1
1970	5	1
1971	1	1
1972	1	1
1973	2	1
1974	4	1
1975	2	1
1976	2	1
1977	2	1
1978	7	2
1979	1	1
1980	9	2
1981	46	2

Boycott's First-class Hundreds

	Score	For	Against	Ground	Year
1	145	Yorkshire	Lancashire	Sheffield	1963
2	113	Yorkshire	Lancashire	Manchester	1963
3	165*	Yorkshire	Leicestershire	Scarborough	1963
4	151	Yorkshire	Middlesex	Leeds	1964
5	131	Yorkshire	Lancashire	Manchester	1964
6	151*	Yorkshire	Leicestershire	Leicester	1964
7	122	Yorkshire	Australians	Bradford	1964
8	113	ENGLAND	AUSTRALIA	THE OVAL	1964
9	177	Yorkshire	Gloucestershire	Bristol	1964
10	193*	MCC	Eastern Province	Port Elizabeth	1964

	Score	For	Against	Ground	Year
11	106	MCC	Western Province	Cape Town	1964
12	114	MCC	Invitation XI	Cape Town	1965
13	117	ENGLAND	SOUTH AFRICA	PORT ELIZABETH	1965
14	156	MCC	Combined XI	Hobart	1966
15	123	Yorkshire	MCC	Lord's	1966
16	136*	Yorkshire	Warwickshire	Birmingham	1966
17	164	Yorkshire	Sussex	Hove	1966
18	103	Yorkshire	Nottinghamshire	Sheffield	1966
19	105	Yorkshire	Nottinghamshire	Sheffield	1966
20	131	T. N. Pearce's XI	West Indies	Scarborough	1966
21	102	Yorkshire	Glamorgan	Harrogate	1967
22	246*	ENGLAND	INDIA	LEEDS	1967
23	220*	Yorkshire	Northamptonshire	Sheffield	1967
24	128	Yorkshire	Pakistan	Leeds	1967
25	135	MCC	President's XI	Bridgetown	1967
26	165	MCC	Leeward Islands	Antigua	1968
27	243	MCC	Barbados	Bridgetown	1968
28	116	ENGLAND	WEST INDIES	GEORGETOWN	1968
29	100	Yorkshire	Sussex	Bradford	1968
30	132	Yorkshire	Leicestershire	Leicester	1968
31	180*	Yorkshire	Warwickshire	Middlesbrough	1968
32	125	Yorkshire	Gloucestershire	Bristol	1968
33	114*	Yorkshire	Leicestershire	Sheffield	1968
34	102*	Yorkshire	MCC	Scarborough	1968
35	115*	England XI	Rest of the World XI	Scarborough	1968
36	128	ENGLAND	WEST INDIES	MANCHESTER	1969
37	106	ENGLAND	WEST INDIES	LORD'S	1969
38	105*	Yorkshire	Somerset	Leeds	1969
39	148	Yorkshire	Kent	Sheffield	1970
40	260*	Yorkshire	Essex	Colchester	1970
41	157	England	Rest of the World XI	The Oval	1970
42	147*	An England XI	An England Under 25 XI	Scarborough	1970
43	173	MCC	South Australia	Adelaide	1970
44	129*	MCC	New South Wales	Sydney	1970

111

	Score	For	Against	Ground	Year
45	124	MCC	Queensland	Brisbane	1970
46	126	MCC	Western Australia	Perth	1970
47	142*	ENGLAND	AUSTRALIA	SYDNEY	1970
48	119*	ENGLAND	AUSTRALIA	ADELAIDE	1970
49	110	Yorkshire	Warwickshire	Middlesbrough	1971
50	112*	Yorkshire	Middlesex	Leeds	1971
51	169	Yorkshire	Nottinghamshire	Leeds	1971
52	121*	ENGLAND	PAKISTAN	LORD'S	1971
53	233	Yorkshire	Essex	Colchester	1971
54	182*	Yorkshire	Middlesex	Lord's	1971
55	112	ENGLAND	PAKISTAN	LEEDS	1971
56	133	Yorkshire	Derbyshire	Scarborough	1971
57	169	Yorkshire	Lancashire	Sheffield	1971
58	151	Yorkshire	Leicestershire	Bradford	1971
59	111	Yorkshire	Hampshire	Bournemouth	1971
60	138*	Yorkshire	Warwickshire	Birmingham	1971
61	124*	Yorkshire	Northamptonshire	Harrogate	1971
62	107	Northern Transvaal	Rhodesia	Pretoria	1972
63	122*	Yorkshire	Somerset	Taunton	1972
64	105	Yorkshire	Lancashire	Leeds	1972
65	100	Yorkshire	Nottinghamshire	Worksop	1972
66	204*	Yorkshire	Leicestershire	Leicester	1972
67	121	Yorkshire	Essex	Chelmsford	1972
68	105	Yorkshire	Hampshire	Southampton	1972
69	141*	Yorkshire	Cambridge University	Cambridge	1973
70	101	Yorkshire	Lancashire	Manchester	1973
71	114	Derrick Robins' XI	West Indies	Eastbourne	1973
72	115	ENGLAND	NEW ZEALAND	LEEDS	1973
73	129	Yorkshire	Nottingham	Bradford	1973
74	261*	England	West Indies Board of Control President's XI	Bridgetown	1974
75	133*	England	Guyana	Georgetown	1974
76	122	ENGLAND	WEST INDIES	PORT-OF-SPAIN	1974
77	140	Yorkshire	Cambridge University	Cambridge	1974
78	160*	England	The Rest	Worcester	1974
79	116	England	The Rest	Worcester	1974

	Score	For	Against	Ground	Year
80	149*	Yorkshire	Derbyshire	Sheffield	1974
81	117	Yorkshire	Sussex	Leeds	1974
82	142*	Yorkshire	Surrey	Bradford	1974
83	152*	Yorkshire	Worcestershire	Worcester	1975
84	141	Yorkshire	Gloucestershire	Bristol	1975
85	173*	Yorkshire	Middlesex	Scarborough	1975
86	139	Yorkshire	Nottinghamshire	Sheffield	1975
87	201	Yorkshire	Middlesex	Lord's	1975
88	105*	Yorkshire	Lancashire	Leeds	1975
89	161*	Yorkshire	Gloucestershire	Leeds	1976
90	207*	Yorkshire	Cambridge University	Cambridge	1976
91	141	Yorkshire	Nottinghamshire	Bradford	1976
92	156*	Yorkshire	Glamorgan	Middlesbrough	1976
93	103*	Yorkshire	Lancashire	Manchester	1976
94	139*	Yorkshire	Somerset	Harrogate	1977
95	103	Yorkshire	Australians	Scarborough	1977
96	117	Yorkshire	Middlesex	Lord's	1977
97	154	Yorkshire	Nottinghamshire	Nottingham	1977
98	107	ENGLAND	AUSTRALIA	NOTTINGHAM	1977
99	104	Yorkshire	Warwickshire	Birmingham	1977
100	191	ENGLAND	AUSTRALIA	LEEDS	1977
101	123*	England	United XI	Faisalabad	1977
102	115*	England	N. W. Frontier Governor's XI	Peshawar	1977
103	100*	ENGLAND	PAKISTAN	HYDERABAD	1978
104	115	Yorkshire	Warwickshire	Birmingham	1978
105	113	Yorkshire	Northamptonshire	Northampton	1978
106	103	Yorkshire	New Zealand	Leeds	1978
107	118	Yorkshire	Glamorgan	Sheffield	1978
108	131	ENGLAND	NEW ZEALAND	NOTTINGHAM	1978
109	129	Yorkshire	Nottinghamshire	Scarborough	1978
110	151*	Yorkshire	Derbyshire	Leeds	1979
111	130*	Yorkshire	Somerset	Harrogate	1979
112	167	Yorkshire	Derbyshire	Chesterfield	1979
113	155	ENGLAND	INDIA	BIRMINGHAM	1979
114	175*	Yorkshire	Nottinghamshire	Worksop	1979
115	125	ENGLAND	INDIA	THE OVAL	1979
116	101*	England	Tasmania	Hobart	1979
117	110	England	South Australia	Adelaide	1979

	Score For		Against	Ground	Year
118	135	Yorkshire	Lancashire	Manchester	1980
119	128*	ENGLAND	AUSTRALIA	LORD'S	1980
120	154*	Yorkshire	Derbyshire	Scarborough	1980
121	104*	ENGLAND	WEST INDIES	ANTIGUA	1981
122	124	Yorkshire	Nottinghamshire	Bradford	1981
123	122*	Yorkshire	Derbyshire	Derby	1981
124	137	ENGLAND	AUSTRALIA	THE OVAL	1981
125	101*	England	India Under 22 XI	Pune	1981
126	105	ENGLAND	INDIA	DELHI	1981

Boycott's First-class Hundreds Against Each Team

An England Under 25 XI	147*
Australia	122, 113, 142*, 119*, 103, 107, 191, 128*, 137 (9)
Australian Combined XI	156
Barbados	243
Cambridge University	141, 140, 207* (3)
Derbyshire	133, 149*, 151*, 167, 154*, 122* (6)
Eastern Province	193*
Essex	260*, 233, 121 (3)
Glamorgan	102, 156*, 118 (3)
Gloucestershire	177, 125, 141, 161* (4)
Guyana	133*
Hampshire	111, 105 (2)
India	246*, 155, 125, 105 (4)
India Under 22 XI	101*
Kent	148
Lancashire	145, 113, 131, 169, 105, 101, 105*, 103*, 135 (9)
Leeward Islands	165
Leicestershire	165*, 151*, 132, 114*, 151, 204* (6)
MCC	123, 102* (2)
Middlesex	151, 112*, 182*, 175*, 201*, 117 (6)
N. W. Frontier Governor's XI	115*
New South Wales	129*
New Zealand	115, 103*, 131 (3)
Northamptonshire	220*, 124*, 113 (3)

Nottinghamshire	103, 105, 169, 100, 129, 139, 141, 154, 129, 175*, 124 (11)
Pakistan	128, 121*, 112, 100* (4)
Queensland	124*
Rest of the World XI	115*, 157 (2)
Rhodesia	107
Somerset	105*, 122*, 139*, 130* (4)
South Africa	117
South African Invitation XI	114
South Australia	173, 110 (2)
Surrey	142*
Sussex	164, 100, 117 (3)
Tasmania	101*
The Rest	160*, 116 (2)
United XI	123*
Warwickshire	136*, 180*, 110, 138*, 104, 115 (6)
Western Australia	126
Western Province	106
West Indies	131, 116, 128, 106, 114, 122, 104* (7)
West Indies Board of Control President's XI	135, 261* (2)
Worcestershire	152*

Boycott's Scores of 100 and 0 in the Same Match (First-class)

106	0	MCC	v	Western Province	at	Cape Town, 1964
136*	0	Yorkshire	v	Warwickshire	at	Birmingham, 1966
201	0	Yorkshire	v	Middlesex	at	Lord's, 1975
0	105*	Yorkshire	v	Lancashire	at	Leeds, 1975
0	103	Yorkshire	v	Australians	at	Scarborough, 1977
137	0	ENGLAND	v	AUSTRALIA	at	THE OVAL, 1981

Boycott Carrying His Bat Through a Completed Innings (First-class)

114 out of 289 Yorkshire *v* Leicestershire at Sheffield, 1968
 53 out of 119 Yorkshire *v* Warwickshire at Bradford, 1969
138 out of 232 Yorkshire *v* Warwickshire at Birmingham, 1971
182 out of 320 Yorkshire *v* Middlesex at Lord's, 1971
175 out of 360 Yorkshire *v* Nottinghamshire at Worksop, 1979
 99 out of 215 ENGLAND *v* AUSTRALIA at PERTH, 1979

Boycott's 100 Partnerships in Each Innings for the First Wicket (First-class)

105 105 with K. Taylor Yorkshire *v* Leicestershire at Leicester, 1963
107 103 with J. EDRICH ENGLAND *v* AUSTRALIA at ADELAIDE, 1971
104 104 with R. Lumb Yorkshire *v* Sussex at Leeds, 1974

Boycott's Pair

0, 0, Yorkshire *v* Kent at Bradford, 1967

Boycott's Two Hundreds in a Match (First-class)

| 103 | 105 | Yorkshire | *v* Nottinghamshire | Sheffield, 1966 |
| 160* | 116 | England | *v* The Rest | Worcester, 1974 |

Boycott's Scores of a Hundred and a Fifty in a Match (First-class)

54	122	Yorkshire	*v* Australia	Bradford, 1964
123	68	Yorkshire	*v* MCC	Lord's, 1966
131	65	T. N. Pearce's XI	*v* West Indies	Scarborough, 1966
93	115*	An England XI	*v* Rest of the World XI	Scarborough, 1966
77	142*	ENGLAND	*v* AUSTRALIA	SYDNEY, 1971
58	119*	ENGLAND	*v* AUSTRALIA	ADELAIDE, 1971
61	110	Yorkshire	*v* Warwickshire	Middlesbrough, 1971
88	112*	Yorkshire	*v* Middlesex	Leeds, 1971

138*	84	Yorkshire	v Warwickshire	Birmingham, 1971
100	75*	Yorkshire	v Nottinghamshire	Worksop, 1972
121	86	Yorkshire	v Essex	Chelmsford, 1972
114	74*	Derrick Robins' XI	v West Indies	Eastbourne, 1972
99	112	ENGLAND	v WEST INDIES	PORT-OF-SPAIN, 1974
139*	60	Yorkshire	v Somerset	Harrogate, 1977
117	54	Yorkshire	v Middlesex	Lord's, 1977
107	80*	ENGLAND	v AUSTRALIA	NOTTINGHAM, 1977
79	100*	ENGLAND	v PAKISTAN	HYDERABAD, 1978
167	57*	Yorkshire	v Derbyshire	Chesterfield, 1979
110	63*	England	v South Australia	Adelaide, 1979
62	128*	ENGLAND	v AUSTRALIA	LORD'S, 1980

Boycott's Two Fifties in a Match (First-class)

76	53	Yorkshire	v Somerset	Taunton, 1963
62	80*	ENGLAND	v WEST INDIES	PORT-OF-SPAIN, 1968
60	50*	MCC	v Guyana	Georgetown, 1968
70	50	ENGLAND	v AUSTRALIA	PERTH, 1970
61	92	ENGLAND	v NEW ZEALAND	LORD'S, 1973
69	66	Yorkshire	v Derbyshire	Chesterfield, 1974
66	64	Yorkshire	v Warwickshire	Birmingham, 1975
70	74	Yorkshire	v Northampton-shire	Bradford, 1977
87	87	England	v President's Young West Indies XI	Point-a-Pierre, 1981
66	73*	England	v West Zone	Baroda, 1981

Boycott's Scores of Ninety (First-class)

99*	ENGLAND	v	AUSTRALIA	PERTH, 1979
99	Yorkshire	v	Derbyshire	Chesterfield, 1970
99	ENGLAND	v	WEST INDIES	PORT-OF-SPAIN, 1974
98*	Yorkshire	v	Gloucestershire	Bristol, 1967
98	Yorkshire	v	Lancashire	Manchester, 1970
98	England	v	Jamaica	Kingston, 1981
97	ENGLAND	v	WEST INDIES	THE OVAL, 1973
95	Yorkshire	v	Somerset	Hull, 1965
95	Yorkshire	v	Gloucestershire	Cheltenham, 1979
94	MCC	v	South Australia	Adelaide, 1965
94	Yorkshire	v	Lancashire	Leeds, 1970
93	An England XI	v	Rest of the World XI	Scarborough, 1968
93	Yorkshire	v	West Indies	Scarborough, 1973
93	ENGLAND	v	WEST INDIES	PORT-OF-SPAIN, 1974
92	Yorkshire	v	Surrey	The Oval, 1965
92	MCC	v	South Australia	Adelaide, 1970
92	ENGLAND	v	NEW ZEALAND	LORD'S, 1973
92	Yorkshire	v	Lancashire	Manchester, 1975
92	Yorkshire	v	Essex	Middlesbrough, 1975
90*	England	v	Tasmania	Hobart, 1979
90	Yorkshire	v	Middlesex	Lord's, 1963
90	Yorkshire	v	Hampshire	Bournemouth, 1967
90	ENGLAND	v	WEST INDIES	BRIDGETOWN, 1968

Boycott's Hundred Partnerships (First-class)

Score	Wicket	Partner	For	Against	Venue	Year
100	1st	Sharpe	Yorkshire	Hampshire	Bournemouth	1967
100	2nd	Padgett	Yorkshire	Warwickshire	Middlesbrough	1971
101	3rd	FLETCHER	ENGLAND	WEST INDIES	PORT-OF-SPAIN	1974
102	1st	Lumb	Yorkshire	Oxford University	Oxford	1981
103	1st	Leadbeater	Yorkshire	Oxford University	Oxford	1969
103	1st	EDRICH	ENGLAND	AUSTRALIA	ADELAIDE	1971
103	2nd	Lumb	Yorkshire	Derbyshire	Scarborough	1975
104	1st	Luckhurst	England	Rest of the World	Leeds	1970
104	1st	Lumb (1st inns)	Yorkshire	Sussex	Leeds	1974
104	1st	Lumb (2nd inns)	Yorkshire	Sussex	Leeds	1974
105	1st	Taylor (1st inns)	Yorkshire	Leicestershire	Leicester	1963
105	1st	Taylor (2nd inns)	Yorkshire	Leicestershire	Leicester	1963
105	1st	Sharpe	Yorkshire	Australia	Sheffield	1968
105	2nd	Padgett	Yorkshire	Leicestershire	Leicester	1968
105*	1st	AMISS	ENGLAND	WEST INDIES	BIRMINGHAM	1973
105	2nd	Hampshire	Yorkshire	Nottinghamshire	Sheffield	1975
105	1st	Brearley	England	N.W. Frontier Governor's XI	Peshawar	1978
106	1st	Lumb	Yorkshire	Northamptonshire	Middlesbrough	1979
106	3rd	WOOLMER	ENGLAND	WEST INDIES	NOTTINGHAM	1980

Score	Wicket	Partner	For	Against	Venue	Year
106*	2nd	Fletcher	England	India Under 22 XI	Pune	1981
107	1st	Russell	MCC	Combined XI	Hobart	1966
107	3rd	GRAVENEY	ENGLAND	INDIA	LEEDS	1967
107	1st	EDRICH	ENGLAND	AUSTRALIA	ADELAIDE	1971
108	1st	Sharpe	Yorkshire	Gloucestershire	Bristol	1964
108	10th	Bore	Yorkshire	Nottinghamshire	Bradford	1973
109	1st	Sharpe	Yorkshire	Warwickshire	Middlesbrough	1968
109	3rd	Padgett	Yorkshire	Derbyshire	Chesterfield	1970
109	3rd	Hampshire	Yorkshire	Somerset	Taunton	1972
109	1st	Lumb	Yorkshire	Northamptonshire	Bradford	1977
110	3rd	Barrington	MCC	Leeward Islands	Antigua	1968
110	3rd	Hampshire	Yorkshire	Gloucestershire	Bristol	1968
110	2nd	Denness	MCC	Jamaica	Kingston	1974
110	2nd	Athey	England	Leeward Islands	Montserrat	1981
111	2nd	DEXTER	ENGLAND	AUSTRALIA	MANCHESTER	1964
111	1st	GOOCH	ENGLAND	NEW ZEALAND	NOTTINGHAM	1978
111*	1st	Lumb	Yorkshire	Leicestershire	Leicester	1980
112	1st	EDRICH	ENGLAND	WEST INDIES	MANCHESTER	1969
112	1st	AMISS	ENGLAND	NEW ZEALAND	LORD'S	1973
112*	4th	Roope	England	N.W. Frontier Governor's XI	Peshawar	1977
112	4th	Athey	Yorkshire	Derbyshire	Chesterfield	1979
113	1st	Tavaré	England	India Under 22 XI	Pune	1981

Score	Wicket	Partner	For	Against	Venue	Year
114	2nd	Parfitt	MCC	South African Universities	Pietermaritzburg	1964
114	1st	Sharpe	Yorkshire	Sussex	Leeds	1970
114	1st	Lumb	Yorkshire	Warwickshire	Bradford	1978
115	2nd	GRAVENEY	ENGLAND	WEST INDIES	LORD'S	1966
115	3rd	GATTING	ENGLAND	AUSTRALIA	THE OVAL	1981
116	4th	Stott	Yorkshire	Glamorgan	Cardiff	1963
116	1st	Hampshire	Yorkshire	Cambridge University	Cambridge	1965
116	1st	Edrich	MCC	South Australia	Adelaide	1965
116	1st	LUCKHURST	ENGLAND	AUSTRALIA	SYDNEY	1971
116	1st	GOOCH	ENGLAND	AUSTRALIA	MELBOURNE	1980
116	2nd	TAVARÉ	ENGLAND	INDIA	DELHI	1981
118	2nd	COWDREY	ENGLAND	WEST INDIES	BRIDGETOWN	1968
119*	1st	Edrich	MCC	Guyana	Georgetown	1968
119	1st	Sharpe	Yorkshire	Lancashire	Leeds	1972
119	3rd	FLETCHER	ENGLAND	NEW ZEALAND	LEEDS	1973
119	1st	AMISS	ENGLAND	WEST INDIES	BIRMINGHAM	1973
120	1st	BARBER	ENGLAND	SOUTH AFRICA	DURBAN	1964
120	1st	Barber	MCC	New South Wales	Sydney	1966
120	2nd	Love	Yorkshire	Glamorgan	Middlesbrough	1976
120*	4th	GATTING	ENGLAND	AUSTRALIA	LORD'S	1980
121	1st	Brearley	President's of MCC XI	Australia	Lord's	1964

121

Score	Wicket	Partner	For	Against	Venue	Year
122	1st	Leadbeater	Yorkshire	Middlesex	Lord's	1977
122	3rd	Hampshire	Yorkshire	Middlesex	Lord's	1977
123	1st	Taylor	Yorkshire	Middlesex	Leeds	1964
123	1st	Taylor	Yorkshire	Leicestershire	Leicester	1966
123	2nd	Lloyd	England	The Rest	Worcester	1974
123	6th	KNOTT	ENGLAND	AUSTRALIA	LEEDS	1977
123	3rd	GOWER	ENGLAND	AUSTRALIA	LORD'S	1981
124	1st	Bolus	MCC	Australians	Lord's	1964
124	1st	Edrich	MCC	Barbados	Bridgetown	1968
124	1st	LUCKHURST	ENGLAND	PAKISTAN	LORD'S	1971
124	1st	Larkins	England	New South Wales	Canberra	1980
125	3rd	Padgett	An England XI	An England Under 25 XI	Scarborough	1968
125	1st	EDRICH	ENGLAND	NEW ZEALAND	LORD'S	1969
126	3rd	DEXTER	ENGLAND	NEW ZEALAND	LORD'S	1965
126	4th	SHARPE	ENGLAND	WEST INDIES	LORD'S	1969
126	1st	Sharp	Yorkshire	Sri Lanka	Sheffield	1981
127	1st	Sharpe	Yorkshire	Gloucestershire	Harrogate	1967
127*	1st	Edrich	MCC	West Indies	Lord's	1969
127	1st	Lumb	Yorkshire	Hampshire	Sheffield	1975
127*	1st	Gooch	England	North Zone	Jammu	1981
128	1st	Sharpe	Yorkshire	Glamorgan	Swansea	1964
128	1st	Taylor	Yorkshire	Worcestershire	Kidderminster	1967

Score	Wicket	Partner	For	Against	Venue	Year
128	2nd	Milburn	MCC	Barbados	Bridgetown	1968
128	3rd	GRAVENEY	ENGLAND	WEST INDIES	MANCHESTER	1969
129	1st	Taylor	Yorkshire	Surrey	Bradford	1964
129	2nd	Padgett	Yorkshire	Essex	Hull	1964
129	1st	Edrich	T. N. Pearce's XI	Pakistan	Scarborough	1967
129	2nd	Padgett	Yorkshire	Essex	Colchester	1971
129	1st	Amiss	MCC	Trinidad	Port-of-Spain	1974
129	2nd	RADLEY	ENGLAND	NEW ZEALAND	NOTTINGHAM	1978
130	1st	Lumb	Yorkshire	Lancashire	Manchester	1974
131	3rd	Hampshire	Yorkshire	New Zealand	Leeds	1978
131*	7th	Miller	England	South Australia	Adelaide	1979
132	2nd	MILBURN	ENGLAND	AUSTRALIA	LORD'S	1968
132	1st	GOOCH	ENGLAND	INDIA	DELHI	1981
133	4th	D'OLIVEIRA	ENGLAND	AUSTRALIA	SYDNEY	1971
133	3rd	Gower	England	South Australia	Adelaide	1978
133	1st	Lumb	Yorkshire	Oxford University	Oxford	1980
134*	2nd	Sharpe	Yorkshire	Gloucestershire	Bristol	1967
134	1st	Lumb	Yorkshire	Warwickshire	Birmingham	1971
134	1st	Rose	England	President's Young West Indies XI	Point-a-Pierre	1981
135	1st	Sharpe	Yorkshire	Nottinghamshire	Sheffield	1966
135	1st	Taylor	Yorkshire	Sussex	Hove	1966

Score	Wicket	Partner	For	Against	Venue	Year
135	4th	D'OLIVEIRA	ENGLAND	PAKISTAN	LEEDS	1971
135	1st	Hampshire	Yorkshire	Northamptonshire	Bradford	1977
135	6th	Carrick	Yorkshire	Gloucestershire	Cheltenham	1979
136	2nd	Sharpe	Yorkshire	Derbyshire	Sheffield	1973
136	3rd	Hampshire	Yorkshire	Surrey	Bradford	1973
137	2nd	Leadbeater	Yorkshire	Lancashire	Manchester	1975
138	1st	Barber	MCC	South Australia	Adelaide	1965
138	3rd	Fletcher	MCC	South Australia	Adelaide	1970
139	1st	Prideaux	T. N. Pearce's XI	West Indies	Scarborough	1966
139	2nd	BARRINGTON	ENGLAND	INDIA	LEEDS	1967
139	3rd	Hampshire	Yorkshire	Nottinghamshire	Leeds	1971
142	5th	Close	Yorkshire	Warwickshire	Middlesbrough	1968
144	1st	Close	Yorkshire	Derbyshire	Chesterfield	1966
144	3rd	Sharpe	Yorkshire	Essex	Colchester	1970
144	1st	Lumb	Yorkshire	Lancashire	Leeds	1975
144	6th	Bairstow	Yorkshire	Nottinghamshire	Worksop	1979
144	1st	GOOCH	ENGLAND	WEST INDIES	ANTIGUA	1981
145	1st	Lumb	Yorkshire	Derbyshire	Leeds	1979
145	3rd	GOOCH	ENGLAND	INDIA	BIRMINGHAM	1979
148	4th	GOWER	ENGLAND	AUSTRALIA	PERTH	1978
150	2nd	Sharpe	Yorkshire	Northamptonshire	Harrogate	1971
151	4th	Close	Yorkshire	Gloucestershire	Bristol	1964

124

Score	Wicket	Partner	For	Against	Venue	Year
153	1st	Sharpe	Yorkshire	Middlesex	Scarborough	1970
154	4th	Parks	MCC	Orange Free State	Bloemfontein	1964
154	3rd	d'Oliveira	MCC	Barbados	Bridgetown	1968
154	3rd	Fletcher	England	Rest of the World	The Oval	1970
154	1st	BREARLEY	ENGLAND	AUSTRALIA	NOTTINGHAM	1977
156	2nd	Dexter	MCC	Border	East London	1964
156	2nd	Knott	MCC	Leeward Islands	Antigua	1968
157	4th	BARRINGTON	ENGLAND	SOUTH AFRICA	PORT ELIZABETH	1964
157	3rd	Hampshire	Yorkshire	MCC	Scarborough	1968
157	3rd	Fletcher	An England XI	An England Under 25 XI	Scarborough	1970
158	3rd	Hampshire	Yorkshire	Glamorgan	Harrogate	1967
158	2nd	Sharpe	Yorkshire	Oxford University	Oxford	1973
158	1st	Lumb	Yorkshire	Nottinghamshire	Sheffield	1975
158	4th	Love	Yorkshire	Nottinghamshire	Bradford	1981
160	1st	Woodford	Yorkshire	Derbyshire	Chesterfield	1971
161*	1st	EDRICH	ENGLAND	AUSTRALIA	MELBOURNE	1971
161	1st	Woodford	Yorkshire	Warwickshire	Middlesbrough	1971
162*	6th	Binks	Yorkshire	Northamptonshire	Sheffield	1967
162	1st	Edrich	MCC	South Australia	Adelaide	1970
163	2nd	Johnson	Yorkshire	Essex	Middlesbrough	1975
165	1st	Lumb	Yorkshire	Derbyshire	Scarborough	1973
167	4th	Love	Yorkshire	Nottinghamshire	Scarborough	1978

Score	Wicket	Partner	For	Against	Venue	Year
168	1st	Sharpe	Yorkshire	Sussex	Bradford	1968
168	4th	Fletcher	MCC	West Indies Board of Control President's XI	Bridgetown	1974
169*	3rd	Hampshire	Yorkshire	Middlesex	Leeds	1971
171	1st	LUCKHURST	ENGLAND	AUSTRALIA	PERTH	1970
171	1st	Lumb	Yorkshire	Derbyshire	Chesterfield	1974
172	1st	EDRICH	ENGLAND	WEST INDIES	BRIDGETOWN	1968
172	2nd	COWDREY	ENGLAND	WEST INDIES	GEORGETOWN	1968
172*	1st	Amiss	Derrick Robins XI	West Indies	Eastbourne	1973
173	1st	Gooch	England	Trinidad	Port-of-Spain	1981
174	1st	Brearley	England	South Australia	Adelaide	1979
175	2nd	Padgett	Yorkshire	Derbyshire	Scarborough	1971
176	3rd	Love	Yorkshire	Somerset	Harrogate	1977
176	1st	Leadbeater	Yorkshire	Nottinghamshire	Nottingham	1977
177	1st	Taylor	Yorkshire	MCC	Lord's	1966
178	1st	Lumb	Yorkshire	Lancashire	Manchester	1973
178	1st	Lumb	Yorkshire	Lancashire	Manchester	1980
180*	4th	Leadbeater	Yorkshire	Cambridge University	Cambridge	1976
181	1st	Lumb	Yorkshire	Hampshire	Southampton	1972
182	3rd	Hampshire	Yorkshire	Leicestershire	Bradford	1971
182	1st	Lumb	Yorkshire	Middlesex	Lord's	1975

Score	Wicket	Partner	For	Against	Venue	Year
184	3rd	Hampshire	Yorkshire	Derbyshire	Derby	1981
185	1st	BREARLEY	ENGLAND	PAKISTAN	HYDERABAD	1978
186	3rd	Hampshire	Yorkshire	Lancashire	Sheffield	1971
186	1st	Lumb	Yorkshire	Middlesex	Scarborough	1975
186*	1st	Gooch	England	South Zone	Hyderabad	1981
190	2nd	Sharpe	Yorkshire	Lancashire	Manchester	1963
190	2nd	Padgett	Yorkshire	Warwickshire	Birmingham	1966
191	1st	Amiss	MCC	Guyana	Georgetown	1974
191	3rd	Love	Yorkshire	Warwickshire	Birmingham	1977
191	4th	GOWER	ENGLAND	INDIA	BIRMINGHAM	1979
198	2nd	Gower	England	President's Young West Indies XI	Port-of-Spain	1981
202	2nd	Athey	Yorkshire	Northamptonshire	Northampton	1978
205*	4th	Sharpe	Yorkshire	Leicestershire	Leicester	1964
205	2nd	Sharpe	Yorkshire	Kent	Sheffield	1970
206	1st	Lumb	Yorkshire	Glamorgan	Sheffield	1978
209	1st	Amiss	MCC	Trinidad	Port-of-Spain	1974
209	1st	AMISS	ENGLAND	WEST INDIES	PORT-OF-SPAIN	1974
210	1st	Sharpe	Yorkshire	Pakistan	Leeds	1967
212	4th	Hampshire	Yorkshire	Essex	Colchester	1970
215	1st	Luckhurst	MCC	Western Australia	Perth	1970
215	6th	KNOTT	ENGLAND	AUSTRALIA	NOTTINGHAM	1977

Score	Wicket	Partner	For	Against	Venue	Year
225*	2nd	Rose	England	United Bank XI	Faiselabad	1977
228	1st	Luckhurst	MCC	New South Wales	Sydney	1970
228	1st	Lumb	Yorkshire	Gloucestershire	Bristol	1975
233	1st	Lumb	Yorkshire	Cambridge University	Cambridge	1973
234	1st	BARBER	ENGLAND	AUSTRALIA	SYDNEY	1966
236	1st	Taylor	Yorkshire	Lancashire	Manchester	1964
240	1st	Sharpe	Yorkshire	Essex	Colchester	1971
242	2nd	Edrich	MCC	Queensland	Brisbane	1970
243	2nd	Love	Yorkshire	Nottinghamshire	Bradford	1976
249	4th	Stott	Yorkshire	Lancashire	Sheffield	1963
249	2nd	Cowdrey	MCC	President's XI	Bridgetown	1968
252	4th	D'OLIVEIRA	ENGLAND	INDIA	LEEDS	1967
252	1st	Amiss	MCC	West Indies Board of Control President's XI	Bridgetown	1974
264	1st	Lumb	Yorkshire	Gloucestershire	Leeds	1976
278	4th	M. J. K. Smith	MCC	Eastern Province	Port Elizabeth	1964
288	1st	Lumb	Yorkshire	Somerset	Harrogate	1979

Boycott's Innings in Australia Against Each Team (First-class, excluding Test Matches)

Team	Matches	Innings	Not Outs	Runs	Highest Score	Average	Hundreds	Fifties	Catches	Ducks
Combined XI	2	2	0	230	156	115·00	1	1	0	0
New South Wales	4	8	2	318	129*	53·00	1	2	3	0
Queensland	4	7	1	251	124*	41·83	1	1	2	1
South Australia	7	13	3	740	173	74·00	2	5	2	1
Tasmania	2	2	2	191	101*	—	1	1	0	0
Victoria	1	2	0	44	40	22·00	0	0	0	0
Western Australia	2	4	0	152	126	38·00	1	0	1	0
TOTALS	22	38	8	1,926	173	64·20	7	10	8	2

Boycott's Innings in Australia, including Test Matches, on Each Ground (First-class)

Ground	Matches	Innings	Not Outs	Runs	Highest Score	Average	Hundreds	Fifties	Catches	Ducks
Adelaide	10	19	4	1,006	173	67·06	3	6	4	1
Brisbane	7	13	2	441	124*	40·09	1	2	3	1
Canberra	1	2	0	53	51	26·50	0	1	0	0
Hobart	3	3	2	347	156	347·00	2	1	0	0
Launceston	1	1	0	74	74	74·00	0	1	0	0
Melbourne	6	12	2	296	76*	29·60	0	2	1	0
Perth	5	10	1	471	126	52·33	1	4	3	1
Sydney	8	15	3	634	142*	52·83	2	3	6	1
TOTALS	41	75	14	3,322	173	54·45	9	20	17	4

Boycott's Bowling in Australia Against Each Team (First-class excluding Test Matches)

Team	Overs	Maidens	Runs	Wickets	Average	Best Bowling
Combined XI	7	0	39	0	—	—
New South Wales	4	0	37	1	37·00	1–37
Queensland	6	2	19	0	—	—
South Australia	10	0	50	0	—	—
Tasmania	1	0	4	0	—	—
Victoria	0·4	0	1	0	—	—
Western Australia	3	0	23	1	23·00	1–23
TOTALS	31·4	2	173	2	86·50	1–23

Boycott's Bowling in Australia, including Test Matches, on Each Ground (First-class)

Ground	Overs	Maidens	Runs	Wickets	Average	Best Bowling
Adelaide	17	3	83	0	—	—
Brisbane	10	2	35	0	—	—
Hobart	8	0	43	0	—	—
Melbourne	9·4	0	33	2	16·50	2–32
Perth	4	0	30	1	30·00	1–23
Sydney	8	1	51	1	51·00	1–37
TOTALS	56·4	6	275	4	68·75	2–32

Boycott's Innings in India, including Test Matches, on Each Ground (First-class)

Ground	Matches	Innings	Not Outs	Runs	Highest Score	Average	Hundreds	Fifties	Catches	Ducks
Bangalore	1	2	0	86	50	43·00	0	1	1	0
Baroda	1	2	1	139	73*	139·00	0	2	1	0
Bombay	2	4	1	128	60	42·66	0	1	1	0
Calcutta	1	2	0	24	18	12·00	0	0	0	0
Delhi	1	2	1	139	105	139·00	1	0	0	0
Hyderabad	1	1	1	55	55*	—	0	1	0	0
Jammu	1	2	1	94	59*	94·00	0	1	0	0
Pune	1	1	1	101	101*	—	1	0	0	0
TOTALS	9	16	6	766	105	76·60	2	6	3	0

Boycott's Innings in India Against Each Team (First-class excluding Test Matches)

Team	Matches	Innings	Not Outs	Runs	Highest Score	Average	Hundreds	Fifties	Catches	Ducks
India Under 22 XI	1	1	1	101	101*	—	1	0	0	0
North Zone	1	2	1	94	59*	94.00	0	1	0	0
South Zone	1	1	1	55	55*	—	0	1	0	0
West Zone	1	2	1	139	73*	139.00	0	2	1	0
TOTALS	4	6	4	389	101*	194.50	1	4	1	0

Boycott's Innings in New Zealand Against Each Team (First-class excluding Test Matches)

Team	Matches	Innings	Not Outs	Runs	Highest Score	Average	Hundreds	Fifties	Catches	Ducks
Auckland	1	2	0	57	32	28.50	0	0	0	0
Canterbury	1	1	0	11	11	11.00	0	0	1	0
Otago	1	2	0	51	37	25.50	0	0	0	0
President's XI	1	1	0	51	51	51.00	0	1	1	0
Young New Zealand	1	1	0	5	5	5.00	0	0	0	0
TOTALS	5	7	0	175	51	25.00	0	1	2	0

Boycott's Innings in New Zealand, including Test Matches, on Each Ground (First-class)

Ground	Matches	Innings	Not Outs	Runs	Highest Score	Average	Hundreds	Fifties	Catches	Ducks
Auckland	2	3	0	111	54	37.00	0	1	0	0
Christchurch	3	5	0	53	26	10.60	0	0	1	0
Dunedin	2	3	0	56	37	18.66	0	0	2	0
Temuka	1	1	0	5	5	5.00	0	0	0	0
Wellington	2	3	0	129	77	43.00	0	1	3	0
TOTALS	10	15	0	354	77	23.60	0	2	6	0

Boycott's Bowling in New Zealand Against Each Team (First-class, excluding Test Matches)

Team	Overs	Maidens	Runs	Wickets	Average	Best Bowling
President's XI	27	13	41	1	41·00	1–27
TOTALS	27	13	41	1	41·00	1–27

Boycott's Bowling in New Zealand, including Test Matches, on Each Ground (First-class)

Ground	Overs	Maidens	Runs	Wickets	Average	Best Bowling
Christchurch	12	6	30	0	—	—
Wellington	27	13	41	1	41·00	1–27
TOTALS	39	19	71	1	71·00	1–27

Boycott's Innings in Pakistan Against Each Team (First-class, excluding Test Matches)

Team	Matches	Innings	Not Outs	Runs	Highest Score	Average	Hundreds	Fifties	Catches	Ducks
BCCP Patrons XI NW Frontier	1	2	0	10	8	5·00	0	0	1	0
Governor XI	1	1	1	123	123*	—	1	0	0	0
United XI	1	1	1	115	115*	—	1	0	0	0
TOTALS	3	4	2	248	123*	124·00	2	0	1	0

Boycott's Innings in Pakistan, including Test Matches, on Each Ground (First-class)

Ground	Matches	Innings	Not Outs	Runs	Highest Score	Average	Hundreds	Fifties	Catches	Ducks
Faisalabad	1	1	1	123	123*	—	1	0	0	0
Hyderabad	1	2	1	179	100	179·00	1	1	0	0
Karachi	1	2	0	87	56	43·50	0	1	0	0
Lahore	1	1	0	63	63	63·00	0	1	0	0
Peshawar	1	1	1	115	115*	—	1	0	0	0
Rawalpindi	1	2	0	10	8	5·00	0	0	1	0
TOTALS	6	9	3	577	123*	96·17	3	3	1	0

Boycott's Bowling in Pakistan Against Each Team (First-class, excluding Test Matches)

Team	Overs	Maidens	Runs	Wickets	Average	Best Bowling
United XI	1	0	1	0	—	—
TOTALS	1	0	1	0	—	—

Boycott's Bowling in Pakistan, including Test Matches, on Each Ground (First-class)

Ground	Overs	Maidens	Runs	Wickets	Average	Best Bowling
Faisalabad	1	0	1	0	—	—
Lahore	3	0	4	0	—	—
TOTALS	4	0	5	0	—	—

133

Boycott's Innings in South Africa Against Each Team (First-class, excluding Test Matches)

Team	Matches	Innings	Not Outs	Runs	Highest Score	Average	Hundreds	Fifties	Catches	Ducks
Border	1	2	1	79	56	79·00	0	1	1	0
Eastern Province	1	1	1	193	193*	—	1	0	0	0
Invitation X1	1	2	0	127	114	63·50	1	0	1	0
Natal	1	2	1	22	14	22·00	0	0	0	0
Orange Free State	1	2	0	100	73	50·00	0	1	0	0
Rhodesia	1	2	0	21	17	10·50	0	0	0	0
S A Colts	1	2	0	91	53	45·50	0	1	1	0
S A Universities	1	1	0	81	81	81·00	0	1	1	0
Transvaal	1	1	0	17	17	17·00	0	0	1	0
Western Province	1	2	0	106	106	53·00	1	0	0	1
TOTALS	10	17	3	837	193*	59·78	3	4	5	1

Boycott's Innings in South Africa, including Test Matches, on Each Ground (First-class)

Ground	Matches	Innings	Not Outs	Runs	Highest Score	Average	Hundreds	Fifties	Catches	Ducks
Benoni	1	2	0	91	53	45·50	0	1	1	0
Bloemfontein	1	2	0	100	73	50·00	0	1	0	0
Cape Town	3	6	1	249	114	49·80	2	0	1	1
Durban	2	3	1	95	73	47·50	0	1	0	0
East London	1	2	1	79	56	79·00	0	1	1	0
Johannesburg	3	4	1	102	76*	34·00	0	1	1	0
Pietermaritzburg	1	1	0	81	81	81·00	0	1	1	0
Port Elizabeth	2	3	1	317	193*	158·50	2	0	2	0
Salisbury	1	2	0	21	17	10·50	0	0	0	0
TOTALS	15	25	5	1,135	193*	56·75	4	6	7	1

Boycott's Bowling in South Africa Against Each Team (First-class, excluding Test Matches)

Team	Overs	Maidens	Runs	Wickets	Average	Best Bowling
Invitation XI	33	8	105	3	35·00	3–69
TOTALS	33	8	105	3	35·00	3–69

Boycott's Bowling in South Africa, including Test Matches, on Each Ground (First-class)

Ground	Overs	Maidens	Runs	Wickets	Average	Best Bowling
Cape Town	53	13	152	6	25·33	3–47
Johannesburg	13	4	28	0	—	—
Port Elizabeth	28	7	82	2	41·00	1–13
TOTALS	94	24	262	8	32·75	3–47

Boycott's Innings in the West Indies Against Each Team (First-class, excluding Test Matches)

Team	Matches	Innings	Not Outs	Runs	Highest Score	Average	Hundreds	Fifties	Catches	Ducks
Barbados	3	5	0	341	243	68·20	1	1	0	0
Guyana	2	3	2	243	133*	243·00	1	2	0	0
Jamaica	2	3	2	185	98	185·00	0	2	1	0
Leeward Islands	2	3	0	252	165	84·00	1	1	0	0
President's Young West Indies XI	1	2	0	174	87	87·00	0	2	0	0
Trinidad	3	4	0	146	70	36·50	0	1	0	0
West Indies Board of Control President's XI	2	2	1	396	261*	396·00	2	0	1	0
Windward Islands	1	2	0	16	12	8·00	0	0	0	0
TOTALS	16	24	5	1,753	261*	92·26	5	9	2	0

Boycott's Innings in the West Indies, including Test Matches, on Each Ground (First-class)

Ground	Matches	Innings	Not Outs	Runs	Highest Score	Average	Hundreds	Fifties	Catches	Ducks
Antigua	2	3	1	307	165	153·50	2	0	1	0
Bridgetown	8	12	1	851	261*	77·36	3	2	2	1
Georgetown	4	6	2	404	133*	101·00	2	2	1	0
Kingston	5	9	2	327	98	46·71	0	3	1	1
Montserrat	1	2	0	87	72	43·50	0	1	0	0
Point-a-Pierre	1	2	0	174	87	87·00	0	2	0	0
Port-of-Spain	8	13	1	766	112	63·83	1	7	2	0
St Lucia	1	2	0	16	12	8·00	0	0	0	0
TOTALS	30	49	7	2,932	261*	69·80	8	17	7	2

Boycott's Bowling in the West Indies Against Each Team (First-class, excluding Test Matches)

Team	Overs	Maidens	Runs	Wickets	Average	Best Bowling
Barbados	3	2	8	0	—	—
Jamaica	8	1	25	1	25·00	1–25
Trinidad	11·3	3	27	2	13·50	1–9
TOTALS	22·3	6	60	3	20·00	1–9

Boycott's Bowling in the West Indies, including Test Matches, on Each Ground (First-class)

Ground	Overs	Maidens	Runs	Wickets	Average	Best Bowling
Antigua	3	2	5	0	—	—
Bridgetown	3	2	8	0	—	—
Kingston	8	1	25	1	25·00	1–25
Port-of-Spain	11·3	3	27	2	13·50	1–9
TOTALS	25·3	8	65	3	21·66	1–9

Boycott's Innings in Test Cricket, Season by Season

Season	Matches	Innings	Not Outs	Runs	Highest Score	Average	Hundreds	Fifties	Catches	Ducks
1964 A	4	6	0	291	113	48·50	1	1	0	0
1964–65 S A	5	8	2	298	117	49·66	1	2	2	0
1965 N Z	2	4	1	157	76	52·33	0	1	0	0
1965 S A	2	4	0	75	31	18·75	0	0	0	1
1965–66 A	5	9	2	300	84	42·85	0	3	1	0
1965–66 N Z	2	3	0	13	5	4·33	0	0	2	0
1966 W I	4	7	0	186	71	26·57	0	2	0	1
1967 I	2	3	1	277	246*	138·50	1	0	2	0
1967 P	1	2	1	16	15	16·00	0	0	0	0
1967–68 W I	5	8	1	463	116	66·14	1	4	1	1
1968 A	3	5	0	162	49	32·40	0	0	1	0
1969 W I	3	6	1	270	128	54·00	2	0	0	1
1969 N Z	3	5	0	101	47	20·20	0	0	0	2
1970–71 A	5	10	3	657	142*	93·85	2	5	4	0
1971 P	2	3	1	246	121*	123·00	2	0	0	0
1971 I	1	2	0	36	33	18·00	0	0	1	0
1972 A	2	4	0	72	47	18·00	0	0	0	0
1973 N Z	3	5	0	320	115	64·00	1	3	1	0
1973 W I	3	5	1	202	97	50·50	0	2	2	0
1973–74 W I	5	9	0	421	112	46·77	1	3	2	0
1974 I	1	2	0	16	10	8·00	0	0	1	0
1977 A	3	5	2	442	191	147·33	2	1	0	0
1977–78 P	3	5	1	329	100*	82·25	1	3	0	0
1977–78 N Z	3	5	0	166	77	33·20	0	2	2	0
1978 N Z	2	3	0	159	131	53·00	1	0	0	0
1978–79 A	6	12	0	263	77	21·91	0	1	2	1
1979 I	4	5	0	378	155	75·60	2	0	1	0
1979–80 A	3	6	1	176	99*	35·20	0	1	2	1
1980 I	1	2	1	65	43*	65·00	0	0	0	0
1980 W I	5	10	1	368	86	40·88	0	3	0	0
1980 A	1	2	1	190	128*	190·00	1	1	0	0
1980–81 W I	4	8	1	295	104*	42·14	1	1	2	1
1981 A	6	12	0	392	137	32·66	1	1	2	1
1981–82 I	4	8	1	312	105	45·00	1	2	2	0
TOTALS	108	193	23	8,114	246*	47·72	22	42	33	10
1970 Rest of the World	2	4	0	260	157	65·00	1	1	3	0

Boycott's Innings against Each Country in Test Matches

Country	Matches	Innings	Not Outs	Runs	Highest Score	Average	Hundreds	Fifties	Catches	Ducks
Australia	38	71	9	2,945	191	47·50	7	14	12	3
India	13	22	3	1,084	246*	57·05	4	2	7	0
New Zealand	15	25	1	916	131	38·16	2	6	5	2
Pakistan	6	10	3	591	121*	84·42	3	3	0	0
South Africa	7	12	2	373	117	37·30	1	2	2	1
West Indies	29	53	5	2,205	128	45·93	5	15	7	4
TOTALS	108	193	23	8,114	246*	47·72	22	42	33	10

Boycott's Scores in Test Matches

	Scores		Opponents	Venue	Season
1	48	—	Australia	Trent Bridge	1964
2	38	3		Headingley	
3	58	—		Old Trafford	
4	30	113		The Oval	
5	73	—	South Africa	Durban	1964–65
6	4	—		Johannesburg	
7	15	1*		Cape Town	
8	5	76*		Johannesburg	
9	117	7		Port Elizabeth	
10	23	44*	New Zealand	Edgbaston	1965
11	14	76		Lord's	
12	31	28	South Africa	Lord's	1965
13	0	16		Trent Bridge	
14	45	63*	Australia	Brisbane	1965–66
15	51	5*		Melbourne	
16	84	—		Sydney	
17	22	12		Adelaide	
18	17	1		Melbourne	
19	4	4	New Zealand	Christchurch	1965–66
20	5	—		Dunedin	
21	60	25	West Indies	Lord's	1966
22	0	71		Trent Bridge	
23	12	14		Headingley	
24	4	—		The Oval	
25	246*	—	India	Headingley	1967

	Scores		Opponents	Venue	Season
26	25	6		Edgbaston	
27	15	1	Pakistan	Trent Bridge	1967
28	68	—	West Indies	Port-of-Spain	1967–68
29	17	0		Kingston	
30	90	—		Bridgetown	
31	62	80*		Port-of-Spain	
32	116	30		Georgetown	
33	35	11	Australia	Old Trafford	1968
34	49	—		Lord's	
35	36	31		Edgbaston	
36	128	1*	West Indies	The Oval	1969
37	23	106		Lord's	
38	12	0		Headingley	
39	0	47	New Zealand	Lord's	1969
40	0	—		Trent Bridge	
41	46	8		The Oval	
42	37	16	Australia	Brisbane	1970–71
43	70	50		Perth	
44	77	142*		Sydney	
45	12	76*		Melbourne	
46	58	119*		Adelaide	
47	121*	—	Pakistan	Lord's	1971
48	112	13		Headingley	
49	3	33	India	Lord's	1971
50	8	47	Australia	The Oval	1972
51	11	6		Lord's	
52	51	1	New Zealand	Trent Bridge	1973
53	61	92		Lord's	
54	115	—		Headingley	
55	97	30	West Indies	The Oval	1973
56	56*	—		Edgbaston	
57	4	15		Lord's	
58	6	93	West Indies	Port-of-Spain	1973–74
59	68	6		Kingston	
60	10	13		Bridgetown	
61	15	—		Georgetown	
62	99	112		Port-of-Spain	
63	10	6	India	The Oval	1974
64	107	80*	Australia	Trent Bridge	1977
65	191	—		Headingley	
66	39	25*		The Oval	
67	63	—	Pakistan	Lahore	1977–78
68	79	100*		Hyderabad	
69	31	56		Karachi	

	Scores		Opponents	Venue	Season
70	77	1	New Zealand	Wellington	1977–78
71	8	26		Christchurch	
72	54	—		Auckland	
73	131	—	New Zealand	Trent Bridge	1978
74	24	4		Lord's	
75	11	16	Australia	Brisbane	1978–79
76	77	23		Perth	
77	1	38		Melbourne	
78	8	0		Sydney	
79	6	49		Adelaide	
80	19	13		Sydney	
81	155	—	India	Edgbaston	1979
82	32	—		Lord's	
83	31	—		Headingley	
84	35	125		The Oval	
85	0	99*	Australia	Perth	1979–80
86	8	18		Sydney	
87	44	7		Melbourne	
88	22	43*	India	Bombay	1980
89	36	75	West Indies	Trent Bridge	1980
90	8	49*		Lord's	
91	5	86		Old Trafford	
92	53	5		The Oval	
93	4	47		Headingley	
94	62	128*	Australia	Lord's	1980
95	30	70	West Indies	Port-of-Spain	1980–81
96	0	1		Bridgetown	
97	38	104*		Antigua	
98	40	12		Kingston	
99	27	4	Australia	Trent Bridge	1981
100	17	60		Lord's	
101	12	46		Headingley	
102	13	29		Edgbaston	
103	10	37		Old Trafford	
104	137	0		The Oval	
105	60	3	India	Bombay	1981–82
106	36	50		Bangalore	
107	105	34*		Delhi	
108	18	6		Calcutta	

Boycott's Test Match Innings on Each Ground

Ground	Matches	Innings	Not Outs	Runs	Highest Score	Average	Hundreds	Fifties	Catches	Ducks
Adelaide	3	6	1	266	119*	53·20	1	1	2	0
Antigua	1	2	1	142	104*	142·00	1	0	1	0
Auckland	1	1	0	54	54	54·00	0	1	0	0
Bangalore	1	2	0	86	50	43·00	0	1	1	0
Bombay	2	4	1	128	60	42·66	0	1	1	0
Bridgetown	3	5	0	114	90	22·80	0	1	1	1
Brisbane	3	6	1	190	63*	38·00	0	1	1	0
Calcutta	1	2	0	24	18	12·00	0	0	0	0
Cape Town	1	2	1	16	15	16·00	0	0	0	0
Christchurch	2	4	0	42	26	10·50	0	0	0	0
Delhi	1	2	1	139	105	139·00	1	0	0	0
Dunedin	1	1	0	5	5	5·00	0	0	2	0
Durban	1	1	0	73	73	73·00	0	1	0	0
Edgbaston	6	10	2	418	155	52·25	1	1	3	0
Georgetown	2	3	0	161	116	53·66	1	0	1	0
Headingley	10	16	2	903	246*	64·50	4	0	1	1
Hyderabad	1	2	1	179	100	179·00	1	1	0	0
Johannesburg	2	3	1	85	76*	42·50	0	1	0	0
Karachi	1	2	0	87	56	43·50	0	1	0	0
Kingston	3	6	0	142	68	23·66	0	1	0	1
Lahore	1	1	0	63	63	63·00	0	1	0	0
Lord's	16	29	2	1,183	128*	43·81	3	6	2	1
Melbourne	5	10	2	252	76*	31·50	0	2	1	0
Old Trafford	7	13	1	442	128	36·83	1	2	2	0
Perth	3	6	1	319	99*	63·80	0	4	2	1
Port Elizabeth	1	2	0	124	117	62·00	1	0	2	0
Port-of-Spain	5	9	1	620	112	77·50	1	6	2	0
Sydney	5	9	1	369	142*	46·12	1	2	3	1
The Oval	8	15	1	747	137	53·35	3	2	1	1
Trent Bridge	10	17	2	663	131	44·20	2	4	2	3
Wellington	1	2	0	78	77	39·00	0	1	2	0
TOTALS	108	193	23	8,114	246*	47·72	22	42	33	10

Boycott's Bowling in Test Matches, Season by Season

Season	Overs	Maidens	Runs	Wickets	Average	Best Bowling
1964 A	1	0	3	0	—	—
1964–65 S A	61	16	157	5	31·40	3–47
1965 NZ		*did not bowl*				
1965 S A	26	10	60	0	—	—
1965–66 A	23	4	89	2	44·50	2–32
1965–66 NZ	12	6	30	0	—	—
1966 WI		*did not bowl*				
1967 I		*did not bowl*				
1967 P		*did not bowl*				
1967–68 WI		*did not bowl*				
1968 A		*did not bowl*				
1969 WI		*did not bowl*				
1969 NZ		*did not bowl*				
1970–71 A	1	0	7	0	—	—
1971 P		*did not bowl*				
1971 I		*did not bowl*				
1972 A		*did not bowl*				
1973 NZ		*did not bowl*				
1973 WI		*did not bowl*				
1973–74 WI		*did not bowl*				
1974 I		*did not bowl*				
1977 A		*did not bowl*				
1977–78 P	3	0	4	0	—	—
1977–78 NZ		*did not bowl*				
1978 NZ		*did not bowl*				
1978–79 A	1	0	6	0	—	—
1979 I	7	3	8	0	—	—
1979–80 A		*did not bowl*				
1980 I		*did not bowl*				
1980 WI	7	2	11	0	—	—
1980 A		*did not bowl*				
1980–81 WI	3	2	5	0	—	—
1981 A	3	2	2	0	—	—
1981–82 I		*did not bowl*				
TOTALS	148 (944 balls)	45	382	7	54·57	3–47

Boycott's Bowling in Test Matches Against Each Country

Country	Overs	Maidens	Runs	Wickets	Average	Best Bowling
Australia	29	6	107	2	53·50	2–32
India	7	3	8	0	—	—
New Zealand	12	6	30	0	—	—
Pakistan	3	0	4	0	—	—
South Africa	87	26	217	5	43·40	3–47
West Indies	10	4	16	0	—	—
TOTALS	148	45	382	7	54·57	3–47

Boycott's Bowling in Test Matches on Each Ground

Ground	Overs	Maidens	Runs	Wickets	Average	Best Bowling
Adelaide	7	3	33	0	—	—
Antigua	3	2	5	0	—	—
Birmingham	5	1	8	0	—	—
Brisbane	4	0	16	0	—	—
Cape Town	20	5	47	3	15·66	3–47
Christchurch	12	6	30	0	—	—
Johannesburg	13	4	28	0	—	—
Lahore	3	0	4	0	—	—
Leeds	5	4	2	0	—	—
Lord's	7	2	11	0	—	—
Manchester	1	0	3	0	—	—
Melbourne	9	0	32	2	16·00	2–32
Nottingham	26	10	60	0	—	—
Perth	1	0	7	0	—	—
Port Elizabeth	28	7	82	2	41·00	1–13
Sydney	4	1	14	0	—	—
TOTALS	148	45	382	7	54·57	3–47

Boycott's Innings in Test Matches Against Australia

Season	Matches	Innings	Not Outs	Runs	Highest Score	Average	Hundreds	Fifties	Catches	Ducks
1964	4	6	0	291	113	48·50	1	1	0	0
1965–66	5	9	2	300	84	42·85	0	3	1	0
1968	3	5	0	162	49	32·40	0	0	1	0
1970–71	5	10	3	657	142*	93·85	2	5	4	0
1972	2	4	0	72	47	18·00	0	0	0	0
1977	3	5	2	442	191	147·33	2	1	0	0
1978–79	6	12	0	263	77	21·91	0	1	2	1
1979–80	3	6	1	176	99*	35·20	0	1	2	1
1980	1	2	1	190	128*	190·00	1	1	0	0
1981	6	12	0	392	137	32·66	1	1	2	1
TOTALS	38	71	9	2945	191	47·50	7	14	12	3

Runs in England 1,549   Runs in Australia 1,396

Boycott's Bowling in Test Matches Against Australia

Season	Overs	Maidens	Runs	Wickets	Average	Best Bowling
1964	1	0	3	0	—	—
1965–66	23	4	89	2	44·50	2·32
1968		did not bowl				
1970–71	1	0	7	0	—	—
1972		did not bowl				
1977		did not bowl				
1978–79	1	0	6	0	—	—
1979–80		did not bowl				
1980		did not bowl				
1981	3	2	2	0	—	—
TOTALS	29	6	107	2	53·50	2·32

Boycott's Innings in Test Matches Against India

Season	Matches	Innings	Not Outs	Runs	Highest Score	Average	Hundreds	Fifties	Catches	Ducks
1967	2	3	1	277	246*	138·50	1	0	2	0
1971	1	2	0	36	33	18·00	0	0	1	0
1974	1	2	0	16	10	8·00	0	0	1	0
1979	4	5	0	378	155	75·60	2	0	1	0
1980	1	2	1	65	43*	65·00	0	0	0	0
1981–82	4	8	1	312	105	45·00	1	2	2	0
TOTALS	13	22	3	1,084	246*	57·05	4	2	7	0

Runs in England 707   Runs in India 377

Boycott's Bowling in Test Matches Against India

Season	Overs	Maidens	Runs	Wickets	Average	Best Bowling
1967		did not bowl				
1971		did not bowl				
1974		did not bowl				
1979	7	3	8	0	—	—
1980		did not bowl				
1981–82		did not bowl				
TOTALS	7	3	8	0	—	—

Boycott's Innings in Test Matches Against New Zealand

Season	Matches	Innings	Not Outs	Runs	Highest Score	Average	Hundreds	Fifties	Catches	Ducks
1965	2	4	1	157	76	52·33	0	1	0	0
1965–66	2	3	0	13	5	4·33	0	0	2	0
1969	3	5	0	101	47	20·20	0	0	0	2
1973	3	5	0	320	115	64·00	1	3	1	0
1977–78	3	5	0	166	77	33·20	0	2	2	0
1978	2	3	0	159	131	53·00	1	0	0	0
TOTALS	15	25	1	916	131	38·16	2	6	5	2

Runs in England 737   Runs in New Zealand 179

Boycott's Bowling in Test Matches Against New Zealand

Season	Overs	Maidens	Runs	Wickets	Average	Best Bowling
1965		*did not bowl*				
1965–66	12	6	30	0	—	—
1969		*did not bowl*				
1973		*did not bowl*				
1977–78		*did not bowl*				
1978		*did not bowl*				
TOTALS	12	6	30	0	—	—

Boycott's Innings in Test Matches Against Pakistan

Season	Matches	Innings	Not Outs	Runs	Highest Score	Average	Hundreds	Fifties	Catches	Ducks
1967	1	2	1	16	15	16·00	0	0	0	0
1971	2	3	1	246	121*	123·00	2	0	0	0
1977–78	3	5	1	329	100*	82·25	1	3	0	0
TOTALS	6	10	3	591	121*	84·42	3	3	0	0

Runs in England 262   Runs in Pakistan 329

Boycott's Bowling in Test Matches Against Pakistan

Season	Overs	Maidens	Runs	Wickets	Average	Best Bowling
1967		did not bowl				
1971		did not bowl				
1977–78	3	0	4	0	—	—
TOTALS	3	0	4	0	—	—

Boycott's Innings in Test Matches Against South Africa

Season	Matches	Innings	Not Outs	Runs	Highest Score	Average	Hundreds	Fifties	Catches	Ducks
1964–65	5	8	2	298	117	49·66	1	2	2	0
1965	2	4	0	75	31	18·75	0	0	0	1
TOTALS	7	12	2	373	117	37·30	1	2	2	1

Runs in England 75   Runs in South Africa 298

Boycott's Bowling in Test Matches Against South Africa

Season	Overs	Maidens	Runs	Wickets	Average	Best Bowling
1964–65	61	16	157	5	31·40	3–47
1965	26	10	60	0	—	—
TOTALS	87	26	217	5	43·40	3–47

Boycott's Innings in Test Matches Against the West Indies

Season	Matches	Innings	Not Outs	Runs	Highest Score	Average	Hundreds	Fifties	Catches	Ducks
1966	4	7	0	186	71	26·57	0	2	0	1
1967–68	5	8	1	463	116	66·14	1	4	1	1
1969	3	6	1	270	128	54·00	2	0	0	1
1973	3	5	1	202	97	50·50	0	2	2	0
1973–74	5	9	0	421	112	46·77	1	3	2	0
1980	5	10	1	368	86	40·88	0	3	0	0
1980–81	4	8	1	295	104*	42·14	1	1	2	1
TOTALS	29	53	5	2,205	128	45·93	5	15	7	4

Runs in England 1,026   Runs in West Indies 1,179

Boycott's Bowling in Test Matches Against the West Indies

Season	Overs	Maidens	Runs	Wickets	Average	Best Bowling
1966		did not bowl				
1967–68		did not bowl				
1969		did not bowl				
1973		did not bowl				
1973–74		did not bowl				
1980	7	2	11	0	—	—
1980–81	3	2	5	0	—	—
TOTALS	10	4	16	0	—	—

Boycott's Modes of Dismissal in Test Matches

Season	Bowled	Caught	Hit Wicket	LBW	Run Out	Stumped
1964 A	2	4	0	0	0	0
1964–65 S A	0	5	0	1	0	0
1965 N Z	0	2	0	1	0	0
1965 S A	1	3	0	0	0	0
1965–66 A	1	4	0	2	0	0
1965–66 N Z	1	1	0	0	1	0

Season	Bowled	Caught	Hit Wicket	LBW	Run Out	Stumped
1966 W I	1	5	0	1	0	0
1967 I	1	0	0	0	0	1
1967 P	1	0	0	0	0	0
1967–68 W I	3	2	0	2	0	0
1968 A	0	4	0	1	0	0
1969 W I	0	3	0	2	0	0
1969 NZ	3	2	0	0	0	0
1970–71 A	0	5	0	0	1	1
1971 P	0	2	0	0	0	0
1971 I	0	2	0	0	0	0
1972 A	2	1	0	1	0	0
1973 NZ	0	3	0	1	1	0
1973 W I	0	4	0	0	0	0
1973–74 W I	2	7	0	0	0	0
1974 I	0	1	0	1	0	0
1977 A	0	3	0	0	0	0
1977–78 P	2	1	0	0	1	0
1977–78 NZ	1	2	0	1	1	0
1978 NZ	1	2	0	0	0	0
1978–79 A	1	6	0	4	1	0
1979 I	1	2	0	2	0	0
1979–80 A	2	2	0	1	0	0
1980 I	0	1	0	0	0	0
1980 W I	1	6	0	1	1	0
1980 A	0	1	0	0	0	0
1980–81 W I	1	6	0	0	0	0
1981	1	8	0	3	0	0
1981–82 I	1	4	0	2	0	0
TOTALS	30	104	0	27	7	2

Boycott's Opening Partners in Test Matches

F. Titmus	2	(innings)	B. Luckhurst	12
J. Edrich	35		D. Amiss	19
B. Barber	26		M. Brearley	21
K. Barrington	1		B. Rose	6
J. Murray	2		D. Randall	3
W. Russell	3		G. Gooch	49
C. Milburn	6		A. Butcher	2
C. Cowdrey	2		W. Larkins	2

Bowlers Who Have Dismissed Boycott the Most in Test Matches

M. Holding	7	R. Collinge	5
D. Lillee	7	C. Croft	5
G. Sobers	7	L. Gibbs	5
T. Alderman	6	Kapil Dev	5
J. Gleeson	6	W. Hall	4
A. Hurst	6	R. Hogg	4
G. McKenzie	6	B. Julien	4
R. Motz	6	K. Boyce	3

Players Who Have Caught Boycott the Most in Test Matches

R. Marsh	8 (+1*st*)	A. Dick	2
Deryck Murray	8	F. Engineer	2 (+1*st*)
E. Barlow	3	M. Findley	2
J. Garner	3	S. Gavaskar	2
K. Hughes	3	R. Hadlee	2
A. Kallicharran	3	B. Jarman	2
R. Kanhai	3	S. Kirmani	2
R. McCosker	3	G. McKenzie	2
R. Simpson	3	David Murray	2
A. Border	2	J. Parker	2
B. Congdon	2	I. Redpath	2
		st = stumped	

Boycott's Records

During Boycott's career, to the end of the 1981–82 season, he had achieved the following records:

First Class

40,152 runs – 12th highest run scorer
126 hundreds – eighth highest century maker
22 times 1,000 runs in a season – equal sixth
1,000 runs in four different countries – only three batsmen have done this:

Sobers	WI, E, I, A
Cowdrey	E, SA, WI, A
Boycott	E, SA, WI, A

Only player to average 100 in a season twice, the only Englishman to do it at all

Eleven consecutive averages of over 50 in an English season

56·31 career average – 2nd highest for a player scoring over 25,000 runs

He has been on trophy-winning sides with Yorkshire on seven occasions, five County Championships and two Gillette Cups

Tests

8,114 runs – highest run getter

22 hundreds – equal fourth highest century maker, equal first for England

48 hundred partnerships – the highest

64 scores of over fifty – the highest

2,205 runs *v* West Indies – highest by an Englishman

2,945 runs *v* Australia – second highest by an Englishman

Second player to play 100 Tests after Cowdrey

Batted in most innings – 193

Most tests by a Yorkshireman

246* – 36th highest score in Test cricket, also the top score in an England–India Test match

Highest average in an England–Australia series – 147·33

Batted on all five days of a Test match

Only player to score 100th 100 in a Test match

Equal 7th wicket stand of 215 with Knott for England against Australia

100s	*v*			
	Australia	7—equal	4th
	India	4—	1st
	New Zealand	2—equal	6th
	Pakistan	2—equal	2nd
	West Indies	5—equal	2nd

Two 99s in Test matches – equal with M. Smith

Only player to score 99 not out in a Test match

One of 3 batsmen to have scored 100s against six countries, the others being Barrington and Cowdrey

One of 2 batsmen to have scored 100s on all six Test match grounds in England, the other being Barrington

Boycott and Edrich are only the 3rd English pair to score a 100 partnership in both innings

One-day Games

Gillette Cup

1963

1   Yorkshire *v* **Sussex**
at Hove   *June 12*
Sussex won by 22 runs

270   63·3 overs   *run out*   71
292   64 overs   0*ct*

1964

2   Yorkshire *v* **Middlesex**
at Lord's   *May 27*
Middlesex won by 61 runs

90   46 overs   *b* Bennett   16
151   52·2 overs   0*ct*

1965

3   Yorkshire *v* **Leicestershire**
at Leicester   *May 22*
Yorkshire won by 6 wickets

170–4   53·2 overs   *lbw* Cross   56
168   49·4 overs   0*ct*
10–1–33–1 (Hallam bowled)

3RD ROUND
4   Yorkshire *v* **Somerset**
at Taunton   *June 23*
Yorkshire won by 7 wickets

64–3   31·5 overs   *not out*   23
63   36·2 overs   0*ct*

THE FINAL
5   Yorkshire *v* **Surrey**
at Lord's   *September 4*
Yorkshire won by 175 runs

317–4   60 overs   *ct* Storey
b Barrington   146
142   40·4 overs   0*ct*

1966

6   Yorkshire *v* **Somerset**
at Taunton   *May 21*
Somerset won by 40 runs

150   50·1 overs   *ct* Clayton
b Alley   21
190–7   60 overs   0*ct*   3–0–12–0

1967

7   Yorkshire *v* **Cambridge
University**
at Castleford   *May 25*
Yorkshire won by 6 wickets

46–4   6·5 overs   *did not bat*
43–8   10 overs   0*ct*

3RD ROUND
8   Yorkshire *v* **Lancashire**
at Manchester   *June 14*
Lancashire won by 4 runs

190   59·2 overs   *ct* Sullivan
b Lever   19
194   57·5 overs   0*ct*

1968

9   Yorkshire *v* **Warwickshire**
at Birmingham   *May 25, 27, 28*
Warwickshire won by 4 wickets

171–9   60 overs   *run out*   10
172–6   57·5 overs   0*ct*

1969

10   Yorkshire *v* **Norfolk**
at Lakenham   *May 10, 11*
Yorkshire won by 89 runs

167   44·4 overs   *ct* Mattocks
b Moore   33
78   50·4 overs   0*ct*

11   Yorkshire *v* **Lancashire**
at Manchester   *June 7*
Yorkshire won by 7 wickets

174–3   48·5 overs   *ct* Sullivan
b Lever   58
173–8   60 overs   0*ct*

12   Yorkshire *v* **Surrey**
at The Oval   *July 2*
Yorkshire won by 138 runs

272   59·4 overs   *ct* Younis
b Gibson   92
134   41·3 overs   0*ct*

13   Yorkshire *v* **Nottinghamshire**
at Scarborough   *July 30*
Yorkshire won by 68 runs

191   59·4 overs   *ct* Murray
b Stead   0
123   50·5 overs   0*ct*

1970

14   Yorkshire *v* **Surrey**
at Harrogate   *April 25, 26, 27*
Surrey won by 58 runs

76   29·4 overs   *b* Willis   10
134–8   60 overs   0*ct*

1971

15   Yorkshire *v* **Kent**
at Canterbury   *June 12*
Kent won by 6 wickets

148   59·2 overs
ct Luckhurst   *b* Julien   46
149–4   42·4 overs   0*ct*

1972

16   Yorkshire *v* **Warwickshire**
at Leeds   *July 5*
Warwickshire won by 4 wickets

173   60 overs   *retired hurt*   12
176   58 overs   0*ct*

1973

17   Yorkshire *v* **Durham**
at Harrogate   *June 30*
Durham won by 5 wickets

135   58·4 overs   *b* Wilkinson   14
138–5   51·3 overs   0*ct*

1974

18   Yorkshire *v* **Hampshire**
at Bradford   *July 10, 11*
Yorkshire won by 41 runs

233–6   60 overs   *lbw* Taylor   22
192   54·5 overs   1*ct*
(Roberts   *b* Leadbeater)

19   Yorkshire *v* **Lancashire**
at Leeds   *July 31, August 1*
Lancashire won by 32 runs

173   54·3 overs   *ct* Engineer
b Lever   39
205   59 overs   0*ct*

1975

20   Yorkshire *v* **Leicestershire**
at Leeds   *July 16*
Leicestershire won by 1 wicket

109   48·5 overs
lbw McVicker   24
111–9   52·3 overs   0*ct*

1976

21   Yorkshire *v* **Gloucestershire**
at Leeds   *July 14*
Gloucestershire won by 4 wickets

232–9   60 overs   *run out*   38
233–6   55 overs   0*ct*

1977

22   Yorkshire *v* **Hampshire**
at Bournemouth   *July 13, 14*
Hampshire won by 86 runs

175   53·3 overs   *b* Taylor   24
261   60 overs   0*ct*

1978

23   Yorkshire *v* **Durham**
at Middlesbrough   *July 7*
Yorkshire won by 113 runs

249–6   45 overs   *ct* Harland
b Wilkinson   18
136–7   45 overs   1*ct* (Birtwisle
b Oldham)

2ND ROUND
24   Yorkshire *v* **Nottinghamshire**
at Bradford   *July 19, 20*
Yorkshire won by 1 wicket

226–9   59·3 overs   *b* Birch   62
225–7   60 overs   2*ct* (Rice
b Stevenson, Smedley
b Sidebottom)

QUARTER FINAL
25   Yorkshire *v* **Sussex**
at Leeds   *August 4*
Sussex won by 9 runs

59–8   10 overs   *not out*   2
68–6   10 overs   0*ct*

1979

26   Yorkshire *v* **Durham**
at Chester-le-Street   *July 18*
Yorkshire won by 4 wickets

214–6   59·1 overs   *ct* Greenword
b Kippax   92
213–9   60 overs   1*ct* (Romaines
b Cooper)

QUARTER FINAL
27   Yorkshire *v* **Middlesex**
at Lord's   *August 8, 9*
Middlesex won by 70 runs

146   54·3 overs   *run out*   26
216   60 overs   0*ct*

1980

28   Yorkshire *v* **Kent**
at Leeds   *July 16*
Yorkshire won by 46 runs

279–6   60 overs   *b* Woolmer   87
233   56 overs   0*ct*   12–0–53–1
(Hills   *ct* Stevenson)

QUARTER FINAL
29   Yorkshire *v* **Hampshire**
at Southampton   *July 30*
Yorkshire won by 7 wickets

197–3   54·5 overs
lbw Stevenson   7
196   58 overs   0*ct*   9–2–33–1
(Nicholas   *st* Bairstow)

SEMI-FINAL
30   Yorkshire *v* **Surrey**
at The Oval   *August 13, 14*
Surrey won by 4 wickets

135   53·5 overs   *lbw* Clarke   5
136–6   47·5 overs
0*ct*   5–1–11–0

Boycott's Innings in the Gillette Cup, Season by Season

Season	Matches	Innings	Not Outs	Runs	Highest Score	Average	Hundreds	Fifties	Catches	Ducks
1963	1	1	0	71	71	71·00	0	1	0	0
1964	1	1	0	16	16	16·00	0	0	0	0
1965	3	3	1	225	146	112·50	1	1	0	0
1966	1	1	0	21	21	21·00	0	0	0	0
1967	2	1	0	19	19	19·00	0	0	0	0
1968	1	1	0	10	10	10·00	0	0	0	0
1969	4	4	0	183	92	45·75	0	2	0	1
1970	1	1	0	10	10	10·00	0	0	0	0
1971	1	1	0	46	46	46·00	0	0	0	0
1972	1	1	1	12	12*	—	0	0	0	0
1973	1	1	0	14	14	14·00	0	0	0	0
1974	2	2	0	61	39	30·50	0	0	1	0
1975	1	1	0	24	24	24·00	0	0	0	0
1976	1	1	0	38	38	38·00	0	0	0	0
1977	1	1	0	24	24	24·00	0	0	0	0
1978	3	3	1	82	62	41·00	0	1	3	0
1979	2	2	0	118	92	59·00	0	1	1	0
1980	3	3	0	99	87	33·00	0	1	0	0
TOTALS	30	29	3	1,073	146	41·26	1	7	5	1

Gold Awards
v Surrey at Lord's, 1965
v Durham at Chester-le-Street, 1979

Boycott's Innings in the Gillette Cup Against Each Team

Team	Matches	Innings	Not Outs	Runs	Highest Score	Average	Hundreds	Fifties	Catches	Ducks
Cambridge University	1	0	—	—	—	—	—	—	0	—
Durham	3	3	0	124	92	41·33	0	1	2	0
Gloucestershire	1	1	0	38	38	38·00	0	0	0	0
Hampshire	3	3	0	53	24	17·66	0	0	1	0
Kent	2	2	0	133	87	66·50	0	1	0	0
Lancashire	3	3	0	116	58	38·66	0	1	0	0
Leicestershire	2	2	0	80	56	40·00	0	1	0	0
Middlesex	2	2	0	42	26	21·00	0	0	0	0
Norfolk	1	1	0	33	33	33·00	0	0	0	0
Nottinghamshire	2	2	0	62	62	31·00	0	1	2	1
Somerset	2	2	1	44	23*	44·00	0	0	0	0
Surrey	4	4	1	253	146	84·33	1	1	0	0
Sussex	2	2	0	73	71	36·50	0	1	0	0
Warwickshire	2	2	1	12	12	12·00	0	0	0	0
TOTALS	30	29	3	1,073	146	41·26	1	7	5	1

Boycott's Innings in the Gillette Cup on Each Ground

Ground	Matches	Innings	Not Outs	Runs	Highest Score	Average	Hundreds	Fifties	Catches	Ducks
Birmingham	1	1	0	10	10	10·00	0	0	0	0
Bournemouth	1	1	0	24	24	24·00	0	0	0	0
Bradford	2	2	0	84	62	42·00	0	1	3	0
Canterbury	1	1	0	46	46	46·00	0	0	0	0
Castleford	1	0	—	—	—	—	—	—	0	—
Chester-le-Street	1	1	0	92	92	92·00	0	1	1	0
Harrogate	2	2	0	24	14	12·00	0	0	0	0
Hove	1	1	0	71	71	71·00	0	1	0	0
Lakenham	1	1	0	33	33	33·00	0	0	0	0
Leeds	6	6	2	202	87	50·50	0	1	0	0
Leicester	1	1	0	56	56	56·00	0	1	0	0
Lord's	3	3	0	188	146	62·66	1	0	0	0
Manchester	2	2	0	77	58	38·50	0	1	0	0

Ground	Matches	Innings	Not Outs	Runs	Highest Score	Average	Hundreds	Fifties	Catches	Ducks
Middlesbrough	1	1	0	18	18	18·00	0	0	1	0
Scarborough	1	1	0	0	0	—	0	0	0	1
Southampton	1	1	0	7	7	7·00	0	0	0	0
Taunton	2	2	1	44	23*	44·00	0	0	0	0
The Oval	2	2	0	97	92	48·50	0	1	0	0
TOTALS	30	29	3	1,073	146	41·26	1	7	5	1

Boycott's Bowling in the Gillette Cup, Season by Season

Season	Overs	Maidens	Runs	Wickets	Average	Best Bowling
1965	10	1	33	1	33·00	1–33
1966	3	0	12	0	—	—
1980	26	3	97	2	48·50	1–33
TOTALS	39	4	142	3	47·33	1–33

Boycott did not bowl in any other season

Boycott's Bowling in the Gillette Cup against Each Team

Team	Overs	Maidens	Runs	Wickets	Average	Best Bowling
Hampshire	9	2	33	1	33·00	1–33
Kent	12	0	53	1	53·00	1–53
Leicestershire	10	1	33	1	33·00	1–33
Somerset	3	0	12	0	—	—
Surrey	5	1	11	0	—	—
TOTALS	39	4	142	3	47·33	1–33

Boycott's Bowling in the Gillette Cup on Each Ground

Ground	Overs	Maidens	Runs	Wickets	Average	Best Bowling
Leeds	12	0	53	1	53·00	1–53
Leicester	10	1	33	1	33·00	1–33
Southampton	9	2	33	1	33·00	1–33
Taunton	3	0	12	0	—	—
The Oval	5	1	11	0	—	—
TOTALS	39	4	142	3	47·33	1–33

Boycott's Modes of Dismissal in the Gillette Cup

Season	Bowled	Caught	Hit Wicket	LBW	Run Out	Stumped
1963	0	0	0	0	1	0
1964	1	0	0	0	0	0
1965	0	1	0	1	0	0
1966	0	1	0	0	0	0
1967	0	1	0	0	0	0
1968	0	0	0	0	1	0
1969	0	4	0	0	0	0
1970	1	0	0	0	0	0
1971	0	1	0	0	0	0
1972	0	0	0	0	0	0
1973	1	0	0	0	0	0
1974	0	1	0	1	0	0
1975	0	0	0	1	0	0
1976	0	0	0	0	1	0
1977	1	0	0	0	0	0
1978	1	1	0	0	0	0
1979	0	1	0	0	1	0
1980	1	0	0	2	0	0
TOTALS	6	11	0	5	4	0

Nat West Trophy

1981

1   Yorkshire v **Kent**
at Canterbury   *July 11*
Kent won by 6 wickets

222–6   60 overs   *b* Cowdrey   32
223–4   57·2 overs   0*ct*

Boycott's Innings in the Nat West Trophy

	Matches	Innings	Not Outs	Runs	Highest Score	Average	Hundreds	Fifties	Catches	Ducks
1981 Kent Canterbury	1	1	0	32	32	32·00	0	0	0	0

Mode of Dismissal: bowled

John Player League

1969

1   Yorkshire v **Middlesex**
at Lord's   *April 27*
Middlesex won by 43 runs

94   32·2 overs   *run out*   3
137–8   40 overs   0*ct*

2   Yorkshire v **Glamorgan**
at Neath   *May 4*
Yorkshire won by 4 wickets

91–6   28·3 overs   *ct* A. Jones
b Nash   18
90   28 overs   0*ct*

3   Yorkshire v **Sussex**
at Huddersfield   *June 1*
Yorkshire won by 7 runs

89–7   19 overs   *ct* Parks
b A. Buss   35
82–7   19 overs   2*ct* (Suttle
b Old, Greig   *b* Nicholson)

4   Yorkshire v **Essex**
at Hull   *June 22*
Essex won by 85 runs

88   32 overs   *b* East   13
173–8   40 overs   1*ct* (Fletcher
b Hutton)

5   Yorkshire v Derbyshire
at Sheffield   *July 20*
Yorkshire won by 9 runs

157–6   38 overs   *ct* Taylor
b Ward   8
148–8   38 overs   2*ct* (Page
b Stringer, Morgan   *b* Old)

6   Yorkshire v Leicestershire
at Scarborough   *August 17*
Leicestershire won by 25 runs

161–7   40 overs   *not out*   73
186–8   40 overs   0*ct*

7   Yorkshire v Northamptonshire
at Bradford   *August 31*
Yorkshire won by 39 runs

169–8   39 overs   *ct* Johnson
b Crump   2
130–9   39 overs   1*ct* (Willey
b Cope)

1970

8   Yorkshire v Derbyshire
at Chesterfield   *May 3*
Derbyshire won by 40 runs

154–4   40 overs   *b* Wilkins   32
194–5   40 overs   2*ct*
(Wilkins *b* Nicholson, Page
b Wilson) 8–0–34–1 (D. Smith
ct Leadbeater)

9   Yorkshire v Glamorgan
at Bradford   *May 17*
Glamorgan won by 1 run

181–6   40 overs   *ct* Kingston
b Nash   12
182–4   40 overs   0*ct*

10   Yorkshire v Nottinghamshire
at Sheffield   *May 24*
Nottinghamshire won by 2 wickets

235–6   39 overs   *ct* Hassan
b Stead   27
236–8   38·5 overs   0*ct*
8–0–36–1 (Harris bowled)

11   Yorkshire v Hampshire
at Hull   *June 7*
Hampshire won by 141 runs

74–9   40 overs   *b* White   4
215–2   40 overs   0*ct*   4–0–26–0

12   Yorkshire v Leicestershire
at Leicester   *June 14*
Yorkshire won by 1 run

182–7   40 overs   *ct* Tolchard
b Spencer   1
181–8   40 overs   0*ct*

13   Yorkshire v Warwickshire
at Birmingham   *June 21*
Warwickshire won by 7 wickets

186–9   40 overs   *ct* Brown
b Ibadulla   73
191–3   38 overs   0*ct*

14   Yorkshire v Sussex
at Middlesbrough   *July 12*
Yorkshire won by 25 runs

207   40 overs   *ct-b* Greig   53
182   36·4 overs   1*ct* (Greenidge
b Woodford) 3–0–25–0

15   Yorkshire v Kent
at Leeds   *July 19*
Yorkshire won by 2 wickets

198–8   39·5 overs   *ct* Ealham
b Asif   24
197–6   40 overs   0*ct*

16   Yorkshire v Essex
at Colchester   *July 26*
Yorkshire won by 43 runs

189–4   31·4 overs   *ct-b* Lever   98
146–8   31·4 overs   1*ct* (Taylor
b Old)

17   Yorkshire v Surrey
at Scarborough   *August 9*
Surrey won by 96 runs

91   30·1 overs   *ct* Storey
b Arnold   0
187   39·3 overs   1*ct* (Intikhab
b Old)

18 Yorkshire _v_ Gloucestershire
at Gloucester _August 23_
Gloucestershire won by 45 runs

136–6 40 overs _ct_ Westley
_b_ Procter 72
181–6 40 overs 0_ct_

19 Yorkshire _v_ Lancashire
at Manchester _August 30_
Lancashire won by 7 wickets

165 37·5 overs _ct_ Bond
_b_ Shuttleworth 81
166–3 35·5 overs 0_ct_

20 Yorkshire _v_ Middlesex
at Bradford _September 6_
No Result

did not bat
0–0 1·1 overs 0_ct_

1971

21 Yorkshire _v_ Warwickshire
at Middlesbrough _May 9_
Yorkshire won by 106 runs

230–7 40 overs _ct_ Jameson
_b_ Hemmings 93
124 37·4 overs 2_ct_ (M. Smith
_b_ Hutton, A. Smith _b_ Schofield)

22 Yorkshire _v_ Middlesex
at Lord's _May 16_
Middlesex won by 27 runs

126 35·5 overs _ct-b_ Jones 23
153–7 39 overs 0_ct_

23 Yorkshire _v_ Leicestershire
at Hull _June 27_
Yorkshire won by a faster scoring
rate over 23 overs

226–4 37 overs _ct_ Tolchard
_b_ McKenzie 46
92–5 23 overs 0_ct_

24 Yorkshire _v_ Kent
at Maidstone _July 4_
Kent won by 83 runs

137–6 39 overs _ct_ Shepherd
_b_ Woolmer 16
220–9 39 overs 0_ct_

25 Yorkshire _v_ Lancashire
at Leeds _July 18_
Lancashire won by 48 runs

191–7 40 overs _b_ Simmons 62
239–4 40 overs 1_ct_
(Engineer _b_ Cooper)

26 Yorkshire _v_ Essex
at Bradford _August 1_
Essex won by 4 wickets

91 36·3 overs _ct_ Taylor
_b_ Edmeades 15
95–6 34·5 overs 1_ct_ (Turner
_b_ Woodford)

27 Yorkshire _v_ Sussex
at Hove _August 29_
Yorkshire won by 39 runs

147–6 34 overs _ct_ A. Buss
_b_ Snow 54
108 31 overs 0_ct_

28 Yorkshire _v_ Hampshire
at Bournemouth _September 5_
Hampshire won by a faster scoring
rate over 34 overs

202–5 40 overs _ct-b_ Jesty 61
176–4 34 overs 0_ct_

29 Yorkshire _v_ Northamptonshire
at Bradford _September 12_
Yorkshire won by 30 runs

169 40 overs _ct-b_ Breakwell 73
139–6 40 overs 0_ct_

1972

30 Yorkshire _v_ Glamorgan
at Swansea _May 14_
Yorkshire won by 6 wickets

116–4 36·5 overs _ct_ Fredericks
_b_ Solanky 41
113 39·2 overs 1_ct_ (Nash
_b_ Hutton)

31 Yorkshire v Derbyshire
at Bradford   *May 28*
Yorkshire won by 7 wickets

110–3   26·2 overs   *run out*   34
109   26·3 overs   0*ct*

32 Yorkshire v Worcestershire
at Worcester   *June 4*
Worcestershire won by 4 wickets

135   39·2 overs
lbw d'Oliveira   16
136–6   36·2 overs   0*ct*

33 Yorkshire v Somerset
at Sheffield   *June 18*
Yorkshire won by 8 wickets

106–2   20·1 overs   *not out*   52
103–8   21 overs   2*ct* (Kitchen
b Nicholson, Langford
b Nicholson)

34 Yorkshire v Lancashire
at Manchester   *July 2*
Yorkshire won by 8 wickets

178–2   38·1 overs   *run out*   32
177–7   40 overs   1*ct* (Bond
b Nicholson)

35 Yorkshire v Hampshire
at Bradford   *August 13*
Hampshire won by 3 wickets

161–9   40 overs   *b* O'Sullivan   12
165–7   39·1 overs   0*ct*

36 Yorkshire v Kent
at Folkestone   *August 20*
Kent won by 9 wickets

159–9   39 overs   *ct* Asif
b Shepherd   40
163–1   34·5 overs   1*ct*
(Johnson   *b* Hutton)

37 Yorkshire v Gloucestershire
at Tewkesbury   *September 3*
Yorkshire won by 8 wickets

91–2   29·2 overs   *b* Hewitt   29
90   39·1 overs   1*ct*
(Graveney   *b* Cooper)

38 Yorkshire v Surrey
at The Oval   *September 10*
Yorkshire won by 4 wickets

152–6   38·3 overs   *b* Arnold   0
148–9   39 overs   0*ct*

1973

39 Yorkshire v Glamorgan
at Colwyn Bay   *April 29*
Yorkshire won by 24 runs

186–5   40 overs   *not out*   104
162–6   40 overs   0*ct*

40 Yorkshire v Nottinghamshire
at Nottingham   *May 6*
Yorkshire won by 7 wickets

135–3   32·1 overs   *not out*   72
134–8   34 overs   1*ct*
(Frost   *b* Nicholson)

41 Yorkshire v Worcestershire
at Worcester   *May 13*
Worcestershire won by 24 runs

71–5   10 overs   *b* Holder   13
95–4   10 overs   0*ct*

42 Yorkshire v Lancashire
at Leeds   *May 27*
Lancashire won by 6 wickets

109–8   40 overs   *lbw* Lee   10
112–4   33·5 overs   0*ct*

43 Yorkshire v Northamptonshire
at Northampton   *June 3*
Yorkshire won by 8 wickets

142–2   33·3 overs   *ct* Bedi
b Cottam   42
140   39·1 overs   0*ct*

44 Yorkshire v Warwickshire
at Birmingham   *June 17*
Yorkshire won by 43 runs

230–8   40 overs
ct-b Hemmings   67
187   39·4 overs   2*ct*
(M. Smith   *b* Cooper,
Whitehouse   *b* Cooper)

45 Yorkshire v Kent
at Dover *July 15*
Kent won by 9 wickets

116–9 33 overs *b* Asif 23
119–1 23·4 overs 0*ct*

46 Yorkshire v Derbyshire
at Scarborough *July 22*
Yorkshire won by 87 runs

174–6 40 overs *b* Buxton 82
87 30 overs 0*ct*

47 Yorkshire v Essex
at Hull *August 19*
Yorkshire won by 5 wickets

124–5 35 overs *b* Edmeades 31
120 38 overs 1*ct* (Pont
b Robinson)

48 Yorkshire v Hampshire
at Bradford *September 2*
Yorkshire won by a faster scoring
rate

85–5 19·2 overs *ct* O'Sullivan
b Herman 0
121–4 30 overs 0*ct*

1974

49 Yorkshire v Glamorgan
at Hull *May 19*
Glamorgan won by 6 wickets

154–8 40 overs *ct* Llewellyn
b Solanky 13
155–4 39 overs 1*ct* (Lewis
b Robinson)

50 Yorkshire v Lancashire
at Manchester *May 26*
Yorkshire won by 37 runs

191–9 40 overs *ct* Lyon
b Lever 0
154 38·2 overs 1*ct*
(Sullivan *b* Old)

**51 Yorkshire v
Northamptonshire**
at Huddersfield *June 2*
Yorkshire won by 59 runs

186–6 40 overs *not out* 108
127 34·4 overs 1*ct* (Steele
b Robinson)

52 Yorkshire v Middlesex
at Leeds *June 23*
Yorkshire won by 125 runs

148 38·2 overs *st* Murray
b Edmonds 48
23 19·4 overs 0*ct*

53 Yorkshire v Essex
at Colchester *June 30*
Yorkshire won by 4 wickets

124–6 39·4 overs *ct* Gooch
b Acfield 22
123 40 overs 1*ct* (Fletcher
b Hutton)

54 Yorkshire v Leicestershire
at Leicester *July 28*
Leicestershire won by 4 wickets

187 40 overs *b* McVicker 75
190–6 40 overs 0*ct*

55 Yorkshire v Nottinghamshire
at Scarborough *August 4*
Yorkshire won by 25 runs

186–9 40 overs *ct* Harris
b Taylor 11
161 38·5 overs 1*ct* (White
b Nicholson)

56 Yorkshire v Kent
at Leeds *August 11*
Yorkshire won by 45 runs

178–9 40 overs *b* Woolmer 30
133 37 overs 1*ct* (Shepherd
b Hutton)

57 **Yorkshire** *v* **Derbyshire**
at Chesterfield   *August 18*
Yorkshire won by 4 wickets

139–6   35·3 overs   *ct* Cartwright
b Venkataraghavan   46
138–8   37 overs   0*ct*

58 **Yorkshire** *v* **Gloucestershire**
at Bristol   *August 25*   No Result

55–1   17·2 overs   *ct* Procter
b Knight   10

1975

59 **Yorkshire** *v* **Derbyshire**
at Huddersfield   *May 11*
Yorkshire won by 104 runs

220–4   39 overs   *ct* Harvey-
Walker   *b* Russell   58
116–8   39 overs   0*ct*

60 **Yorkshire** *v* **Kent**
at Canterbury   *May 18*
Kent won by 6 wickets

115   39·3 overs   *b* Shepherd   24
116–4   36·1 overs   0*ct*

61 **Yorkshire** *v* **Warwickshire**
at Birmingham   *May 25*
Warwickshire won by 8 wickets

217–3   40 overs   *ct* Amiss
b Hemmings   65
218–2   37·1 overs   2*ct* (Jameson
b Nicholson, Amiss   *b* Old)

62 **Yorkshire** *v* **Leicestershire**
at Hull   *June 1*
Yorkshire won by 13 runs

154–9   40 overs   *ct-b* Steele   32
141   39·1 overs   0*ct*

63 **Yorkshire** *v* **Worcestershire**
at Worcester   *June 8*
Yorkshire won by 9 wickets

123–1   27·5 overs   *not out*   71
122   38·5 overs   0*ct*

64 **Yorkshire** *v* **Somerset**
at Bradford   *June 22*
Yorkshire won by 12 runs

172   40 overs   *ct* Richards
b Jennings   47
160   39 overs   0*ct*

65 **Yorkshire** *v* **Surrey**
at Scarborough   *June 29*
Yorkshire won by 6 wickets

159–4   32·3 overs
ct Skinner   *b* Roope   20
158   40 overs   3*ct* (Edrich
b Robinson, Butcher   *b* Old,
Arnold   *b* Stevenson)

66 **Yorkshire** *v* **Northamptonshire**
at Northampton   *July 20*
Northamptonshire won by 17 runs

112   28 overs   *ct-b* Cottam   58
129–8   30 overs   1*ct* (Steele
b Old)

67 **Yorkshire** *v* **Middlesex**
at Lord's   *July 27*
Yorkshire won by 10 wickets

144–0   36·5 overs   *not out*   60
143–7   40 overs   1*ct*
(Butcher   *b* Stevenson)

68 **Yorkshire** *v* **Glamorgan**
at Cardiff   *August 3*
Yorkshire won by 2 wickets

150–8   38·4 overs   *ct* Cordle
b Armstrong   1
146   39·4 overs   3*ct* (A. Jones
b Old, Majid   *b* Cooper,
E. Jones   *b* Cooper)

69 **Yorkshire** *v* **Hampshire**
at Bradford   *August 10*
Hampshire won by 2 wickets

138   36·2 overs
ct Stephenson   *b* Taylor   30
139–8   39·5 overs   0*ct*

70 Yorkshire _v_ Gloucestershire
at Scarborough   _August 24_
Yorkshire won by 11 runs

200–1   40 overs   _ct_ Zaheer
_b_ Knight   99
189–8   40 overs   0_ct_

71 Yorkshire _v_ Nottinghamshire
at Nottingham   _August 31_
Nottinghamshire won by 47 runs

147   36·1 overs   _ct_ Hassan
_b_ White   23
194–7   40 overs   1_ct_ (Rice
_b_ Stevenson)

72 Yorkshire _v_ Essex
at Bradford   _September 14_
Yorkshire won by 9 wickets

195–1   39·2 overs   _not out_   78
191   40 overs   1_ct_ (Edmeades
_b_ Stevenson)

1976

73 Yorkshire _v_ Surrey
at The Oval   _April 25_
Surrey won by 6 wickets

219–7   39 overs   _b_ Intikhab   14
220–4   37·5 overs   0_ct_

74 Yorkshire _v_ Gloucestershire
at Bristol   _May 9_
Yorkshire won by 36 runs

172–9   40 overs   _run out_   55
136   33·1 overs   0_ct_

75 Yorkshire _v_ Lancashire
at Manchester   _May 16_
Yorkshire won by 3 wickets

127–7   39·1 overs
retired hurt   18
123–8   40 overs   0_ct_

76 Yorkshire _v_ Somerset
at Glastonbury   _July 18_
Somerset won by 6 wickets

205–2   40 overs   _not out_   82
207–4   38 overs   0_ct_

77 Yorkshire _v_ Derbyshire
at Chesterfield   _August 1_
Derbyshire won by 7 wickets

197–7   40 overs   _ct_ Barlow
_b_ Stevenson   46
198–3   37·5 overs   0_ct_

78 Yorkshire _v_ Nottinghamshire
at Scarborough   _August 8_
Yorkshire won by 9 wickets

222–1   38·5 overs   _not out_   89
218–7   40 overs   0_ct_

79 Yorkshire _v_ Leicestershire
at Leicester   _August 15_
Leicestershire won by 6 runs

173–6   40 overs   _b_ McVicker   19
179   39·3 overs   0_ct_

80 Yorkshire _v_ Glamorgan
at Leeds   _August 22_
Yorkshire won by 5 wickets

190–5   39·2 overs   _b_ Allin   13
188–6   40 overs   0_ct_

81 Yorkshire _v_ Middlesex
at Bradford   _August 29_
Yorkshire won by 10 wickets

135–0   27·5 overs   _not out_   56
134–9   40 overs   0_ct_

82 Yorkshire _v_ Essex
at Leyton   _September 5_
Essex won by 12 runs

142   38·2 overs   _b_ Lever   0
154   38·4 overs   1_ct_ (Fosh
_b_ Robinson)

1977

83 Yorkshire _v_ Gloucestershire
at Bradford   _May 1_   No Result

did not bat
84–2   24 overs   0_ct_

84 Yorkshire *v* **Sussex**
at Hove   *May 8*
Sussex won by 5 wickets

172–3   40 overs   *ct* M. Buss
b Phillipson   36
175–5   39 overs   1*ct* (Knight
b Robinson)

85 Yorkshire *v* **Worcestershire**
at Worcester   *May 15*
Yorkshire won by 6 wickets

140–4   34·5 overs   *not out*   79
139–9   40 overs   2*ct*
(Humphries   *b* Old, Inchmore
b Old)

86 Yorkshire *v* **Hampshire**
at Huddersfield   *May 22*
Hampshire won by 129 runs

120   30·3 overs   *ct* Roberts
b Murtagh   72
249–5   40 overs   1*ct* (Richards
b Sidebottom)

87 Yorkshire *v* **Glamorgan**
at Cardiff   *May 29*
Glamorgan won by 23 runs

188–9   40 overs   *ct* E. Jones
b Cordle   9
211–5   40 overs   0*ct*

88 Yorkshire *v* **Nottinghamshire**
at Nottingham   *June 12*   No result

did not bat
98   39·4 overs   0*ct* 8–2–15–1
(Rice   *ct* Lumb)

89 Yorkshire *v* **Somerset**
at Scarborough   *June 19*
Somerset won by 84 runs

110   37 overs   *ct* Botham
b Jennings   45
194–8   40 overs   0*ct*

90 Yorkshire *v* **Derbyshire**
at Hull   *June 26*
Derbyshire won by 2 runs

138–7   40 overs   *ct* Taylor
b Barlow   11
140   40 overs   0*ct*

91 Yorkshire *v* **Lancashire**
at Leeds   *July 10*
Yorkshire won by 6 wickets

225–4   38·1 overs   *b* Hogg   76
223–4   40 overs   2*ct*
(D. Lloyd   *b* Sidebottom,
Hayes   *b* Ramage)

92 Yorkshire *v* **Northamptonshire**
at Milton Keynes   *July 17*
No result

166–7   36 overs   *ct* Sharp
b Hodgson   0
40–0   6·3 overs   0*ct*

93 Yorkshire *v* **Kent**
at Canterbury   *July 24*
Kent won by 51 runs

102   34·2 overs   *ct* Knott
b Jarvis   11
153–8   40 overs   1*ct* (Ealham
b Sidebottom) 5–3–5–0

94 Yorkshire *v* **Middlesex**
at Lord's   *August 7*   No result

19–2   4 overs   *run out*   8

1978

95 Yorkshire *v* **Derbyshire**
at Huddersfield   *May 14*
Derbyshire won by 54 runs

117   28·4 overs   *ct* Wright
b Barlow   2
171–6   30 overs   1*ct* (Miller
b Old)

96 Yorkshire *v* **Somerset**
at Bristol (Imperial)   *June 25*
Somerset won by 16 runs

184–7   40 overs   *not out*   20
200–7   40 overs   0*ct*

97 Yorkshire v Kent
at Canterbury *July 2*
Yorkshire won by 85 runs

199 40 overs *run out* 25
114 32·4 overs 0*ct*

98 Yorkshire v Warwickshire
at Leeds *July 9*
Yorkshire won by 5 wickets

162–5 39 overs *ct* Perryman
b Hemmings 14
160–7 40 overs 2*ct*
(Abberley *b* Sidebottom,
Kallicharran *b* Athey)

99 Yorkshire v Middlesex
at Lord's *July 30*
Yorkshire won by 4 wickets

132–6 19·1 overs *not out* 0
130–6 20 overs 0*ct*

100 Yorkshire v Hampshire
at Portsmouth *August 6*
Hampshire won by 86 runs

130 28·2 overs *st* Stephenson
b Rice 40
216–4 34 overs 0*ct*

101 Yorkshire v Nottinghamshire
at Scarborough *August 20*
Yorkshire won by 6 wickets

135–4 26·3 overs
ct-b Tunnicliffe 21
131–7 27 overs 1*ct* (Birch
b Stevenson)

102 Yorkshire v Surrey
at The Oval *September 3*
Surrey won by 9 wickets

158 38·1 overs
lbw Jackman 19
162–1 34·2 overs 0*ct*
0·2–0–4–0

1979

103 Yorkshire v Nottinghamshire
at Nottingham *May 13*
Yorkshire won by 7 wickets

145–3 36 overs *ct* French
b Rice 47
140 35·1 overs 0*ct*

104 Yorkshire v Glamorgan
at Bradford *May 27*
Yorkshire won by 9 wickets

78–1 22·4 overs *not out* 37
77–8 28 overs 0*ct* 4–1–5–2
(Ontong *ct* Athey, Richards
bowled)

105 Yorkshire v Surrey
at Hull *June 3*
Yorkshire won by 6 wickets

129–4 35·5 overs *ct* Butcher
b Thomas 13
128–3 40 overs 0*ct*

106 Yorkshire v Somerset
at Scarborough *July 1*
Somerset won by 6 wickets

128 37·4 overs *ct* Taylor
b Botham 7
132–4 31·1 overs 0*ct*
2–0–13–0

107 Yorkshire v Essex
at Colchester *July 22*
Yorkshire won by 9 runs

142–8 38 overs *ct* Smith
b Turner 16
133 37·1 overs 1*ct* (Pont
b Oldham)

108 Yorkshire v Middlesex
at Scarborough *July 29*
Middlesex won by 43 runs

162–9 35 overs *ct* Gould
b Jones 26
205–4 35 overs 0*ct* 1–0–3–0

109 Yorkshire v Gloucestershire
at Cheltenham *August 12*
Gloucestershire won by 6 wickets

181–8   40 overs   *ct* Procter
b Partridge   18
183–4   39·1 overs   0*ct*
6·1–0–32–1 (Procter bowled)

110 Yorkshire v Lancashire
at Bradford *August 26*   No result

12–1   5 overs   *not out*   5
137–3   36 overs   0*ct*

1980

111 Yorkshire v Worcestershire
at Bradford *May 4*
Worcestershire won by 7 wickets

191–6   40 overs   *ct* Humphries
b Inchmore   66
195–3   38·1 overs   0*ct*

112 Yorkshire v Warwickshire
at Huddersfield *May 11*
Warwickshire won by 5 wickets

223–8   40 overs   *retired*   37
225–5   37·3 overs   0*ct*
6–0–29–1 (Amiss bowled)

113 Yorkshire v Somerset
at Taunton *May 18*
Somerset won by 7 wickets

158–9   40 overs   *run out*   3
159–3   37·3 overs   0*ct*

114 Yorkshire v Sussex
at Middlesbrough *June 1*
Sussex won by 3 wickets

138–6   28 overs   *ct* Mendis
b Imran   38
139–7   27·2 overs   1*ct*
(Le Roux   *b* Stevenson)

115 Yorkshire v Glamorgan
at Swansea *June 15*
Glamorgan won by a faster scoring
rate

139–7   25 overs   *not out*   19
101–6   16·3 overs   0*ct*

116 Yorkshire v Hampshire
at Basingstoke *June 29*
Yorkshire won by 10 runs

177–8   40 overs   *ct-b* Malone   2
167   39·3 overs   0*ct*   8–2–21–0

117 Yorkshire v Derbyshire
at Leeds *August 3*
Yorkshire won by a faster scoring
rate

138–6   36 overs   *b* Wood   11
145–9   40 overs   0*ct*   8–0–31–1
(Steele bowled)

118 Yorkshire v Lancashire
at Manchester *August 24*
Lancashire won by 1 run

161   40 overs   *ct* Allott
b O'Shaughnessy   50
162–7   40 overs   0*ct*

1981

119 Yorkshire v Kent
at Huddersfield *May 17*
Kent won on a faster scoring rate

79–7   21 overs   *ct* Shepherd
b Jarvis   17
223–6   33 overs   1*ct* (Rowe
ct-b) 2–0–15–1 (Rowe *ct-b*)

120 Yorkshire v Leicestershire
at Leeds *May 24*
Yorkshire won by 5 runs

147   33 overs   *b* Parsons   1
142   32·5 overs   0*ct*

121 Yorkshire v Middlesex
at Bradford   *May 31*   No result

45–4   7·5 overs   *did not bat*
85–6   13 overs   0ct

122 Yorkshire v Worcestershire
at Worcester   *June 28*
Yorkshire won by 9 wickets

215–1   39 overs   *not out*   91
212–6   40 overs   0ct

123 Yorkshire v Essex
at Chelmsford   *July 26*
Essex won by 73 runs

177   37·4 overs   *ct* Fletcher
b East   22
250–3   40 overs   1*ct* (Gooch
b Ramage)

Boycott's Innings in the John Player League, Season by Season

Season	Matches	Innings	Not Outs	Runs	Highest Score	Average	Hundreds	Fifties	Catches	Ducks
1969	7	7	1	152	73*	25·33	0	1	6	0
1970	13	12	0	477	98	39·75	0	5	5	1
1971	9	9	0	443	93	49·22	0	5	4	0
1972	9	9	1	256	52*	32·00	0	1	6	1
1973	10	10	2	444	104*	55·50	1	3	4	1
1974	10	10	1	363	108*	40·33	1	1	6	1
1975	14	14	3	666	99	60·54	0	7	12	0
1976	10	10	4	392	89*	65·33	0	4	1	1
1977	12	10	1	347	79*	38·55	0	3	7	1
1978	8	8	2	141	40	23·50	0	0	4	0
1979	8	8	2	169	47	28·16	0	0	1	0
1980	8	8	2	226	66	37·66	0	2	1	0
1981	5	4	1	131	91*	43·66	0	1	2	0
TOTALS	123	119	20	4,207	108*	42·49	2	33	59	6

Boycott's Innings in the John Player League Against Each Team

Team	Matches	Innings	Not Outs	Runs	Highest Score	Average	Hundreds	Fifties	Catches	Ducks
Derbyshire	10	10	0	330	82	33·00	0	2	6	0
Essex	9	9	1	295	98	36·87	0	2	9	1
Glamorgan	10	10	3	267	104*	38·14	1	0	4	0
Gloucestershire	7	6	0	283	99	47·16	0	3	1	0
Hampshire	8	8	0	221	72	27·62	0	2	1	1
Kent	9	9	0	210	40	23·33	0	0	4	0
Lancashire	9	9	2	334	81	47·71	0	4	5	1
Leicestershire	7	7	1	247	75	41·16	0	2	0	0
Middlesex	10	8	3	224	60*	44·80	0	2	1	0
Northamptonshire	6	6	1	283	108*	56·60	1	2	3	1
Nottinghamshire	8	7	2	290	89*	58·00	0	2	4	0
Somerset	7	7	3	256	82*	64·00	0	2	2	0
Surrey	6	6	0	66	20	11·00	0	0	4	2
Sussex	5	5	0	216	54	43·20	0	2	5	0
Warwickshire	6	6	1	349	93	69·80	0	4	8	0
Worcestershire	6	6	3	336	91*	112·00	0	4	2	0
TOTALS	123	119	20	4,207	108*	42·49	2	33	59	6

Boycott's Innings in the John Player League on Each Ground

Ground	Matches	Innings	Not Outs	Runs	Highest Score	Average	Hundreds	Fifties	Catches	Ducks
Basingstoke	1	1	0	2	2	2·00	0	0	0	0
Birmingham	3	3	0	205	75	68·33	0	3	4	0
Bournemouth	1	1	0	61	61	61·00	0	1	0	0
Bradford	17	14	4	467	78*	46·70	0	4	3	1
Bristol	3	3	1	85	55	42·50	0	1	0	0
Canterbury	3	3	0	60	25	20·00	0	0	1	0
Cardiff	2	2	0	10	9	5·00	0	0	3	0
Chelmsford	1	1	0	22	22	22·00	0	0	1	0
Cheltenham	1	1	0	18	18	18·00	0	0	0	0

Ground	Matches	Innings	Not Outs	Runs	Highest Score	Average	Hundreds	Fifties	Catches	Ducks
Chesterfield	3	3	0	124	46	41·33	0	0	2	0
Colchester	3	3	0	136	98	45·33	0	1	3	0
Colwyn Bay	1	1	1	104	104*	—	1	0	0	0
Dover	1	1	0	23	23	23·00	0	0	0	0
Folkestone	1	1	0	40	40	40·00	0	0	1	0
Glastonbury	1	1	1	82	82*	—	0	1	0	0
Gloucester	1	1	0	72	72	72·00	0	1	0	0
Hove	2	2	0	90	54	45·00	0	1	1	0
Huddersfield	7	7	2	329	108*	65·80	1	2	6	0
Hull	8	8	0	163	46	20·37	0	0	3	0
Leeds	10	10	0	289	76	28·90	0	2	6	0
Leicester	3	3	0	95	75	31·66	0	1	0	0
Leyton	1	1	0	0	0	—	0	0	1	1
Lord's	5	5	2	94	60*	31·33	0	1	1	0
Maidstone	1	1	0	16	16	16·00	0	2	0	0
Manchester	5	5	1	181	81	45·25	0	2	2	1
Middlesbrough	3	3	0	184	93	61·33	0	1	4	0
Milton Keynes	1	1	0	0	0	—	0	0	0	1
Neath	1	1	0	18	18	18·00	0	0	0	0
Northampton	2	2	0	100	58	50·00	0	1	1	0
Nottingham	4	3	1	142	72*	71·00	0	1	2	0
Portsmouth	1	1	0	40	40	40·00	0	0	0	0
Scarborough	11	11	2	473	99	52·55	0	4	6	1
Sheffield	3	3	1	87	52*	43·50	0	1	4	0
Swansea	2	2	1	60	41	60·00	0	0	1	0
Taunton	1	1	0	3	3	3·00	0	0	0	0
Tewkesbury	1	1	0	29	29	29·00	0	0	1	0
The Oval	3	3	0	33	19	11·00	0	0	0	1
Worcester	5	5	3	270	91*	135·00	0	2	2	0
TOTALS	123	119	20	4,207	108*	42·49	2	33	59	6

Boycott's Bowling in the John Player League, Season by Season

Season	Overs	Maidens	Runs	Wickets	Average	Best Bowling
1970	23	0	121	2	60·50	1–34
1977	13	5	20	1	20·00	1–15
1978	0·2	0	4	0	—	—
1979	13·1	1	53	3	17·66	2–5
1980	22	2	81	2	40·50	1–29
1981	2	0	15	1	15·00	1–15
TOTALS	73·3	8	294	9	32·66	2–5

Boycott did not bowl in any other season

Boycott's Bowling in the John Player League Against Each Team

Team	Overs	Maidens	Runs	Wickets	Average	Best Bowling
Derbyshire	16	0	65	2	32·50	1–31
Glamorgan	4	1	5	2	2·50	2–5
Gloucestershire	14·1	2	53	1	53·00	1–31
Hampshire	4	0	26	0	—	—
Kent	7	3	20	1	20·00	1–15
Middlesex	1	0	3	0	—	—
Nottinghamshire	16	2	51	2	22·50	1–15
Somerset	2	0	13	0	—	—
Surrey	0·2	0	4	0	—	—
Sussex	3	0	25	0	—	—
Warwickshire	6	0	29	1	29·00	1–29
TOTALS	73·3	8	294	9	32·66	2–5

Boycott's Bowling in the John Player League on Each Ground

Ground	Overs	Maidens	Runs	Wickets	Average	Best Bowling
Basingstoke	8	2	21	0	—	—
Bradford	4	1	5	2	2·50	2–5
Canterbury	5	3	5	0	—	—
Cheltenham	6·1	0	32	1	32·00	1–32
Chesterfield	8	0	34	1	34·00	1–34
Huddersfield	8	0	44	2	22·00	1–15
Hull	4	0	26	0	—	—
Leeds	8	0	31	1	31·00	1–31
Middlesbrough	3	0	25	0	—	—
Nottingham	8	2	15	1	15·00	1–15
Scarborough	3	0	16	0	—	—
Sheffield	8	0	36	1	36·00	1–36
The Oval	0·2	0	4	0	—	—
TOTALS	73·3	8	294	9	32·66	2–5

Boycott's Modes of Dismissal in the John Player League

Season	Bowled	Caught	Hit Wicket	LBW	Run Out	Stumped
1969	1	4	0	0	1	0
1970	2	10	0	0	0	0
1971	1	8	0	0	0	0
1972	3	2	0	1	2	0
1973	4	3	0	1	0	0
1974	2	6	0	0	0	1
1975	1	10	0	0	0	0
1976	4	1	0	0	1	0
1977	1	7	0	0	1	0
1978	0	3	0	1	1	1
1979	0	6	0	0	0	0
1980	1	4	0	0	1	0
1981	1	2	0	0	0	0
TOTALS	21	66	0	3	7	2

Benson and Hedges Cup

1972

1 Yorkshire _v_ **Lancashire**
at Bradford   _April 29, 30, May 1_
Yorkshire won by 9 wickets

84–1   41·1 overs   _b_ Wood   28
82   47·2 overs   0ct

2 Yorkshire _v_ **Derbyshire**
at Chesterfield   _May 15_
Yorkshire won by 6 wickets

128–4   47·1 overs   _not out_   58
127   53·5 overs   2ct (Wilkins
_b_ Old, Ward   _b_ Nicholson)

3 Yorkshire _v_ **Nottinghamshire**
at Nottingham   _June 3_
Nottinghamshire won by 3 wickets

122–8   55 overs   _ct_ Sobers
_b_ White   32
123–7   52·2 overs   0ct

4 Yorkshire _v_ **Sussex**
at Bradford   _June 14, 15_
Yorkshire won by 5 wickets

89–5   51 overs   _run out_   24
85   51·1 overs   1ct (Graves
_b_ Wilson)

5 Yorkshire _v_ **Gloucestershire**
at Leeds   _June 28_
Yorkshire won by 7 wickets

134–3   48·4 overs   _not out_   75
131   55 overs   0ct

1973

6 Yorkshire _v_ **Derbyshire**
at Bradford   _May 7_
Yorkshire won by 5 wickets

109–5   48·2 overs   _ct_ Hendrick
_b_ Rumsey   11
108   52·4 overs   1ct (Bolus
_b_ Carrick)

7 Yorkshire _v_ **Lancashire**
at Manchester   _May 12_
Lancashire won by 7 wickets

125   54·1 overs   _ct_ Pilling
_b_ Wood   8
131–3   47·5 overs   0ct

8 Yorkshire _v_ **Minor Counties
(North)**
at Chester-le-Street   _May 19_
Yorkshire won by 9 wickets

144–1   43·1 overs   _not out_   83
140–9   55 overs   0ct

9 Yorkshire _v_ **Nottinghamshire**
at Hull   _June 2_
Yorkshire won by 8 wickets

209–2   52·5 overs
lbw Sobers   44
208–2   55 overs   0ct

1974

10 Yorkshire _v_ **Minor Counties
(North)**
at Leeds   _April 27_
Yorkshire won by 9 wickets

110–1   48·5 overs   _not out_   56
109   54·5 overs   1ct (Wing
_b_ Bore)

11 Yorkshire _v_ **Derbyshire**
at Chesterfield   _May 6_
Yorkshire won by 2 wickets

154–8   54·4 overs   *ct* Ward
b Tunnicliffe   53
153   52·2 overs   0*ct*

12   Yorkshire *v* Lancashire
at Bradford   *June 1*
Lancashire won by 3 wickets

188–8   55 overs   *st* Lyon
b Wood   36
189–7   54·5 overs   1*ct* (Wood
b Bore)

13   Yorkshire *v* Surrey
at The Oval   *June 12*
Surrey won by 24 runs

201   52·5 overs   *b* Jackman   5
225–7   55 overs   0*ct*

1975

14   Yorkshire *v* Lancashire
at Manchester   *April 26*
Lancashire won by 78 runs

137–7   55 overs
lbw Ratcliffe   47
215–6   55 overs   1*ct* (Hayes
b Nicholson)

15   Yorkshire *v* Derbyshire
at Bradford   *May 5*
Yorkshire won by 60 runs

162–8   55 overs   *st* Taylor
b Swarbrook   51
102   46 overs   0*ct*

**16   Yorkshire *v* Minor Counties
(North)**
at Scunthorpe   *May 10*
Yorkshire won by 36 runs

218–3   55 overs   *b* Maslin   54
182   51·5 overs   0*ct*

17   Yorkshire *v* Nottinghamshire
at Barnsley   *May 21*
Yorkshire won by 8 wickets

138–2   42·3 overs   *ct* Harris
b Wilkinson   59
137–9   55 overs   0*ct*

18   Yorkshire *v* Middlesex
at Lord's   *June 4*
Middlesex won by 4 wickets

182   55 overs   *ct* Murray
b Lamb   58
183–6   54·1 overs   0*ct*

1976

19   Yorkshire *v* Kent
at Canterbury   *April 24*
Yorkshire won by 9 wickets

152–1   46·2 overs   *not out*   86
148–9   47·5 overs   0*ct*

20   Yorkshire *v* Surrey
at Bradford   *May 3, 4*
Surrey won by 7 wickets

122–9   55 overs
lbw Butcher   25
126–3   48·4 overs   1*ct*
(Howarth   *b* Cooper)

21   Yorkshire *v* Sussex
at Hove   *May 8*
Yorkshire won by 38 runs

217–5   55 overs   *ct* Groome
b Snow   6
179   48·5 overs   1*ct* (Graves
b Cooper)

1977

22   Yorkshire *v* Middlesex
at Lord's   *April 23, 24*
Middlesex won by 12 runs

182   53·2 overs   *ct* Radley
b Gatting   7
194–7   55 overs   0*ct*

23   Yorkshire *v* Northamptonshire
at Middlesbrough   *April 30*
Northamptonshire won by 6 wickets

216–7   55 overs   *ct* Sharp
b Dye   102
217–4   55 overs   0*ct*

24   Yorkshire v Minor Counties (East)
at Jesmond   *May 14*
Yorkshire won by 51 runs

218–9   55 overs   *ct* Robinson
b O'Brien   73
167   49·5 overs   0*ct*   4–0–14–0

25   Yorkshire v Essex
at Barnsley   *May 23*
Yorkshire won by 7 wickets

144–3   44·4 overs   *not out*   74
143   51·4 overs   0*ct*

1978

26   Yorkshire v Kent
at Canterbury   *April 22*
Kent won by 46 runs

114   51 overs   *ct* Tavaré
b Woolmer   20
160   52·3 overs   0*ct*

27   Yorkshire v Essex
at Harrogate   *May 2*
Yorkshire won by 26 runs

90–3   10 overs   *did not bat*
64–5   10 overs   0*ct*

28   Yorkshire v Surrey
at Barnsley   *May 13, 15*
Surrey won by 1 wicket

150   51·3 overs   *ct* Richards
b Baker   9
151–9   54·2 overs   0*ct*

29   Yorkshire v Nottinghamshire
at Nottingham   *May 20*
Nottinghamshire won by 19 runs

168–9   55 overs   *b* Cooper   15
187–9   55 overs   0*ct*   5–1–9–0

1979

30   Yorkshire v Nottinghamshire
at Bradford   *May 5, 7, 8*
No result

198–7   55 overs   *ct* Tunnicliffe
b Hemmings   45
8–0   4 overs   0*ct*

31   Yorkshire v Minor Counties (North)
at Jesmond   *May 12*
Yorkshire won by 10 wickets

86–0   30·5 overs   *not out*   53
85   42·5 overs   1*ct* (Riddell
b Carrick)

32   Yorkshire v Kent
at Leeds   *May 19*
Yorkshire won by 56 runs

189–8   55 overs   *ct* Knott
b Hills   27
133   47·1 overs   1*ct* (Knott
b Cooper)

33   Yorkshire v Middlesex
at Lord's   *May 23, 24, 25*
No result

did not bat
175–7   55 overs
0*ct*   6–0–17–0

QUARTER FINAL
34   Yorkshire v Middlesex
at Lord's   *June 6*
Yorkshire won by 4 wickets

108–6   47 overs   *b* Daniel   3
107   49 overs   1*ct* (Edmonds
b Carrick) 4–2–4–0

1980

35   Yorkshire v Warwickshire
at Leeds   *May 10*
Warwickshire won by 1 wicket

268–4   55 overs   *run out*   40
269–9   44·5 overs
0*ct*   3–0–16–1 (Amiss bowled)

36   Yorkshire *v* **Worcestershire**
at Worcester   *May 17*
Worcestershire won by 4 wickets

269–6   55 overs   *ct* Hemsley
b Alleyne   142
270–6   54 overs
0*ct*   5–0–25–0

37   Yorkshire *v* **Combined Universities**
at The Parks   *May 20, 21*
Yorkshire won by 9 wickets

151–1   39·3 overs   *not out*   69
150–7   55 overs
0*ct*   7–0–20–1 (Orders
st Bairstow)

38   Yorkshire *v* **Northamptonshire**
at Bradford   *May 22*
Northamptonshire won by 2 runs

203–8   55 overs   *ct* Sharp
b Sarfraz   0
205–9   55 overs
0*ct*   7–1–23–0

1981

39   Yorkshire *v* **Derbyshire**
at Derby   *May 9, 11*
Yorkshire won by 1 wicket

203–9   53·4 overs
b Tunnicliffe   31
202–8   55 overs
0*ct*   3–0–16–0

40   Yorkshire *v* **Warwickshire**
at Birmingham   *May 19*
Yorkshire won by 10 runs

221   54·3 overs   *lbw* Willis   9
211   54·3 overs   1*ct* (Din
b Sidebottom)

41   Yorkshire *v* **Scotland**
at Bradford   *May 21, 22*
Yorkshire won by 42 runs

228–6   55 overs   *run out*   3
186   51·3 overs
0*ct*   5–0–20–0

42   Yorkshire *v* **Somerset**
at Leeds   *June 24*
Somerset won by 3 wickets

221–9   55 overs   *ct* Rose
b Marks   21
223–7   53·5 overs
0*ct*   7–0–37–0

Boycott's Innings in the Benson and Hedges Cup, Season by Season

Season	Matches	Innings	Not Outs	Runs	Highest Score	Average	Hundreds	Fifties	Catches	Ducks
1972	5	5	2	217	75*	72·33	0	2	3	0
1973	4	4	1	146	83*	48·66	0	1	1	0
1974	4	4	1	150	56*	50·00	0	2	2	0
1975	5	5	0	269	59	53·80	0	4	1	0
1976	3	3	1	117	86*	58·50	0	1	2	0
1977	4	4	1	256	102	85·33	1	2	0	0
1978	4	3	0	44	20	14·66	0	0	0	0
1979	5	4	1	128	53*	42·66	0	1	3	0
1980	4	4	1	251	142	83·66	1	1	0	1
1981	4	4	0	64	31	16·00	0	0	1	0
TOTALS	42	40	8	1,642	142	51·31	2	14	13	1

Gold Awards

v *Gloucestershire at Leeds, 1972*
v *Minor Counties (North) at Leeds, 1974*
v *Nottinghamshire at Barnsley, 1975*
v *Minor Counties (East) at Jesmond, 1977*
v *Northamptonshire at Middlesbrough, 1977*
v *Essex at Barnsley, 1977*
v *Minor Counties (North) at Jesmond, 1979*

Boycott's Innings in the Benson and Hedges Cup Against Each Team

Team	Matches	Innings	Not Outs	Runs	Highest Score	Average	Hundreds	Fifties	Catches	Ducks
Combined Universities	1	1	1	69	69*	—	0	1	0	0
Derbyshire	5	5	1	204	58*	51·00	0	3	3	0
Essex	2	1	1	74	74*	—	0	1	0	0
Gloucestershire	1	1	1	75	75*	—	0	1	0	0
Kent	3	3	1	133	86*	66·50	0	1	1	0
Lancashire	4	4	0	119	47	29·75	0	0	2	0

Team	Matches	Innings	Not Outs	Runs	Highest Score	Average	Hundreds	Fifties	Catches	Ducks
Middlesex	4	3	0	68	58	22·66	0	1	1	0
Minor Counties (East)	1	1	0	73	73	73·00	0	1	0	0
Minor Counties (North)	4	4	3	246	83*	246·00	0	4	2	0
Northamptonshire	2	2	0	102	102	51·00	1	0	0	1
Nottinghamshire	5	5	0	195	59	39·00	0	1	0	0
Scotland	1	1	0	3	3	3·00	0	0	0	0
Somerset	1	1	0	21	21	21·00	0	0	0	0
Surrey	3	3	0	39	25	13·00	0	0	1	0
Sussex	2	2	0	30	24	15·00	0	0	2	0
Warwickshire	2	2	0	49	40	24·50	0	0	1	0
Worcestershire	1	1	0	142	142	142·00	1	0	0	0
TOTALS	42	40	8	1,642	142	51·31	2	14	13	1

Boycott's Innings in the Benson and Hedges Cup on Each Ground

Ground	Matches	Innings	Not Outs	Runs	Highest Score	Average	Hundreds	Fifties	Catches	Ducks
Barnsley	3	3	1	142	74*	71·00	0	2	0	0
Birmingham	1	1	0	9	9	9·00	0	0	1	0
Bradford	9	9	0	223	51	24·77	0	1	4	1
Canterbury	2	2	1	106	86*	106·00	0	1	0	0
Chesterfield	2	2	1	111	58*	111·00	0	2	2	0
Chester-le-Street	1	1	1	83	83*	—	0	1	0	0
Derby	1	1	0	31	31	31·00	0	0	0	0
Harrogate	1	0	—	—	—	—	—	—	—	—
Hove	1	1	0	6	6	6·00	0	0	1	0
Hull	1	1	0	44	44	44·00	0	0	0	0
Jesmond	2	2	1	126	73	126·00	0	2	1	0
Leeds	5	5	2	219	75*	73·00	0	2	2	0
Lord's	4	3	0	68	58	22·66	0	1	1	0
Manchester	2	2	0	55	47	27·50	0	0	1	0
Middlesbrough	1	1	0	102	102	102·00	1	0	0	0

Ground	Matches	Innings	Not Outs	Runs	Highest Score	Average	Hundreds	Fifties	Catches	Ducks
Nottingham	2	2	0	47	32	23·50	0	0	0	0
The Oval	1	1	0	5	5	5·00	0	0	0	0
The Parks	1	1	1	69	69*	—	0	1	0	0
Scunthorpe	1	1	0	54	54	54·00	0	1	0	0
Worcester	1	1	0	142	142	142·00	1	0	0	0
TOTALS	42	40	8	1,642	142	51·31	2	14	13	1

Boycott's Bowling in the Benson and Hedges Cup, Season by Season

Season	Overs	Maidens	Runs	Wickets	Average	Best Bowling
1977	4	0	14	0	—	—
1978	5	1	9	0	—	—
1979	10	2	21	0	—	—
1980	22	1	84	2	42·00	1–16
1981	15	0	73	0	—	—
TOTALS	56	4	201	2	100·50	1–16

Boycott did not bowl in any other season

Boycott's Bowling in the Benson and Hedges Cup on Each Ground

Ground	Overs	Maidens	Runs	Wickets	Average	Best Bowling
Bradford	12	1	43	0	—	—
Derby	3	0	16	0	—	—
Jesmond	4	0	14	0	—	—
Leeds	10	0	53	1	53·00	1–16
Lord's	10	2	21	0	—	—
Nottingham	5	1	9	0	—	—
The Parks	7	0	20	1	20·00	1–20
Worcester	5	0	25	0	—	—
TOTALS	56	4	201	2	100·50	1–16

Boycott's Bowling in the Benson and Hedges Cup Against Each Team

Team	Overs	Maidens	Runs	Wickets	Average	Best Bowling
Combined Universities	7	0	20	1	20·00	1–20
Derbyshire	3	0	16	0	—	—
Middlesex	10	2	21	0	—	—
Minor Counties (East)	4	0	14	0	—	—
Northamptonshire	7	1	23	0	—	—
Nottinghamshire	5	1	9	0	—	—
Scotland	5	0	20	0	—	—
Somerset	7	0	37	0	—	—
Warwickshire	3	0	16	1	16·00	1–16
Worcestershire	5	0	25	0	—	—
TOTALS	56	4	201	2	100·50	1–16

Boycott's Modes of Dismissal in the Benson and Hedges Cup

Season	Bowled	Caught	Hit Wicket	LBW	Run Out	Stumped
1972	1	1	0	0	1	0
1973	0	2	0	1	0	0
1974	1	1	0	0	0	1
1975	1	2	0	1	0	1
1976	0	1	0	1	0	0
1977	0	3	0	0	0	0
1978	1	2	0	0	0	0
1979	1	2	0	0	0	0
1980	0	2	0	0	1	0
1981	1	1	0	1	1	0
TOTALS	6	17	0	4	3	2

One-day Internationals

Prudential Trophy in UK

1972

1 England v Australia
at Manchester *August 24*
England won by 6 wickets

226–4 49·1 overs *ct* Marsh
b Watson 25
222–8 55 overs 0*ct*

2 England v Australia
at Lord's *August 26*
Australia won by 5 wickets

236–9 55 overs *b* Lillee 8
240–5 51·3 overs 0*ct*

3 England v Australia
at Birmingham *August 28*
England won by 2 wickets

180–8 51·3 overs *ct* Massie
b Lillee 41
179–9 55 overs 0*ct*

1973

4 England v New Zealand
at Swansea *July 18*
England won by 7 wickets

159–3 45·3 overs *ct* Turner
b Congdon 20
158 52·5 overs 0*ct*

5 England v New Zealand
At Manchester *July 20*
No result

167–8 48·3 overs
lbw Taylor 15

6 England v West Indies
at Leeds *September 5*
England won by 1 wicket

182–9 54·3 overs *ct* Kanhai
b Holder 0
181 54 overs 0*ct*

1978

7 England v Pakistan
at Manchester *May 24, 25*
England won by 132 runs

217–7 55 overs *ct* Bari
b Sarfraz 3
85 47 overs 0*ct*

1980

8 England v West Indies
at Leeds *May 28, 29*
West Indies won by 24 runs

174 51·1 overs *ct* Kallicharran
b Garner 5
198 55 overs 0*ct*

9 England v West Indies
at Lord's *May 30*
England won by 3 wickets

236–7 54·3 overs *run out* 70
235–9 55 overs 0*ct*

10 England v Australia
at The Oval *August 20*
England won by 23 runs

248–6 55 overs *ct* Hughes
b Lillee 99
225–8 55 overs 0*ct*

11 England v Australia
at Birmingham *August 22*
England won by 47 runs

320–8 55 overs *ct* Marsh
b Border 78
273–5 55 overs 0*ct* 1–0–11–0

1981

12 England v Australia
at Lord's *June 4*
England won by 6 wickets

212–4 51·4 overs *not out* 75
210–7 55 overs 0*ct*

13 England v Australia
at Birmingham *June 6*
Australia won by 2 runs

247 54·5 overs *b* Lawson 14
249–8 55 overs 0*ct*

14 England v Australia
at Leeds *June 8*
Australia won by 71 runs

165 46·5 overs *ct* Marsh
b Hogg 4
236–8 55 overs 0*ct*

One-day Internationals Overseas

1977–78

1 England v Pakistan
at Sialkot *December 30*
England won by 6 wickets

152–4 32·7 overs *did not bat*
151 33·3 overs 0*ct*

2 England v Pakistan
at Lahore *January 13*
Pakistan won by 36 runs

122 31·6 overs *lbw* Sarfraz 6
158–6 35 overs 3*ct*
(Miandad *b* Lever, Raja *b* Cope,
Jamil *b* Old)

1978–79

3 England v Australia
at Sydney *January 13* No result

did not bat
17–1 7·2 overs 0*ct*

4 England v Australia
at Melbourne
January 24
England won by 7 wickets

102–3 28·2 overs *not out* 39
101 33·5 overs 0*ct*

5 England v Australia
at Melbourne *February 4*
Australia won by 4 wickets

212–6 40 overs *lbw* Laughlin 33
215–6 38·6 overs 1*ct* (Hughes
b Lever)

6 England v Australia
at Melbourne *February 7*
Australia won by 6 wickets

94 31·7 overs *ct* Cosier
b Dymock 2
95–4 21·5 overs 0*ct*

1980–81

7 England v West Indies
at St. Vincent *February 4*
West Indies won by 2 runs

125 48·2 overs *ct* Mattis
b Croft 2
127 47·2 overs 0*ct*

8 England v West Indies
at Berbice *February 26*
West Indies won by 6 wickets

137 47·2 overs *b* Richards 7
138–4 39·3 overs 0*ct*

1981–82

9   England v India
at Ahmedabad
November 25
England won by 5 wickets

160–5   43·5 overs   *lbw* Madan
Lal   5
156–7   46 overs   0*ct*

10   England v India
At Jallundur   *December 20*
India won by 6 wickets

161–7   36 overs   *run out*   6
164–4   35·3 overs   0*ct*

Prudential World Cup in UK

1979

1   England v Australia
at Lord's   *June 9*
England won by 6 wickets

160–4   47·1 overs
lbw Hogg   1
159–9   60 overs   0*ct*
6–0–15–2 (Hilditch bowled,
Hughes   *ct* Hendrick)

2   England v Canada
at Manchester   *June 14*
England won by 8 wickets

46–2   13·5 overs   *not out*   14
45   40·3 overs   0*ct*   1–0–3–0

3   England v Pakistan
at Leeds   *June 16*
England won by 14 runs

165–9   60 overs   *lbw* Majid   18
151   56 overs   0*ct*
5–0–14–2 (Bari   *ct* Taylor,
Sikander   *ct* Hendrick)

4   England v New Zealand
at Manchester   *June 20*

England won by 9 runs

221–8   60 overs   *ct* Howarth
b Hadlee   2
212–9   60 overs   0*ct*
9–1–24–1 (Howarth *lbw*)

5   England v West Indies
at Lord's   *June 23*
West Indies won by 92 runs

194   51 overs   *ct* Kallicharran
b Holding   57
286–9   60 overs   0*ct*
6–0–38–0

Benson and Hedges World Series Cup in Australia
1979–80

1   England v Australia
at Melbourne   *December 8*
England won by 3 wickets

209–7   49 overs   *ct* Lillee
b Hogg   68
207–9   50 overs   0*ct*

2   England v Australia
at Sydney   *December 11*
England won by 72 runs

264–7   49 overs   *b* Lillee   105
192   47·2 overs   0*ct*

3   England v West Indies
at Brisbaine   *December 23*
West Indies won by 9 wickets

217–8   50 overs   *ct* Marshall
b Holding   68
218–1   46·5 overs   0*ct*

4   England v Australia
at Sydney   *December 26*
England won by 4 wickets

195–6   45·1 overs   *not out*   86
194–6   47 overs   0*ct*

5   England *v* **West Indies**
at Melbourne   *January 20*
West Indies won by 2 runs

213–7   50 overs   *ct* Haynes
b Roberts   35
215–8   50 overs   0*ct*

6   England *v* **West Indies**
at Sydney   *January 22*
West Indies won by 8 wickets

208–8   50 overs   *ct* Greenidge
b Roberts   63
209–2   47·3 overs   0*ct*

Boycott's Innings in One-day Internationals, Season by Season

Season	Matches	Innings	Not Outs	Runs	Highest Score	Average	Hundreds	Fifties	Catches	Ducks
Prudential Trophy in UK										
1972 A	3	3	0	74	41	24·66	0	0	0	0
1973 NZ	2	2	0	35	20	17·50	0	0	0	0
1973 WI	1	1	0	0	0	0·00	0	0	0	1
1978 P	1	1	0	3	3	3·00	0	0	0	0
1980 WI	2	2	0	75	70	37·50	0	1	0	0
1980 A	2	2	0	177	99	88·50	0	2	0	0
1981 A	3	3	1	93	75*	46·50	0	1	0	0
TOTALS	14	14	1	457	99	35·15	0	4	0	1
One-day Internationals Overseas										
1977–78 P	2	1	0	6	6	6·00	0	0	3	0
1978–79 A	4	3	1	74	39*	37·00	0	0	1	0
1980–81 WI	2	2	0	9	7	4·50	0	0	0	0
1981–82 I	2	2	0	11	6	5·50	0	0	0	0
TOTALS	10	8	1	100	39*	14·28	0	0	4	0
Prudential World Cup in UK										
1979	5	5	1	92	57	23·00	0	1	0	0
Benson and Hedges World Series Cup in Australia										
1979–80	6	6	1	425	105	85·00	1	4	0	0
GRAND TOTALS	35	33	4	1,074	105	37·03	1	9	4	1

Boycott's Man-of-the-Match Awards in One-day Internationals

Prudential Trophy

v West Indies at Lord's, 1980
v Australia at Lord's, 1981

Benson and Hedges World Series Cup

v Australia at Sydney, 1979
v Australia at Sydney, 1979

Boycott's Innings in One-day Internationals Against Each Team

Team	Matches	Innings	Not Outs	Runs	Highest Score	Average	Hundreds	Fifties	Catches	Ducks
Prudential Trophy in UK										
Australia	8	8	1	344	99	49·14	0	3	0	0
New Zealand	2	2	0	35	20	32·50	0	0	0	0
Pakistan	1	1	0	3	3	3·00	0	0	0	0
West Indies	3	3	0	75	70	25·00	0	1	0	1
TOTALS	14	14	1	457	99	35·15	0	4	0	1
One-day Internationals Overseas										
Australia	4	3	1	74	39*	37·00	0	0	1	0
India	2	2	0	11	6	5·50	0	0	0	0
Pakistan	2	1	0	6	6	6·00	0	0	3	0
West Indies	2	2	0	9	7	4·50	0	0	0	0
TOTALS	10	8	1	100	39*	14·28	0	0	4	0
Prudential World Cup in UK										
Australia	1	1	0	1	1	1·00	0	0	0	0
Canada	1	1	1	14	14*	—	0	0	0	0
New Zealand	1	1	0	2	2	2·00	0	0	0	0
Pakistan	1	1	0	18	18	18·00	0	0	0	0
West Indies	1	1	0	57	57	57·00	0	1	0	0
TOTALS	5	5	1	92	57	23·00	0	1	0	0
Benson and Hedges World Series Cup in Australia										
Australia	3	3	1	259	105	129·50	1	2	0	0
West Indies	3	3	0	166	68	55·33	0	2	0	0
TOTALS	6	6	1	425	105	85·00	1	4	0	0

Boycott's Innings in One-day Internationals on Each Ground

Ground	Matches	Innings	Not Outs	Runs	Highest Score	Average	Hundreds	Fifties	Catches	Ducks
Prudential Trophy in UK										
Birmingham	3	3	0	133	78	44·33	0	1	0	0
Leeds	3	3	0	9	5	3·00	0	0	0	1
Lord's	3	3	1	153	75*	76·50	0	2	0	0
Manchester	3	3	0	43	25	14·33	0	0	0	0
Swansea	1	1	0	20	20	20·00	0	0	0	0
The Oval	1	1	0	99	99	99·00	0	1	0	0
TOTALS	14	14	1	457	99	35·15	0	4	0	1
One-day Internationals Overseas										
Ahmedabad	1	1	0	5	5	5·00	0	0	0	0
Berbice	1	1	0	7	7	7·00	0	0	0	0
Jallundur	1	1	0	6	6	6·00	0	0	0	0
Lahore	1	1	0	6	6	6·00	0	0	3	0
Melbourne	3	3	1	74	39*	37·00	0	0	1	0
St. Vincent	1	1	0	2	2	2·00	0	0	0	0
Sialkot	1	0	—	—	—	—	—	—	—	—
Sydney	1	0	—	—	—	—	—	—	—	—
TOTALS	10	8	1	100	39*	14·28	0	0	4	0
Prudential World Cup in UK										
Leeds	1	1	0	18	18	18·00	0	0	0	0
Lord's	2	2	0	58	57	29·00	0	1	0	0
Manchester	2	2	1	16	14*	16·00	0	0	0	0
TOTALS	5	5	1	92	57	23·00	0	1	0	0
Benson and Hedges World Series Cup in Australia										
Brisbane	1	1	0	68	68	68·00	0	1	0	0
Melbourne	2	2	0	103	68	51·50	0	1	0	0
Sydney	3	3	1	254	105	127·00	1	2	0	0
TOTALS	6	6	1	425	105	85·00	1	4	0	0

Boycott's Bowling in One-day Internationals, Season by Season

Season	Overs	Maidens	Runs	Wickets	Average	Best Bowling
Prudential Trophy in UK						
1980	1	0	11	0	—	—
TOTALS	1	0	11	0	—	—
Prudential World Cup in UK						
1979	27	1	94	5	18·80	2–14
TOTALS	27	1	94	5	18·80	2–14

Boycott's Bowling in One-day Internationals Against Each Team

Team	Overs	Maidens	Runs	Wickets	Average	Best Bowling
Prudential Trophy in UK						
Australia	1	0	11	0	—	—
TOTALS	1	0	11	0	—	—
Prudential World Cup in UK						
Australia	6	0	15	2	7·50	2–15
Canada	1	0	3	0	—	—
New Zealand	9	1	24	1	24·00	1–24
Pakistan	5	0	14	2	7·00	2–14
West Indies	6	0	38	0	—	—
TOTALS	27	1	94	5	18·80	2–14

Boycott's Bowling in One-day Internationals on Each Ground

Ground	Overs	Maidens	Runs	Wickets	Average	Best Bowling
Prudential Trophy in UK						
Birmingham	1	0	11	0	—	—
TOTALS	1	0	11	0	—	—
Prudential World Cup in UK						
Leeds	5	0	14	2	7·00	2–14
Lord's	12	0	53	2	26·50	2–15
Manchester	10	1	27	1	27·00	1–24
TOTALS	27	1	94	5	18·80	2–14

Boycott's Modes of Dismissal in One-day Internationals

Season	Bowled	Caught	Hit Wicket	LBW	Run Out	Stumped
Prudential Trophy in UK						
1972	1	2	0	0	0	0
1973	0	2	0	1	0	0
1978	0	1	0	0	0	0
1980	0	3	0	0	1	0
1981	1	1	0	0	0	0
TOTALS	2	9	0	1	1	0
One-day Internationals Overseas						
1977–78	0	0	0	1	0	0
1978–79	0	1	0	1	0	0
1980–81	1	1	0	0	0	0
1981–82	0	0	0	1	1	0
TOTALS	1	2	0	3	1	0
Prudential World Cup in UK						
1979	0	2	0	2	0	0
TOTALS	0	2	0	2	0	0
Benson and Hedges World Series Cup in Australia						
1979–80	1	4	0	0	0	0
TOTALS	1	4	0	0	0	0

Parker & Son Ltd
Oxford 1982

Passed to Jonothan Lechmere
from Peter Bell
26 February 2013.